D0465083

SEAN BEAN
THE BIOGRAPHY

Also by Laura Jackson

Golden Stone
The Untold Life and Mysterious Death
of Brian Jones

Queen and I
The Brian May Story

Daniel Day-Lewis
The Biography

Mercury
The King of Queen

Heart of Stone
The Unauthorized Life of
Mick Jagger

Ewan McGregor
A Force to be Reckoned With

Queen
The Definitive Biography

LAURA JACKSON
SEAN BEAN
THE BIOGRAPHY

PIATKUS

Dedicated to my husband David,
a quite extraordinary man

Copyright © 2000 by Laura Jackson

First published in 2000 by
Judy Piatkus (Publishers) Limited
5 Windmill Street
London W1T 2JA
e-mail: info@piatkus.co.uk

For the latest news and information on all our titles,
visit our website at www.piatkus.co.uk

The moral right of the author has been asserted

A catalogue record for this book is available from the British Library

ISBN 0 7499 2150 1

Edited by Judy Gough
Design by Sara Kidd

This book has been printed on paper manufactured with respect for the environment
using wood from managed sustainable resources.

Typeset by Phoenix Photosetting, Chatham, Kent
Printed and bound in Great Briatin by
Mackays of Chatham PLC, Chatham, Kent

CONTENTS

ACKNOWLEDGEMENTS

Grateful appreciation to everyone whom I interviewed. My thanks for all contributions to: Paul Anderson; Sallie Aprahamian; Dave Bassett; Roy Battersby; Timothy Bentinck; Gabriel Beristain, BSC; Robert Bierman; Barbara Broccoli; Pierce Brosnan; Trevor Byfield; Ted Childs; William Chubb; Martin Clark; Christine Clarke; Tom Clegg; Scott Cleverdon; Michael Cochrane; Terry Coles; Bernard Cornwell; Brian Cox; Brian Croucher; Paul G. Daniels; Ted Danson; Roger Deakins, BSC; Joe Elliott; Julian Fellowes; Gerry Fisher, BSC; Ian Footitt; James Fox; Clive Francis; Dawn French; Nitin Ganatra; Stevie Glover; Malcolm Godfrey; Michael Gough; Julian Grant; Richard Greatrex, BSC; Michael Haggiag; James Andrew Hall; Robert Hamilton; Adrian Hodges; John Hubbard; Tony Imi, BSC; John Kavanagh; John B. Keane; Professor Sir Harold Kroto, FRS; John Levitt; Pamela Lonsdale; Aileen McCracken; John McGlashan, BSC; Andrée Molyneaux; Alex Norton; Maureen Oakes; Daragh O'Malley; Thaddeus O'Sullivan; Cecile Paoli; James Purefoy; Assumpta Serna; Ian Shouler; Beverley Simpkins; Rosemary Anne Sisson; Euan Smith; Paul Street; Muir Sutherland; Professor John Tarn, OBE; David Thewlis; Alex Thomson, BSC; David Troughton; Robin Vidgeon, BSC; Natasha Wagstaff; Stephen Wakelam; George Waring; Paul Wheeler, BSC; Janet Whitaker; Michael Whyte; Saskia Wickham; Sita Williams; Rex Windle; Terry Winsor.

Also thanks for their help to: Athelstan Primary School, Sheffield (Tony Woodward); Barnsley Football Club; Beamish Museum, Co. Durham; BBC Archives Centre (Mike Websell); BBC Information Service; BFI, London; British Library, London; British Society of Cinematographers (Frances Russell); Broadcasting Standards Commission (Lorraine Miller); Carlton TV; Children's Film & Television Foundation Ltd; Chillingham Road Primary School, Newcastle; Citizens' Theatre, Glasgow; *Coventry Evening Telegraph*; *Daily Telegraph*; Directors Guild of Great Britain; 18 Dean Street

Restaurant, Newcastle; Elgin Library staff; Eon Productions (Katherine McCormack); Folio Productions (Becky Clarke); *GQ*; Sandra Gillott, Handsworth Historical Society, Sheffield; Granada Film (Colin Hankins); Granada Television; Gutman Associates; Hartswood Films Ltd (Debbie Vertue, and Kate); ICM, London; *Impact, The Action Movie Magazine*; Independent Newspapers; Irish Film Archive, Dublin; ITV Network (Paul); Jim Henson Productions; Robocop Productions (Robert McNamara); Valerie Kemp (Assistant to Lord Puttnam); London Films Production Ltd (Andrew Luff); LWT (Helen, and Olivia Chalk); Ann McPherson, Elgin; *Newcastle Chronicle & Journal*; Northern Screen Commission (Christine J. Boulby); Chris and Patricia O'Dell; PACT, London; Pinewood Studios, England; *Radio Times*; Rotherham College of Arts and Technology (Nick Henstock); *She*; Sheffield Central Library (Maureen Bailey); Sheffield City Council; Sheffield Hallam University (Natasha Wagstaff, and Professor J.D.A. Widdowson); Sheffield Newspapers Ltd; Sheffield Registrar of Births, Deaths and Marriages; Sheffield United Football Club (Kevin Cookson); *Spotlight*, London; *The Bill* (Julie); The Library Council, Dublin; The Shakespeare Birthplace Trust (Sylvia Morris); The Sharpe Appreciation Society (Christine Clarke); *The Weekly News*; Theatre Museum, London (Janet Birkett); *Time Out*; Toronto Film and Television Commission (Rhonda Silverstone); *TV Times*; Tyne Tees TV (Margaret Brown); *Viz*; Watermill Theatre, Newbury (Jill Fraser).

Special thanks to David for his extraordinary support, and also to my editor Rachel Winning, and all at Piatkus Books.

Sean brings a lovely clarity to his work.
He has such strength and a hard core
flinty edge to him that comes from his
childhood. He's a class act. He's a man
who marches to his own drum. He's never
let go of his roots, his accent or what he's
about.

Pierce Brosnan
June 2000

1

MADE IN SHEFFIELD

BRANDED AS 'undeniably, Britain's greatest living sex bomb', at the beginning of the 21st century Sean Bean tops the list of many casting directors on the lookout for hot British talent. For the forty-one-year-old, Yorkshire-born actor there was no startling catapult to stardom. Fame, for Bean has evolved over an accumulation of striking performances that have illuminated his impressive versatility, across a broad spectrum of roles.

In the phenomenally successful television series *Sharpe* as the romantically dashing nineteenth-century rifleman – embodying one of the best ever television heroes – he stirred the imagination of millions. From the forthright, lustful gamekeeper in *Lady Chatterley* he shocked a nation and went on to acquire a reputation as a sizzling screen heartthrob. While as a vengeful maniac in *Patriot Games* and James Bond's sinister nemesis in *GoldenEye*, he displayed a chillingly lethal appeal. One of the UK's busiest actors, Sean Bean cleverly juggles a unique balance between the big and small screen, which makes him a sought-after star of international standing, who yet still seems somehow to remain tantalisingly accessible.

His success could never have been signposted. There was no theatrical blood in his working-class background, no desperate craving to seek the limelight. Instead, Sean coasted through school before working in a succession of undemanding local jobs. By his own admission, he had never stuck to anything before, so when he took a sudden interest in acting, those around him could have been forgiven for assuming it to be yet another phase. But Bean surprised them, and perhaps himself most of all, by knuckling down with a hitherto unfamiliar determination that would sweep him inexorably towards his future career.

Now highly accomplished and much respected he particularly relishes action roles, while his forte in bringing a palpably attractive menace to the part of a villain was spotted early on in such stand-up performances as the cruel aristocratic rapist Robert Lovelace in the 1991 BBC production *Clarissa*, which led the period drama's director of photography, John McGlashan, to recall of filming its shocking rape scene, 'Sean scared me then.'

That the camera transforms Sean Bean is not in dispute. He has commanding screen authority and at the same time he is unafraid to contrast this aura of strength with a touching vulnerability. Yet off screen he is a shy man devoid of any pretentiousness, who largely shuns the glitzy social scene and makes no apologies for preferring the joys found in traditional male bastions – drinking beer with his mates in the pub and indulging a legendary passion for football. The Press would come to cite this same passion as a major factor in the demise of his second marriage but lately, and with good reason, Bean has come to query the totality of the one-dimensional laddish tag which the media has firmly pinned to him.

One indelible hallmark, however, is his enduring pride in holding fast to his Northern roots. And those rock-solid foundations were laid in Sheffield, England's fourth largest city, world famous for its steel, cutlery and engineering industries. Shaun Mark Bean was born on 17 April 1959 in the family home at 26 Lathkill Road, in the city's Richmond district, the first child of Brian and Rita Bean. The combination of blond hair and remarkably clear pale green eyes made him a striking boy and his strong features would later develop into a prime asset for an actor.

His reign as an only child ended when a baby sister, Lorraine, was born. Rita had been a secretary in a local steelworks office, but had relinquished the chance of a career when Sean was born. She stayed at home to raise her two children and this stability would cultivate the strongly-held traditional views on a mother's role in life that Sean would carry into adulthood. His father, Brian, a steel plater by trade, worked as a welder with the big steel company, Davy United, before going on to establish his own small fabrication and welding firm. And altogether, theirs was a close-knit unit with a strong sense of family values.

With Lorraine's arrival the family, now complete, moved from Lathkill Road to a new home in Retford Road, a comfortable semi-detached council house on the Handsworth estate. A Sheffield suburb about five miles from the city centre, Handsworth had originally been a village in its own right and Retford Road was an arterial road which had once led to the village of Retford. A patchwork of fields rolled out behind the main road, affording the area a spacious fresh-air feel and although it was not a well-to-do district, it was far from being rundown. With its multitude of pubs, clubs, snooker halls and youth clubs there was plenty to do and it provided a friendly environment in which to grow up.

Sean began his education at Handsworth Infants School, one of those old imposing traditional stone-built schools of character with chimney stacks and a bell tower on the roof, and its playground surrounded by black wrought iron railings mounted on thick stone walls. And from there he moved on to the newly built Athelstan Junior in September 1966; a seven-year-old embarking on a four-year span upon which he would later reflect fondly.

Athelstan Junior then had around four hundred pupils. One of Sean's teachers, Ted Danson, recalls those years, 'I taught Sean in Junior 2 and then I had him again in Junior 4. He was a very quiet, shy little boy who avoided the spotlight at all times. He was popular in a group of lads and one of his particular friends was Jimmy Richardson who remained mates with Sean right the way through school. Sean's one ambition in life then was to play football for Sheffield United and that is all he dreamt about, night and day. He would turn up at school in his Sheffield United shirt every chance he got.'

Sean embraced football with an enthusiasm that remains unabated today. Of the city's two professional football teams, Sheffield Wednesday and Sheffield United, it was a Bean family tradition to support the latter. The first time Sean passed through the well-worn turnstiles and joined the faithful streaming on to the Kop (the home side's section of the terraces behind one of the goals where the club's most ardent supporters gather) at the club's ground at Bramall Lane, it was for him a magical experience.

Wrapped up against the cold Sean stood rigid with excitement, his father beside him, his breath clouding the frosty winter air in what seemed to be a gigantic arena. As he gazed around at the stadium's huge, powerfully-lit floodlights, with his young fertile imagination, he would forever remember the scene as resembling a glorious spaceship.

That night's game began a ritual of setting off across the city on match days, whatever the weather, to cheer on 'The Blades', as the team is nicknamed after the pair of crossed cutlasses depicted on the club's insignia. And he would go fully equipped. Not only had he the noisy hand rattle that was popular with football fans in those days, and red and white striped Sheffield United scarves tied round his neck and wrists, but (until he outgrew it) he also carried a sturdy box that his grandfather had made for him to stand on so that he could see the action on the pitch.

Founded in 1889 Sheffield United's fortunes had fluctuated, but when Sean began supporting them they were playing in what was then the English First Division and trying hard to avoid relegation, thus giving the fans much to root for. In 1968 the legendary attacking midfielder Tony Currie joined the club. He was to earn seventeen England caps and, with outstanding ball skills and displaying consummate flair on the pitch, he became United's star player. Little did Sean realise that he would one day have the chance to work with the dazzling footballer who he, like his friends, idolised.

Sean's capacity for such burning enthusiasm was just one of the sparks that lit a passionate and strong personality. He was a typically boisterous lad who played football around the streets, played soldiers and made camps in fields, and dangled recklessly from precarious tree swings in surrounding woods before coming home muddy and exhilarated for his supper.

Maureen Oakes, a Bean family friend recalls Sean's childhood. She says, 'Sean's father, Brian, was my husband's best friend and when he used to come round to the house he would bring Sean with him to play with our sons, Mark and Stuart. We had an ante room, full of toys and the three boys would play in there and out in the back garden and Mark and Stuart would also go round and play at Sean's house.

'He was a lovely little boy. So keen on football and I think what stands out most from those years was actually how knowledgeable Sean was about football and Sheffield United. It was such a surprise to us when he became an actor because he never had shown the slightest inclination towards that as he grew up. I'm so pleased for him but I remember the first time I saw him in *Sharpe* I thought, "That's surely not the little boy who played in our back garden all those times?" '

Although mainly a happy child, he had a wilful side that could erupt angrily if he felt thwarted. On one spectacular occasion a tantrum landed him in hospital with serious injury. It happened one day at home when, having spent hours outside playing with a cousin, the pair were in the lounge making paper shapes. When Sean, tired and a little fractious, wanted the scissors and was not immediately given them, his rage exploded. He began thumping his hand hard on a nearby glazed door, shattering the pane and showering himself with broken glass. A particularly vicious shard dug deep into one of his legs near to a main artery, with the result that blood spurted alarmingly everywhere. Recalling this drama years later, Sean said, 'I don't remember the pain. My uncle wrapped me in towels and rushed me to hospital.' His leg was saved but the injury seriously incapacitated his ability to walk for a long time afterwards and left him with a permanent scar on his thigh that he will sometimes jokingly claim is a shark bite.

In summer 1970 Sean left Athelstan Junior for Brook Comprehensive, a new secondary modern school, where his extremely casual attitude towards education became evident. Throughout his years there he exhibited a cheerful disinterest in school work. He has freely admitted, 'I was too busy reading comics and messing about.' And one of his teachers, Ian Footitt, confirms, 'Sean was usually at school, but not because he wanted to do schoolwork – because that's where his mates were.'

Though that is not to say that he had no interests. Academic study may have missed the spot with him, but he was showing a natural creative bent in a love of painting and drawing; an aptitude for which once won him first prize – a £1.50 voucher. He enjoyed pop music, too, and toyed with the idea of forming a rock band – a notion, however, which never progressed beyond the odd jam session in the bedroom. For Sean ambitions were no more than ideas that flared and died. In time he would come to recognise in himself a pattern of lacking any sense of commitment. That would change, but as yet he had not found what would become the magnet in his life.

In any event, he was in his early teens and having far too much fun. By now he was a football-loving, charismatic tearaway whose blond-haired, green-eyed looks and lively spirit were beginning to make him popular with the opposite sex. He still had not learned to curb his quick temper and he would engage in mild rebellion, getting into fist fights with friends in the school yard, usually over girls – 'a kick around and a thump' as he put it. But he was just as quick at making peace and would be lighting up a cigarette with the same friend out of sight of the teachers.

Outside school it was much of the same thing. Life on the Handsworth estate, with its close community spirit, felt good to Sean. But growing up on a working-class city estate is not for the faint-hearted. From indulging in harmless high jinks such as crashing through neighbours' orderly gardens after dark when the curtains were closed – pranks Sean and his friends called hedge-hopping or cat-creeping – the future screen leader of men became the head of a gang called The Union, whose traditional rival was another local gang dubbed The Firm. Ian Footitt reveals, 'Union gang members used to have a Union card, a little cardboard membership card.'

Sean was not a thug, nor did he become embroiled in any serious trouble. But to the teenager it was an essential part of his adolescence that in a toughish environment he had to be prepared to assert himself. He once recalled, 'It was hard and sometimes violent, but not with knives and things you get now.'

Ian Footitt goes on, 'Sean was a bit more truculent than most, I'd say. But although The Union and The Firm would clash, no one ever got greatly hurt. This was the latter end of the skinhead days and one group would size up to the other. Years later, the first time that I watched Sean as Richard Sharpe with his men seeing off the enemy, I had this clear vision of Sean with The Union, chasing The Firm for their lives across the school yard.'

Irrefutably the one constant thread running through Sean's life remained football. Although a dyed-in-the-wool supporter and spectator of the game, he realised in his early teens that he was not so fanatical about actually playing. He had played inside-right for his school team, but when he discovered the dedication that was required to get down to serious training his interest, in typical fashion, petered out.

Says Ian, 'Sean's main interest in life was football but even here he wasn't a grafter. He'd get lost for a good part of the game and wouldn't be running around like blazes, sweating up. But as soon as the ball came into the right place he would come out of nowhere and score the goal. A chocolate liner, as they say here – someone who moves in after everyone else has done the work and snatches the glory.'

Amid the jostle on the Kop, loudly cheering on his beloved Sheffield United and healthily barracking the opposition, here too passion sometimes spilled over into territorial skirmishes with pockets of visiting fans. Sean was never arrested, but he has owned up to occasionally having been among fans who were separated from a brawl by policemen on match duty and made to back off and cool down. He once said dismissively. 'It were all just kicking and booting and punching, and then it got sorted out.'

His consuming interest in football, however, did not blind him to other sports and at fifteen he picked up on another family tradition. His father, Brian, had won awards for boxing whilst serving in the army and now Sean joined a local boxing club called Croft House. It spurred him into adopting, for the two years he kept up the noble art, a healthier lifestyle in that he drank only milkshakes and temporarily gave up smoking.

Apart from honing his fitness, Sean felt that he benefited from acquiring self-discipline. Boxing gave him the perfect lightning rod to channel any aggression in a controlled situation. But an indication that he saw boxing as being more than just another sport came when he once proudly declared that it was, 'the pinnacle of masculinity and that's something to be proud of'.

Exuding masculinity is something that comes naturally to Sean Bean. In his mid-teens he stood just shy of six feet tall and was built along very lean athletic lines. Favoured with well-defined bone structure and a chiselled jaw he was handsome in an interestingly hewn, wolfish sort of way with an unruly smile that reached, and lit up, his very expressive eyes.

Inwardly, his personality was already one of depth and complexity and in contrast to his tearaway image and his well-established ability to defend himself, he possessed a strong core of gentle sensitivity. His is intrinsically a loyal nature – to his favourite football team, to his family and friends and to the woman in his life at any given time. Despite the fact that he would scrap over girls in the school grounds and that, later on, he acquired a reputation as a smouldering screen lover, privately he would prove to have a stable streak when it came to romance.

His first steady girlfriend was Debra Ann James, two years Sean's junior. Her father was a boilermaker and she was, almost literally, the girl next door as she, along with her family, lived in Retford Road.

When Sean left Brook Comprehensive at sixteen in 1975 he was armed with just two O Levels, one in English and the other in art. He was eager to be free to earn a wage and to establish some independence. Conventional wisdom in those days dictated that for a working-class lad who was not academic, his future lay in learning a trade or in labouring.

But Sean had taken to visiting the cinema. Influenced by the screen stars he watched in the darkened theatres, he began to develop a sharp dress sense that was guaranteed to set him apart. And for a lad who had happily squandered his opportunities at school, the cinema fed the now persistent gnawing feeling deep inside him that he yearned to be different somehow. As yet he could not define it and, accordingly, he could have no firm direction to follow. But it was out there. All he had to do was find it.

2

SQUARE PEG IN A ROUND HOLE

OVER THE YEARS, Sheffield has produced a mini galaxy of talent in the entertainment world, including the famous novelist sisters Margaret Drabble and A.S. Byatt, popular television presenter Michael Palin, rock legend Joe Cocker and the giant heavy metal band Def Leppard, as well as several actors. That the name Sean Bean would come to be added to this impressive celebrity roll-call was not yet apparent.

Now set loose upon the wide world Sean continued his direction-less drift, hopping from one job to another. Local employment prospects in the mid-1970s were becoming strained with industry and commerce going into decline. But although it was getting harder to be able to jack in one job, confident of walking straight into another, from the summer of 1975 over roughly the next eighteen months, Bean did just that.

Memorably, one job lasted a single morning. That was when he took up a post as a porter at a Marks & Spencer department store. Wearing an overall and a white paper hygiene cap, his task was to lug heavy cheeses up from the basement to the shop's delicatessen, but he went home at lunch-time never to return. He later admitted, 'Mum rang to say the smell [of the cheeses] made me sick.'

He had more luck working for the local authority shovelling snow and salting paths in the winter, and cutting hedges and grass in the summer. Even here, though, Sean managed to distinguish himself by building a wall that collapsed within days; his tenure as a Sheffield City Council employee was not destined to last long.

None of this bothered Bean whose free-spirited attitude began causing some tension at home as naturally his parents were frustrated by his endless aimlessness. Although he has long since become close to them Sean has admitted, 'As a teenager there was a bit of distance between me and my family.'

That said, this tension did not prevent Sean from accepting his father's invitation to join his company and learn a trade. Darwin and Bean was a steel fabrication shop which manufactured plant machinery and wielding a welding rod and acetylene torch Sean began his apprenticeship. He is openly proud of his father having built up his own business and part of Sean warmed to the closeness on offer of working alongside Brian for life. But in his heart he knew that this would never satisfy him. He would call it a dirty and dangerous job, but it was not a distaste for getting his hands mucky that put Sean off. It was rather that behind the heavy protective face shield he wore as he toiled, bent over his work bench, his mind was forever elsewhere.

He could not take an interest either when, through his work, he was put on a day-release welding course at the nearby Rotherham College of Arts and Technology as his tutor there, Ian Shouler, recalls. Says Ian, 'Sean was learning to be a structural engineer, but he wasn't into this line at all. He wasn't interested in taking over the family business. I would try to talk to him about it, but he would only ever shrug his shoulders and it was clear that he didn't want to discuss it.

'Then he began missing classes. It got to the point where I phoned his father and told him. And his dad said, "I'll make sure that he gets there next week." Sure enough, the next week this car drove up and Sean got out. But once he had waved goodbye to his mother and she drove off, he promptly walked over to a parked Mini and got in with his girlfriend and they drove off. I saw all this from the window so I rang his father again and said, "Well, you got him here okay. But he's off already!" Even when it came to the end of term exam which took about two and a half hours, Sean asked me right away, "How long do I have to stay for?" I told him he could leave after one hour. He just wasn't cut out for this job and he knew it.'

Sean did, however, glean valuable life experience during the three years or so he spent at the workshop. He gained some maturity in this hard-working environment. Already a guy who called a spade a spade, he was surrounded by equally no-nonsense type men; a good bunch of blokes who, as Bean later reflected, 'didn't take any shit'. He also appreciated the fact that it clearly made no difference to the men that the new recruit was the boss's son.

Grafting meant that it was not hard for Sean to portray the working man authentically, whenever this was required in his future career. Typically he once declared, 'You need a bit of proper work under your belt before you start prancing about being an actor in tights.' Not that becoming an actor had, as yet, entered his head. His conviction that he was not cut out for a life in mundane employment was growing but, if anything, his dreams were anchored in his attraction to art.

At seventeen he had had some of his work displayed for sale in a local building society window in a tentative attempt to test the water with his wares. But he had not been able to make any money from this. Undaunted, he kept his hand in and thus maintained the flame. His welding tutor, Ian Shouler, recalls Sean's artistic flair.

'Sean had quite a talent for art. He would sit and do free-hand sketching and one particular day he drew me, but as an egg shape. In those days I had a goatee beard and he drew this like a dagger jutting right up through the bottom of the egg. There was this dramatic jagged split in the egg shape with blood dripping from it. He was very creative.'

He was music mad by this time too as Ian continues, 'Sean was in his David Bowie phase right then. He had a startling dyed streak right down the front of his hair and had shaved his eyebrows. He didn't half look like Bowie, I must say, with his build and his high cheek-bone structure. But for all his flair, still he was a shy lad. He was a bit of a loner at college, not a good mixer and much more sensitive in nature to the other bread-and-butter future welders.'

Although an important part of Sean remained unfulfilled, on the face of things his life had stabilised. He lived at home, had a secure job learning a trade and enjoyed an active social life. His evenings and weekends were divided between spending time smoking and drinking pints of lager with his mates in the pubs, attending home football games at Bramall Lane or joining the travelling support to Sheffield United's away fixtures, and developing his relationship with his girlfriend Debra, who had also left school and was training locally to be a hairdresser.

But then this regular rhythm began to change when one day, whilst at college, he came across an art class in progress and the old urge to pursue his artistic craving surged to the fore. Only this time the craving would not be suppressed and he now thought he knew what he wanted to do – go to art school.

Finding a college in which he felt comfortable was essential to him but that turned out not to be straightforward. Impatient with posers, Sean preferred a more casual style; indeed even the prospect of conforming to a uniform dress code did not appeal. He tried Granville College, but left at the lunch break on the first day having decided that it was 'wanky'. At another college he stuck it out for one week before baling out of there too. His sights then returned to Rotherham College and by September 1979 having dropped clean out of the welding course he signed up for a Fine Art foundation course, again as a day-release student.

Here he found that he did indeed have a talent but, almost imme-diately, he discovered a class of drama students at work and suddenly his attention was engaged in a way that he had never previously known. An ambition to act had not consciously entered his head, yet he now recognised how potent the lure was to him and he took his first step towards formally training as an actor when again – and for the last time – he switched courses.

His drama tutor at Rotherham College, Paul Daniels, explains, 'Because Sean hadn't achieved a high academic standard at school he signed on for the equivalent of an O Level course that embraced drama, English and art and design. It was a full-time course.'

For a lad who had breezed disinterestedly through secondary school it was not easy making the sudden transition back to full-time student and there was a brief breaking-in period, before he felt in his element. His days included group discussions about the individual merits of a variety of authors and playwrights and the ex-trainee welder now began reading the likes of Oscar Wilde. If it seemed incongruous to others, it was not to Sean.

The works of William Shakespeare made a particular impression on him and he has cited his contact with the play *Macbeth* as having provided the first real trigger; the compellingly powerful tangle of ambition and betrayal fascinated him. The adrenalin rush he experienced told him loud and clear that finally he had found his true goal and buoyed up on a gigantic buzz, he lost no time in sharing this discovery enthusiastically with his parents. Because of all their son's past phases, Brian and Rita Bean were neither surprised at, nor convinced by, this new ambition to be an actor and so they greeted it with a degree of gentle caution.

Sean recalled, 'My family thought the fascination with acting was just another fad.' He understood their thinking and will honestly concede that until then, he had been very fickle; going still further, he has also acknowledged that at this stage his parents probably thought him a little odd at times because of his changeability. His mates baited him, too, to some extent, over what they saw as an unusually effeminate preference for such a bloke's bloke. But it all slid off Bean's back.

However, despite this new creative vitality there were certain aspects about Sean that remained unchanged as tutor Paul Daniels recalls, 'He didn't take to studying. He did it, but he was putting up with it with a sort of, "Oh well, I suppose I'll have to do it" attitude. In his English classes he didn't want to be doing this all over again and even when we were studying a play he didn't stand out.

'When it came to the art and design sessions he was the same. He considered it all very interesting, as long as it was for someone else. There was a particular college play, an open air production of *Murder in the Cathedral*, and for this, one of the tutors set some of the students the task of making loads of macramé pieces for the costumes to weight them down a bit, or to be decorative additions. There were balls and balls of string and tons of tiny different beads. Well, I walked into the room where Sean was one of a small group doing this, and he was clearly thoroughly disgusted, because every time he picked up a bead to thread on to the string he would curse, "Fuckin' macramé!"

'But, as soon as Sean was performing he absolutely shone! He had intuitive stage presence. That look of his. He knew instinctively how to link with an audience, to hook them in. I was astounded at the quality and pace of his development, for instance in voice projection and how he tackled scripts. I was amazed at his level of understanding of quite difficult scripts, at the way he worked them out and brought them to life. And the speed at which he learned lines was frankly incredible.

'He clearly worked hard at handling the scripts but somehow it was never obvious. He just shone whilst performing. As a drama teacher, it's only very occasionally that you get a glimpse of someone who is clearly going to go places but the reason that Sean stands out in my memory to this day is, strangely, not because he went on to become famous. It's because I found it so remarkable to watch a young student literally flower in front of my eyes the way Sean did at Rotherham College.'

Sean's approachability and sense of humour also made him fun to be around. Paul continues, 'Sean was very popular. He's one of the lads. There's no side to him and he was also a great improviser – a very quick thinker, and was at ease bouncing verbally off of those people who could give it back. As an example of his sense of humour I have a clear recollection once of setting the class an exercise where I gave them a last line, and they had to work towards that.

'The line was, "Oh no. Not again." So Sean got in a huddle with three other lads then they all lay down on their backs close to each other and began waving their arms and legs in the air, and for the life of me I couldn't work out what on earth it meant, what they were leading up to. It turned out that they were pretending to be tea bags in a teapot anticipating the boiling water. That was Sean. He could be completely off the wall. He was a typical Sheffield lad. His attitude was, "There's the rules. How can I break 'em!" Yet although he was taking the piss out of my exercise, at the same time he was actually doing it.'

Having patently found his niche, Sean began visiting the theatre and so struck was he by the prospect of becoming an actor that he went through a humble phase of thinking that he would be content simply to perform in local rep. He firmly believed that to actively start out seeking fame would be a guaranteed recipe for failure. And in any event, all he aspired to then, he has maintained, was to 'get a script, get up and do some words'. In reality this was a mirage for Bean's focus had seriously sharpened and the newfound sense of direction was driving him with increasing momentum.

One of his first amateur performances came when the college staged a production of *The Owl and The Pussycat*. But it was the very favourable reaction that his appearance elicited in a version of Joseph Kesselring's black farce *Arsenic and Old Lace* that really spurred him on and he could scarcely wait to land a stage role outside the confines of the college.

That goal was reached when he took part in a production of *Cabaret* (the musical which originated from the Christopher Isherwood book *Goodbye to Berlin*) that was staged in September 1980 at the Rotherham Civic Theatre on Catherine Street, a stone's throw from the college. Fellow cast members included Andrew Bates, Graham Cooper, Caroline Maher, Helen Brown and Jill Taylor, and the play was produced by Paul Daniels.

Paul explains, 'In addition to my work at Rotherham College I also directed and produced with the South Yorkshire Theatre for Youth which, at this point, put on an annual production that we would advertise to my students at college. Four students went forward to do *Cabaret* and Sean was one of them.

'He played Herr Schultz, the male role in *Cabaret* that most stands out in people's minds. It's usually played by a short, dumpy man and here was Sean, a tall, thin lad playing this bespectacled Jewish gentleman. It was a very strong dramatic role that required a lot of control because he has to get the audience's sympathies without wallowing in tears and Sean was outstanding. Indeed, he and Caroline Maher, who acted opposite him as Fräulein Schneider, both gave an extremely beautiful, powerful and emotionally intense, yet controlled, performance.

'It was Sean's first, and probably his only, musical role too. He had to sing "The Pineapple Song" but he kind of cheated, because he *performed* the song, in the sense that he got away with half singing, half saying it. It was an excellent production and the commitment all round was well rewarded.'

It certainly exhilarated Sean. Propelled to new heights, his thoughts inevitably zeroed in on applying for a place at drama school. He had known for a long time that if he was ever going to make anything of himself, then he had to be prepared to leave Sheffield. He was also aware that if he was successful in his bid to enter drama school it would be a very big step and in more ways than one, for there was not only himself to consider. He and Debra had been dating for years and it seemed entirely natural when they decided to get married. They set a wedding date for spring 1981.

Equally, the urge to pursue this potential career was compelling and so, also in early 1981, Sean applied to audition at London's Royal Academy of Dramatic Art. He applied to RADA only because that was the one drama school he had heard of and therefore assumed it to be the place where all British actors received their training. Debra clearly understood his needs, because supportively she subsequently accompanied him to London when he went for his audition.

Euan Smith, who became Sean's tutor at RADA, sat on the drama school board that year. He explains, 'An applicant has to do two pieces at his or her audition, one Shakespeare, one modern, before two directors. That's the first round. Then names are forwarded to a panel on which sits the principal and about four directors. It's a step by step process. A shortlist is eventually drawn up and then working from an absurd marking system, far too complicated to even begin to explain, we arrive at our top thirty. I think you can spot talent that early. It's individuality that stands out and Sean made it.'

Shelving his Sheffield accent during his two audition performances of a piece from Shakespeare and the other from Bertolt Brecht, Sean won – from a field of around eleven thousand that year – a scholarship to RADA for a two-year course commencing that summer. He has described the sensation he experienced on opening the prestigious drama school's acceptance letter as feeling as if he was clutching a ticket to another life.

It was undoubtedly a time of major change in his life. On 11 April 1981, six days before his twenty-second birthday, Sean married his nineteen-year-old childhood sweetheart Debra Ann James in a traditional ceremony in the Church of England Parish Church of St Mary in Handsworth. The happy newlyweds, however, were not to have the greatest start to married life. They had barely four months together before having to confront the vital crossroads before them, and it could only be problematic.

Sean's tantalising future lay waiting for him in London, whilst Debra wanted to continue her hairdressing career in Sheffield. She did not want to move South. They must have discussed it exhaustively, but no matter which way it was looked at, there was no scope for a workable compromise; they could only hope that their marriage would survive the separation.

It was a difficult decision, but the harsh reality was that as a drama student in London Sean would have very little money and they could scarcely have managed on Debra's junior hairdressing wage. There was also the question of where they would live. For Sean, it meant a two-year term which required total commitment and an investment of faith in something that had no guaranteed outcome.

Those same uncertain prospects in a notoriously insecure profession worried Sean's parents. They had fully supported him once they had recognised that he was deadly serious about becoming an actor, but still on that summer's day when they waved him off Brian assured his son that his welding job would always be there for him should the career not work out.

There were those in Sheffield who would have been surprised to learn that Sean had got even this far, as Brook Comprehensive teacher Ian Footitt admits, 'The first time I heard of an actor, from Sheffield called Sean Bean I thought, "It can't be him! Yet with a name like that . . .?" It took me so aback because at school he hadn't been motivated by anything. It's amazing how the hell he ever ended up in acting. Certainly the sort of people he knocked about with had not been the kind to end up as actors.'

For tutor Paul Daniels, it was understandably a different matter. 'Knowing that this lad had had a rough start, we were really thrilled that he could come through Rotherham College of Arts and Technology and secure a place in the most prestigious drama school in the world. It was a plus for the staff and has been a great shot in the arm for our students.

'There was one person, when Sean got accepted by RADA, who

felt that he should've finished his Rotherham College course first and got his qualifications. But he certainly wasn't going to do that. And why should he have? Why should he have put up with another year of study, doing stuff that he hated when he had got where he wanted to be? He had won a place at RADA. I was delighted for him. He'd been a thoughtful lad through it all too and it would show in small touches. For instance, after the success of *Cabaret* he and Caroline Maher gave me a small gift which I've still got. It is a mug with a designed handle. I was so surprised and touched because that doesn't happen often.'

In the intervening period between finishing at Rotherham College and starting at RADA, Sean continued to gain experience by appearing with the Rotherham Rep in a production of the Emlyn Williams' play *A Murder Has Been Arranged*. The Rep's Rex Windle who directed the play recalls, 'Sean played the juvenile lead. I had gone to see his mum and dad first to get their permission to use Sean in the play and I got on very well with them. I used to take Sean to rehearsal and home because he didn't have a car and I remember it took me one day to teach him how to fall over the back of a settee. He's a renegade, Sean, but a nice lad and he was good in the play. On stage you've got to have a spark and he's got that spark.'

Rex Windle, however, has trenchant personal views on what Sean went on to do with that spark. He says, 'To me, you are either an actor, or a screen performer. There's a big difference between actors, and TV and bloody film people and I personally think Sean went wrong by going into television and film. The lad has talent.' Nevertheless, Sean's departure for London loomed closer.

Sean was ready to make the break but it was a wrench to leave behind everything he loved in the world – his young bride, his parents, his lifelong friends and his home town. But the fuel injection he needed to help him take that step was a steely determination to succeed and this he had in abundance. He was fully sensitive to all the emotive personal aspects that resulted from his choice to pursue an acting career right then. But it is also true to say that there was an underpinning truth to it all that he recognised and embraced. And speaking of this life-changing moment he later admitted, 'I wanted to get away. I wanted to *be* somebody.'

3

ROUGH DIAMOND

THE ROYAL ACADEMY of Dramatic Art was founded in 1904 and of the many thousands of would-be actors who have passed through its famous portals on Gower Street, the school has spawned some of Britain's best known and loved screen stars.

The class of 1981 would yield its own share of shining lights for Sean's fellow freshmen included Kenneth Branagh, Fiona Shaw, James Wilby, John Sessions, Janet McTeer and Joely Richardson. Sean's enthusiasm to get started had propelled him to RADA, but once in London, among a multitude of strangers by day and alone in a small bedsit at night, he was astonished by the powerful gut-wrenching feeling of homesickness which engulfed him. He had to struggle hard with a strong desire to leave and go back to Sheffield, and this unnerving tussle took him until practically Christmas to conquer.

Another source of initial insecurity surrounded his Yorkshire accent. Personally he is proud of his roots and had no desire to disguise them, as his mother, Rita Bean, neatly illustrated when she recalled, 'When we used to visit Sean at acting college, I was worried about our accent. But he used to tell us to be ourselves.' Professionally, however, he did briefly consider learning to soften the distinctive enunciation. He had no intention of losing his own sound entirely, for Sean to abandon that would have been to let go of an intrinsic part of his make-up. In any event, at least one of his tutors advised against making this sacrifice and instead encouraged Sean to learn received pronunciation; a technique which would enable him to perform in stage classical roles.

In fact, Bean was to become a master at adopting accents, a skill he would use effectively throughout his film and television career, but the issue of his native tongue was later destined to come to the fore often. Like any other actor, off set he reverts to his natural accent. Yet as fame made him a magnet for the Press, several journalists have overdone the emphasis they place on the way the star speaks; something that has come to faintly irk Bean, who points out that the same people do not find it necessary to make a big deal of the way a Welsh, Irish or Scottish actor talks.

This initial self-consciousness over his accent was probably twinned to his preconceived notion that RADA would be peopled with a discomforting proportion of well-heeled sons and daughters of snobbish parentage, but this was one perception that he was pleased to have proved wrong. On the contrary, once he settled in at the drama school he discovered a cosmopolitan mix of people from a variety of backgrounds and circumstances which suited him so well that he ended up enjoying his years there far more than he had anticipated that he would.

For all that, a cloud did hang over his first term and not an entirely unexpected one. In hindsight, it was maybe naive in the circumstances to expect that his marriage to Debra would survive. They were not only a husband and wife who lived many miles apart, more significantly they occupied two different worlds and regrettably it became obvious that those worlds were destined never to merge.

Perhaps helped by the familiarity and sound mutual respect that can best come from having been childhood sweethearts, there were no fireworks though when, tested by these pressures, the break-up of their relationship became inevitable. Instead, their brief marriage disintegrated discreetly on the joint recognition that their individual paths lay in different directions. Reticent to speak about his private life, Sean has uttered few words concerning his first love but he later said of their decision to wed so young, 'It seemed like the right thing to do. Maybe in London it's trendy to marry later but all my pals in Sheffield were getting married.' Their decision to divorce was likewise mutual and amicable.

Like Sean, Debra has never been inclined to broadcast details of the failure of their marriage but she is said to have made mention in a rare comment to one of the local Sheffield newspapers that she considered the reasons as having been firstly, that they had both been very young, and secondly, that they had not even had the chance of establishing a home base together. She would, however, in addition to keeping in touch with her former inlaws, retain a fondness for her ex-husband and has not begrudged his success.

It is one of life's ironies that when she had accompanied Sean to London the previous spring, Debra had actually met the woman who would next capture his heart. Melanie Hill had auditioned at RADA at the same time as Sean.

At seventeen, fellow drama student Melanie's sheer vivacity caught his eye. With tumbling thick hair and curves in all the right places as far as Sean was concerned – he was supposedly knocked out by her amply proportioned breasts – he could scarcely have failed to be attracted to the radiantly infectious smile that mirrored Melanie's twinkling eyes. Also from the North and five years younger than Sean, she was spirited with a lively sense of humour and eager to make her way in the same profession.

Melanie later described their attraction as, 'Whoosh! Love!'. Unsurprisingly, with such mutual chemistry they quickly became an item and there was the added bonus that on neither side did they come to the relationship with a lot of emotional baggage. True Sean had a broken marriage behind him, but Melanie was only his second steady girlfriend, and Sean was the first man in Melanie's life. She believed in fidelity and his equally ingrained steadiness where his lovelife was concerned would be proved over the fifteen years that they remained together.

Despite his happy state of mind with his newfound love, Sean's temper could still be as volatile as a tinder box. It's not something he is proud of, or enjoys, but he once confessed, 'If I go off, I really can't stop then. I have to get it out of me system.' Euan Smith, his tutor at RADA, recalls this side of Sean's personality, 'He could be argumentative, not with me, but with other students. I saw flashes of it. Sean was quite restless at that time and he's not good with untapped energy so there was an edginess to him.'

On one occasion that short fuse landed Bean in trouble with the law. Along with a mate, he had tried to gate-crash a party and when someone refused entry to the two uninvited students by attempting to shut the door in their faces, Sean lost his temper. He has since owned up publicly to the incident and to his violent reaction thus, 'I ended up whacking the guy a couple of times.' The police became involved and Sean was charged with, and subsequently convicted of, the offence of ABH (Actual Bodily Harm) for which he was fined £50.

This aside however, Sean spent his time profitably exploring the full range of dramatic skills and acquiring the tools he would employ as a versatile actor. During the course of this training, the former boxer discovered that the brute strength that lay in his clenched fists, was more than equalled by the finesse of having a cunningly supple wrist. Sean found that he possessed a special flair for swordplay and he became a dazzling fencer, an art for which he would win prizes and one that would stand him in excellent stead for many future roles.

Bean took part in several productions at RADA which embraced the standard raft of Shakespearean plays, including *King Lear, Twelfth Night, Measure for Measure* and *Much Ado About Nothing*, as well as *The Three Sisters* by Anton Chekhov, and a version of the Richard Bissell Broadway play *The Pajama Game*. In 1982, as a second-year student, Sean took on the lead role of R.P. McMurphy in *One Flew over the Cuckoo's Nest*, based on the novel by Ken Kesey, which had, as a feature film seven years earlier, mopped up the five top Oscars. In this stage version Sean stepped into Jack Nicholson's shoes to play the only sane patient in an asylum who inspires his fellow inmates to better express themselves. For his graduation performance Bean played a character called Pozzo in the play *Waiting for Godot* which earned him a Silver Medal.

Reflecting on Sean's years at RADA, Euan Smith's most abiding memory of him is of his personality. Says Euan, 'Sean was a great practical joker, very funny and with a very individual sense of humour. I recall one of the quirkier things he got up to once was when one Friday afternoon after class was over, out of sheer boredom he and another student, Paul Mooney, stood in the pouring rain in London's Tottenham Court Road and tried to sell the space inside a cardboard box to passing motorists. He could be slightly eccentric in his behaviour sometimes. He was also immensely kind and otherwise quiet about the way he went about things. And a team player too, which is a great thing to be for an actor. Sean always struck me as being a great improvisor in life.'

Sean Bean graduated from RADA in April 1983. Now aged twenty-four he was a young man once again poised on the threshold of a new chapter in his life and one which would test his newly acquired abilities and the depth of his commitment. He already had all the desirable physical attributes and a depth of character that was marked by an unusually still quality, and, intriguingly, he radiated a latent raw, edgy energy that gave off an air of unpredictability. This outward stillness came to be matched by an inward watchfulness which, indeed, is part of an actor's stock in trade, but Sean is naturally an observer of life and of the human condition. By this time he would also come to see a degree of arrogance as being a useful tool in any actor's arsenal.

As it happened, a grain or two of arrogance right then might have come in handy for eager though he was to get out there and gain first-hand experience, it was nevertheless a daunting prospect. What undoubtedly smoothed Sean's transition from drama student to facing the real thing was that he would be working under the direction of Euan Smith who was giving Sean, along with a few other newly graduated actors, his first chance.

It was at this juncture that Sean decided to adopt a professional name and he chose to call himself Shaun Behan. Later, he would revert to his real surname and would amend the spelling of his Christian name to Sean. But it was as Shaun Behan that he made his nerve-racking professional acting debut.

He had been cast as Tybalt in a production of the Shakespearean tragedy *Romeo and Juliet*, which was to be performed at the Watermill Theatre in Newbury, Berkshire. After a four-week rehearsal period, the play was scheduled to run from 10–28 May and for this engagement Bean joined a cast that included Gerrard McArthur, Kathryn Hunter, David Maylan and John Levitt. Bean was thrilled to be getting paid as an actor at last – his weekly wage was £70 – and as in all landmark moments it was the tiniest detail that would forever stand out, as was evident when he later gleefully recalled, 'I remember it was a blue wage packet.'

Veteran actor John Levitt who played Juliet's father, Capulet, clearly remembers Sean Bean's debut. He says, 'Tybalt is one of the best parts in *Romeo and Juliet*, and although it's not a big part, it's one in which a young actor can make his mark. Sean was fine in the play. He wasn't exceptional, but remember he was only a matter of weeks out of RADA and this was his first job. He worked very hard at it though.'

Euan Smith recalls, 'What stood out for me about Sean's perform- ance were the sword fights. He and David Maylan were evenly matched and they went at it so ferociously that they used to plainly terrify the audience.'

In addition to evening performances school matinées were staged one afternoon mid-week, as well as on a Saturday. The rest of the time was spent around Bagnor, the picturesque hamlet deep in the country- side about three miles from Newbury racecourse.

Says Levitt, 'It really is an idyllic setting. There is a pub with a water mill and we mostly lived in at The Watermill Theatre. Sean was put up in a separate nearby bungalow along with the other young cast members, many of whom had graduated with him from RADA, so he was in familiar company.'

During this time John noticed several features about Sean's person- ality. 'He was a very unassuming young man and lacking in any airs and graces. He was not at all boastful – actors straight out of drama school are often full of themselves, even if only in order to keep up their confidence levels. But what especially comes to mind is that Sean struck me strongly as having a unique physical look. His blond hair was very short and his looks were quite outstanding, not in the accepted Hollywood hunk mould – not ultra handsome – but in a striking way. I felt that his was a face born for the camera.

'And I must say he was always extremely laid back. He didn't say a lot. Of course, I didn't see him when he had been drinking, but there was nothing showy about him. He has a natural way of talking both on and off stage and is very natural in his actions too.'

Melanie Hill, flush from winning the Vanburgh Award, had also graduated from RADA and would likewise cut her teeth in the shallows of provincial theatre, but for now she was able to join Sean and did so often according to John Levitt. He recalls, 'Sean was very wrapped up with his girlfriend who was around a great deal. If he was not in rehearsal or on stage, he was with Melanie and they were clearly very close. Whenever you saw them, they were always arm in arm.'

Of Sean's subsequent success, John says, 'I've been very impressed at how his career has flourished. He is very truthful in his performances, utterly believable in whatever he does and is never affected in any way. He has used his own accent in quite a lot of things which is good, because he has his own speech rhythms and that always helps to make it very real. He is a very natural actor in my opinion. I remember years later when I saw him in *Lady Chatterley* when he was quite outstanding as Mellors, and thinking, "My goodness – he hasn't changed at all!" '

The production of *Romeo and Juliet* went on a two-week tour of Sweden but Bean's involvement ended on 28 May, after which he was pitched into the rigours of touring in rep when he swapped the cosy rural setting of Newbury for the urban reality of Glasgow. He spent about six months working north of the Border and during this time the company performed at the Citizens' Theatre in the city's Gorbals Street. From 16–24 September 1983 Bean took the role of a journalist in a production of *The Last Days of Mankind*, written just after the First World War by Karl Kraus. The play had been translated and was being directed here by Robert David MacDonald. Fellow cast members included Ciaran Hinds, Lorcan Cranitch and Gary Oldman.

Thereafter, with the same thirty-odd strong company, Sean plunged directly into *Rosenkavalier*, an adaptation of Hugo von Hofmannsthal's *Der Rosenkavalier*, this time directed by Philip Prowse which ran from 30 September to 15 October and in which 'Shaun Behan' is credited as playing an animal seller.

Whilst these early experiences were essential for planing down the rough edges, touring in rep was no picnic. For Bean, this was just the start of living in cheap lodgings that offered the basics and few home comforts. His recollections would centre on having continually to feed ten pence coins into increasingly greedy slot meters to maintain lighting and heating. But he adapted and had no difficulty in filling his spare time.

He had become an avid reader of novels – he is especially attracted to seafaring tales – and of history. Musically he has catholic tastes that range from Madness to Mozart, from Tamla Motown to brass bands and in essence he lived from day to day content, despite the spartan conditions, to be doing what he wanted to be doing.

There would be no fairytale whirlwind to whisk Sean into the spotlight. Hard slog lay ahead, during which time he would pay his dues whilst refining his craft. But he was up for it. He may have once fleetingly entertained the notion of being happy to paddle in the shallows of local theatre, but now it was a different story. Reflecting on those salad days Sean said, 'I had to start at the bottom of the ladder.' Before long, he was voicing, 'I want to be at the top of what I do.'

4

CHALLENGING TIMES

GETTING HIS FEET WET in television became Sean Bean's next ambition. He had by no means left the theatre years behind him, but 1984 would see him make three small screen appearances, including sampling his first experience of being in a TV movie.

His television debut occurred when he secured a bit part playing a character called Lurch in *Punters*. Also known as *Joey and Spansky*, the comedy play, written by Stephen Wakelam, was to be produced by Andrée Molyneaux and directed by Chris Mensul for the BBC. Filming took roughly four weeks at various locations in Doncaster commencing on 5 February and Bean (he had dropped the professional name of Shaun Behan to become Sean Bean) joined a cast which, in support of Mick Ward and Tom Davidson in the leading roles, included among others Tim Barker, Peter Howitt, Janet Dale and Lesley Clare O'Neill.

Set in South Yorkshire in the late 1970s the play is a subtly intricate portrait of two very different teenage gamblers who go into partnership together. Sean crops up in a group scene in a disco, but although he had only a couple of short lines of dialogue both the play's writer and producer remember him. 'I vividly recall that although Sean was in what would turn out to be quite a distinguished little group of actors, he somehow created a lasting impression,' says Andrée Molyneaux.

Writer Stephen Wakelam's impressions were formed earlier. 'When we gathered at one of the BBC's rehearsal rooms in Acton what stood out for me was that although Sean was perfectly pleasant and did exactly what was asked of him, he said almost nothing at rehearsal. He stood out by being so silent! I once worked with Paul McGann years ago and he was exactly the same – couldn't get a word out of him either. I thought that Paul just hadn't wanted to be bothered talking to some wanky writer but I discovered later that he had been scared stiff. That this was Sean's very first television experience maybe explains it in his case. Or, I don't know, maybe he knew that he was better than having only such a small part as this. Peter Howitt, who went on to do *Sliding Doors* with Gwyneth Paltrow, was with Sean in the disco group scene and though his role was slightly bigger, both had bit parts, and yet both Peter and Sean went on to achieve such success. Heaven knows what happened to our two leads and they had been terrific in the roles.'

There is one aspect of Bean's future fame which has surprised Stephen Wakelam. 'I never imagined that Sean would become a sex symbol. It certainly wasn't obvious then. But it's marvellous what has happened to him since.' Filming ended on 1 March 1984 and the seventy-minute *Punters* was transmitted on the BBC later that year, on 27 November.

It was, then, with this minuscule television experience under his belt that around Easter 1984 Bean walked straight into his first made-for-TV film, and in a more substantial role. The movie was *Winter Flight* which, from a screenplay by Alan Janes and directed by Roy Battersby, was an Enigma Production under the aegis of executive producer David Puttnam.

The story revolved around a timid young airman called Mal, played by Reece Dinsdale, who falls in love with Angie (Nicola Cowper), a barmaid working at an RAF station pub nicknamed The Pigs Bar, and with good reason as its clientele are the toughest men on the base. The sensitive hero soon comes up against the worst specimen among these men, Hooker, played by Bean.

Sean's future reputation as a fine screen villain started with this powerful portrayal of a ruthless hard man, but he had not originally been up for the part as the film's director Roy Battersby recalls, 'There are two particular characters, Hooker and his friend Dave. Hooker is a member of the RAF Police on the base. He's also a leading light in the bar culture and is hard through and through. Dave is hard too, but with a soft side and when casting director Marilyn Johnson, who had seen Sean at drama school, introduced me to Sean it was actually with a view to him playing Hooker's friend. Anyway, we saw Gary Olsen for Hooker and Sean for Dave. But when I met them both, I felt strongly that it would work much better the other way round. I took to Sean at once. I immediately knew that he was Hooker.'

Sean comes into his own early in the movie in a disturbingly brutal scene when Hooker beats up the bookish Mal, then filling a bucket with beer, cigarette ends, spit and even urine he scoops up a pint of this gross cocktail and forces the battered young airman to drink from it before pushing the man's head into the bucket. He is an intimidating character who frightens his faithless girlfriend and, according to the director, no one could have brought more authenticity to a character who also festered with class hang-ups.

Roy Battersby explains, 'By this time Thatcherism was well developed in Britain and the film caught something about this big class question. Mal is from South Yorkshire and he sounds that way so Reece played him as being on the side of the people, working class if you like. Hooker is very much a figure who has found a way into that class horror so at his first meeting with Mal he goes right for him and metes out a convincingly awful humiliation. And Sean clearly understood that class rage – I mean that he understood it viscerally. He didn't need anything explained to him. It is sometimes difficult in England to find actors to portray violent people without the character becoming a caricature. But Sean is one of those actors who had a proper life before coming into acting. The result was that he brought an obvious truthfulness to the part and he acted from the centre. He was very scary, I would say immediately powerful in the role.'

Roy elaborates, 'Sean understands what it is to be dangerous. He gives off this wonderful sense that you don't quite know what the guy is going to do next. And that's a tricky thing to do. Some actors can *act* it, but with Sean it's true. And he will go the whole way. He undeniably has a special quality of the kind that is especially true of screen actors. The great ones have always had a big hinterland there, like you're only seeing a piece of him and you know that there's more that you would like to know about. Spencer Tracy had it and Sean has got that mystery quality too. You can never give it to someone. You cannot put it there. But when it naturally exists, the camera sees it and responds to it.'

Sean's scenes are the moodiest and most menacing moments in this otherwise tender tale of first love and his effective handling of them was the perfect foil to the sweet sensitivity from the two lead actors; which was all the more telling for it having been, for all three actors, their début film performance.

And making the film proved to be a happy time, with many light-hearted behind-the-scenes moments. Further into the movie Sean has another major scene during which his volcanic temper erupts. Having suspected that his girlfriend is two-timing him, through a ground floor window in the accommodation block he spies her in bed with her lover Jack, another airman. Enraged, Hooker hot-wires a JCB and bulldozes Jack's car against the window, which brings the military police down on him. He is eventually wrestled viciously out of the cab and on to the ground by an Alsatian police dog. But as co-star Timothy Bentinck, who played Jack, recalls behind the violent explosion on screen, the cast ended up creased with laughter.

'In the script it said that Hooker, driving the JCB, would smash clean through the wall and deposit the car at the foot of the bed and I had to spring up startled and gasp, "My car!" Well they had weakened the wall in advance and Sean rammed the digger at it once. Nothing happened. Twice, three times he did it and still the wall wouldn't break. The girl and I were not inside the room while all this was going on in case the whole building collapsed and, of course, it was filmed from outside, but the wall just refused to give way. So they decided, instead, to have Sean just smash the car against the window.'

He goes on, 'It's a weird thing. You meet an actress and it's a case of, "Hello, how do you do? Let's get into bed then!" Well on *Winter Flight*, I am not kidding, it was the coldest bed imaginable, in a *freezing* hut in between a perfectly freezing pair of sheets with just one thin RAF blanket and you're supposed to get all friendly, snuggle up and pretend to be making love. Because it was being filmed from the outside, we were alone in the room, which is very strange because normally you're surrounded by a camera crew, which takes away from it being in any way real. Anyway, we couldn't hear the word, "Action" so it was decided to put a walkie-talkie in the room and there was this tentative tap on the door, like someone didn't want to disturb us. We were yelling, "Well come in! Just what do you think we are doing in here, for God's sake?" Still, this red-faced guy rushed in to leave the walkie-talkie and self-consciously rushed out, as if he was intruding on us! We were shouting after him, "Hoy! We're not up to anything!" Through the walkie-talkie everyone outside could hear all this and by now Sean and Reece were rolling around on the ground, absolutely pissing themselves with laughter!'

The productive working environment contributed to bringing out the best in everyone. Roy Battersby explains, 'Sean was well prepared in the sense that he had done all his homework. But I think at that time – and so early in his career – it struck me most that he had guts. Although he was new and felt understandably nervous, still he had the courage to open up to the living moment on set in front of the camera and to respond to it. Now that takes a lot of nerve because it's dangerous. If everything is safely worked out in advance, then you know your trousers are not going to fall down, as it were. But Sean would take a chance. He would pick up on a nuance which meant that he had suddenly discovered a different way of expressing the scene. He had an insight into detecting that moment and it takes bottle to go along with it.

'The other actor I have worked with who is also like that, is Robbie Coltrane. Actors like Sean and Robbie might do two takes and they are okay, but not magical. So they will do another and he might say a line in a different way. Or he hears the same line but with an implication that hadn't seemed to have been there before and it has the effect of correspondingly bringing a new dimension to his response. It's a continuous two-way process between actor and director when it works, but it is also a process that can leave an actor very vulnerable, especially as it may affect the outcome of the whole scene.'

Clearly actor and director had found a rapport. Battersby says, 'The interesting thing is that Sean was excellent at playing this fero-ciously tough guy when in reality he's a total sweetheart. He was smashing to work with, warm and straightforward. There is no bullshit about Sean. It was the same thing as him not being afraid to be vulnerable on set. Off set, if he was concerned or hadn't got it all quite worked out, he would come to me and say as much. He also made me laugh. He doesn't tell jokes as such, but he tells scurrilous stories that are just hilarious. He's a good man.'

That they had made a good film also became clear quite quickly, although one last-minute change had to be made. The director recalls, 'Originally its working title was *The Big Surprise*, based on the fact that Angie is already pregnant when Mal meets her and although they intended passing the baby off as his, the plan goes awry when the baby is born a black child. Then we tested the film with a select audience in one of the preview cinemas in Reading. We showed it with the music and everything, but no title. Everyone seemed to like it then right at the end a guy said, "Oh, by the way, what's it called?" We told him and he promptly asked, "What is the big surprise?" At which point we fell about laughing, as it dawned on us that there could be no surprise big enough to justify it being called that. We did a rethink and because it was set in the RAF in winter and there was a flight in it we decided to call it *Winter Flight*.'

The final product was also a testament to what could be done on a modest budget. 'We did some extraordinary things, considering,' says Roy. 'We had to film base training exercises and raids on the airfield and we were always up against the clock. We shot it at the Duxford RAF Museum airfield in Cambridgeshire and at another airfield in Bedfordshire where we got no cooperation from the RAF at all. But luckily there were some American fighter planes on exercise there at the time. We spoke to the Tower, who very kindly talked to a couple of the American pilots and they did some landings for us, some tricky touch-downs and so on.

'Even though it was all done in an incredibly short space of time I had a very good director of photography, Chris Menges, who won Oscars for both *The Killing Fields* and *The Mission* and had been the brilliant cinematographer on *Kes*. So that was a bonus. In fact, I was surrounded by wonderful people who all understood that we were working on a tight budget.' *Winter Flight* was first aired on Channel 4 television on 20 December 1984. 'It did extremely well,' says Roy

Battersby. 'David Puttnam was very proud of it, it also sold well abroad and the critics liked it, which helps.'

As summer 1984 rolled on Bean returned to the theatre, this time in the joint lead role of Jonathan in the William Douglas Home stage play *David and Jonathan*. Performed at The Redgrave Theatre in Farnham, Surrey and directed by Stephen Barry, it was scheduled to run from 12–30 June. The two-act play about a homosexual wedding was set in the vestry of a Hampshire village church. Sean was one of a small cast which included John McAndrew, co-starring as the epony-mous David, George Waring, Suzie Cerys, Mike Shannon, Michael Cotterill and Charlotte Attenborough. Veteran actor George Waring, who starred as the vicar in the play, remembers this three-week engage-ment.

'William Douglas Home dealt with the topic quite bravely but not, I felt, altogether satisfactorily. It was a very good production though with an absolutely fabulous set – almost like a film set, with the pulpit and that whole part of a church. Sean was splendid in it and although these were early days and he was still very much feeling his way forward in the business, it was obvious that he was going to go places. You can usually tell. Privately though, he didn't care too much for the play. It didn't appeal to him, but he didn't show it. On stage, he gave it everything.'

George describes Sean as being a good company player as well as being good company socially. He says, 'Usually with a play like this you are so knackered at the end of each day that there's not much scope for a social life, but we did have many a boozy time in the pubs. Sean loves a pint and although in lots of ways he is very retiring, he likes joining in with things.'

There was one occasion on which Sean was not especially retiring, though, when he wanted to take part in a particular extra-curricular activity as George Waring recalls, 'Sean is a man who has strong views on things, which he quietly expresses. He's not a loud man. However, he managed to get us thrown out of the prestigious Farnham Tennis Club. The tennis court literally adjoins the theatre and two or three of us decided we would like a game. I got hold of the coach and managed to arrange for a couple of games. Sean said he'd like to come too.

'We all turned up in our conformist whites but Sean wouldn't wear them and he showed up dressed, what can only be described, as a scruff bag. I don't know if he was making a point, or what, but the guy in charge at the club promptly shrieked, "I can't allow *him* on the court!" He was a stickler for the rules and he insisted, "Either he leaves, or you will all have to go!" '

Showing solidarity, the actors all left. Such élitism was like a red rag to a bull to Sean and he did not mince his words in reaction to this edict. According to George, 'Sean said, "If he wants to behave like that, then fuck him!" Of course, I tackled him about it. Part of me was with him, but then again none of the rest of us appreciated being denied the chance to play and I told Sean, "That's all very well, but you've just lost us all the bloody game!" I must say, he was very regretful afterwards.' It wasn't held against him though by his friends and later they all ended up laughing about the incident.

A gala performance on the second night, attended by Princess Margaret, had been a success. Says Waring, 'The charity do was a big event with important theatre critics there, as well as a host of notables. The play went down extremely well and I think Princess Margaret really liked it. The whole cast was introduced to her after the show. But I don't know what Sean felt about performing before royalty – I didn't ask him!'

When his stint at The Redgrave Theatre came to an end, it would be several weeks before Sean's next assignment which saw him appear in a small role in a new police drama called *The Bill*.

Created by Geoff McQueen and directed by John Michael Phillips for Thames Television, this fifty-minute episode called *Long Odds* was the fourth in the first series of what would become a long-running show. Bean's character, Horace Clark, was a shifty looking leather-jacketed bovver boy who was up to no good and when he joined the cast and crew at various London locations over two weeks in September, it reunited him briefly with his *Winter Flight* side-kick Gary Olsen who played PC Dave Litten. When *Long Odds* went out on the ITV network on 6 November 1984 it completed Sean's hat trick of television appearances that year and, indeed, he had to be content with seeing the fruits of his labour on screen for work had again dried up. Over the next couple of years he would experience barren spells, but he never considered packing it in and returning to the 'normal' job awaiting him in Sheffield. During this time Bean declared, 'There are often bad times when you can't get work, but I think I've made the right choice.'

The saviour proved to be the theatre and from early 1985 through into summer Bean took to treading the boards once again. After a lean winter, it geed him up to have a busy time stretch before him, starting in a revival of the Jean Genet play *Deathwatch*. This version was a new translation by the playwright Nigel Williams for the Foco Novo Theatre Company and Sean played Lederer, one of two petty criminals who vie for the attention of a third cellmate, a murderer played by Vincenzo Ricotta.

As Lederer, Bean once again portrayed a nasty jealous type who this time victimises his fellow petty crook Mackie (Jimmy Chisholm). Gary Lilburn played the part of the prison warder. This powerful four-man play was a suffocatingly intense drama, seething with malevolence and sexual tension, all moulded carefully by director Roland Rees to produce raw, incisive performances that attracted many favourable reviews as the touring production, from its opening night on 7 February at the Birmingham Repertory Theatre Studio, moved around the country and ended up at the Young Vic Theatre in London, where it ran from 18 April to 4 May.

Sean remained in the theatre, moving on to take part in a triple bill at the Royal Court Theatre Upstairs in London's Sloane Square. The three productions, all directed by Simon Curtis, were *Who Knew McKenzie* by Brian Hilton, *Stalemate* by Emily Fuller and *Gone* by Elizabeth Krechowiecka in which he played the characters of Terry, an estate agent and Arf, respectively. Between 26 June and 20 July 1985, along with the five other cast members Hetta Charnley, Alan Leith, Elizabeth Bell, Lesley Sharpe and Jonathan Phillips, Sean would go on to complete sixteen performances of this triple bill.

In addition to widening his experience and honing his communication skills, overall these many months touring in rep would be an all-round education for Sean, and it was also a time during which he committed his fair share of gaffes, or suffered some of the familiar ignominies. At the Vanbrugh Theatre in London he realised too late that he had come on stage with his trouser flies conspicuously undone. During a performance of the already bleak *Deathwatch* in Herefordshire the lights failed plunging everyone into pitch darkness, and on at least one occasion Sean fell foul of an uncontrollable fit of the giggles. In a performance of a play called *The Country Wives*, Sean unexpectedly lost the plot and brought the scene to a premature close, thereby throwing the rest of the cast into temporary chaos.

Now that he was working on stage so much, attending the theatre for pleasure had tailed off. Whatever time Sean had to socialise, he wanted to spend it doing something which gave him freedom of mobility – not to be a prisoner in a seat for a set length of time – and preferably somewhere that allowed him to enjoy a pint.

Life in London, now with live-in lover Melanie Hill who was like-wise concentrating on building a career, was still a period of some adjustment for Sean. To Bean there was a discernible difference in personality between some of the people he found himself among and that of his friends back home in Sheffield. He would say in general terms of Southerners, 'People aren't as down to earth.' The links with his family and friends up North remained strong, however, and some-times a mate visited him in London and they would go to a football match together like old times; Sean also tried not to miss Sheffield United's important home games.

With a strong work ethic, though, he was keen to get back in harness and in the ten days following the end of his run in the triple stage bill, Bean was concentrating on preparation for his next role as Terry Donlan in the medical drama *The Practice*. Granada Television were aiming to emulate the Australian drama *A Country Practice* and of the thirteen, fifty-minute episodes made, Sean appeared in two – *I Can Handle It* and *The Tragedy of Heroin* – shown on 13 and 20 June 1986 as part of the second series.

Filming for the two-parter took place between 1 and 28 August at the television company's Manchester studios under the stewardship of directors Pedr James and Dave Richards, with producer Sita Williams also at the helm. As Terry Donlan, Sean's task was to portray an anxious young father living in deprived conditions and with a domestic drama to handle under pressure. And the show's producer remembers his performance well.

'Sean was relatively new to television then but already it was clear that there was something exciting about him. It was a tough, but sympathetic role. His was a deprived family, living in poor conditions and as Terry, Sean had to fight Social Services vigorously. Yet no matter how intense he became, you never lost sympathy for him and this is something I think that Sean has carried with him throughout his career. He conveys that there is an underlying goodness there, some-where. Even when he is portraying a character you ought not to like, he makes something about that character attractive and thereby brings to his portrayal an understanding of why he is as he is, which has the effect that even if the viewer cannot like what he is doing, they cannot entirely bring themselves not to like him a little.'

She goes on, 'Sean already had all that he needed to become the star he is today. He is talented, good-looking and was extremely nice to work with, yes. But he also has quiet strength and charisma. Very few English actors have the kind of charisma that it takes to make them a star. They can be fine actors but lack just that certain something that sets them apart. But Sean has always had that extra ingredient of screen presence that draws people to his character and makes you want to watch him.'

Bean was obviously leaving in his wake a strongly favourable impression with directors and producers as, steadily, he paved the way towards his future success. An important step in that journey took place when Sean set about making his feature film début.

On the strength of seeing Bean's performance in *Deathwatch*, the British director Derek Jarman invited him to audition for one of the main parts in *Caravaggio*, a film centring on the life of the Italian baroque painter Michelangelo Merisi Caravaggio who died a pauper in Tuscany in 1610.

Written by Jarman and produced by Sarah Radclyffe, getting the film off the ground had not been easy. The director often worked with homosexual themes and was a highly controversial figure – he once described himself as emitting 'a whiff of sulphur' – and two of his earlier films, *Jubilee* and *Sebastiane*, had been condemned in the Winston Churchill Obscenity Bill debates as examples of precisely what British citizens should not be exposed to. Dismissive of these charges, Jarman had flared, 'If I didn't exist, then Mary Whitehouse and Winston Churchill would have had to invent me.'

Nevertheless, it had proved to be a struggle to get backing for a film of a seventeenth-century painter's life about which existing documentation made for salacious reading and *Caravaggio* had been a mighty seven years in pre-production; lost years, Jarman dubbed them. Eventually, the British Film Institute stepped in and bankrolled the entire project, but to the restricted tune of £475,000. Not unnerved by the shoestring budget, Jarman maintained, 'Films don't need money, they need minds.'

He certainly had much to exercise his brain, for problems continued when the script required several re-writes before finally the six-week shoot began on 2 September 1985. Doubtless due to the small budget there would be no exterior shots or location filming. The entire movie would be filmed in a large derelict warehouse on the Isle of Dogs, near to London's Limehouse Studios where production designer Christopher Hobbs had built incredible sets which cleverly recreated scenes in Caravaggio's paintings.

The large assembled cast fused fresh young blood with the stability of experience, and brought together the combined talents of Nigel Davenport as Marchese Giustiniani, Michael Gough as Cardinal Del Monte, Robbie Coltrane to play Cardinal Scipione Borghese and Jonathan Hyde as Baglione, among others.

The three key roles were filled by Nigel Terry in the lead role of Caravaggio, Tilda Swinton as Lena, the prostitute lover of Sean's character, Ranuccio Thomasoni. Jarman had video-taped the auditions and in Bean's case he had liked the degree of self-contained distance that he had detected about the actor's demeanour during the moments when he was not performing.

As Ranuccio Thomasoni, Sean had been entrusted with the portrayal of the young, bisexual streetwise hustler whom Caravaggio hires to pose as a model for his painting 'The Calling of St Matthew and the Saint's Martyrdom'. An intense and violent relationship develops between the artist, his model and the model's lover, one of the consequences of which is that Lena is found floating in the River Tiber, and Ranuccio is arrested for her murder. Caravaggio passionately petitions the Pope for clemency for Thomasoni, but when his lover is released and boasts that he had indeed murdered Lena, the artist slits Thomasoni's throat and spends the next four years evading the law.

Bean liked the filmmakers' simplistic approach; the film's somewhat spare script, shot through with expletives and one-liners, meant also that it was short on dialogue and placed more emphasis on action which Sean always prefers.

In his film début he also photographed well. One of the most unusual aspects of *Caravaggio* was the deployment of 'living pictures' where one or more of the cast posed silent and motionless against a particular Christopher Hobbs' set in order to represent a scene in a specific painting. In one striking shot a near naked Sean, wearing only a loin cloth and a headband, stands frozen, sword in hand showing off his tall, lean but tautly muscled physique.

The use of these 'living pictures' was one of the ways in which the central pivot of the film, turning on a tale of jealousy, murder and a triangular love affair, was given a unique treatment. The director explained, 'The narrative is grounded in painting, which is a very silent occupation. The actual paintings themselves are placed, constrained and silent, although there are violent moments in them too.'

To recreate the dramatic contrasts of light and shade, redolent of Caravaggio's work, required the skills of the accomplished cinematographer Gabriel Beristain whose cinematic use of chiaroscuro was so impressive that he subsequently won the Silver Bear award for Cinematography and Visual Style for *Caravaggio* at the Berlin Film Festival.

Gabriel Beristain explains, 'Michelangelo de Caravaggio invented chiaroscuro and many followed his style. I followed his lighting. I studied it, analysed it and finally I let my instinct work. In those days it required careful understanding to use its characteristics properly, but working very close to Chris Hobbs and by shooting several tests I managed to make my Fuji Film a tremendous tool. Chiaroscuro was a theme, a metaphor for the soul of the painter and a vehicle for Derek's poetry.'

Of Sean's first role portraying a bisexual, Gabriel has this to say, 'Sean was incredibly committed to the role of Ranuccio and he gave a flawless performance. He was in control of his physicality and his emotions, so he knew when to give that little extra and when to keep it back. His role was a tough one, a wild horse, and one that needed a strong actor to portray such a complex man, without giving deceiving hints, or taking anything over the top.

'He obviously approached the role of this bisexual rascal who was a powerful boxer and, to the other extreme, a handsome superb model, with great respect. And the demands on Sean were huge – from posing to fighting, from taking coins with his mouth from Nigel Terry's mouth to seducing Tilda, from showing masculinity and bravado to a refined homosexuality. For me, Ranuccio Thomasoni was Sean Bean's masterpiece.'

Beristain's other abiding memory of working with Sean was what he called Bean's complete commitment to his craft and an enormous desire to learn. 'I remember the scene where his character is killed. Sean would observe the stuntman's explanations and then would be perfect with his reactions. He was always polite, obliging and a real professional. He and I both had a little problem with each other's accent, yet even in the complex fist-fighting and knife-fighting scenes in which the actor has to interact with, and be very aware of, the camera, Sean proved that in spite of his little film experience that he would become a consummate screen actor. Sean and I, behind the camera, metaphorically danced in perfect choreography. He led and led well. He got my immediate respect.'

Gabriel says of director Derek Jarman's work on his long-awaited film, 'We were his makers and we knew very well what to do. Derek did not need to talk too much, his presence sufficed. He was the real artist, we were the craftsmen. It was magical. Derek saw the sets, the costumes, my lighting, the acting and tears would come to his eyes. Nothing dramatic, but simply and elegantly Derek let us know that we had managed to give life to his dream. Everybody there believed in

Derek and everybody was underpaid! But I have never experienced a closer collaboration in any film set I have worked on.'

For his part veteran respected actor Michael Gough remembers the way in which no one stood on ceremony whilst making this film. 'I arrived early one day and a paint brush was put in my hand and I had to paint a flat [a bit of scenery].' The entire process had been different from the start as Michael explains, 'When I first met with Derek in his flat, we didn't talk much about *Caravaggio* or acting. We talked about painting and the art of creation.'

Of working on the movie and Sean's performance in particular Michael declares, 'Sean gave a wonderful performance. He is a brave and totally honest actor. I think we all enjoyed working on *Caravaggio*. Derek Jarman chose us because we are who we are, not just actors playing weird people. So apart from choreographing a scene, he encouraged us to go for it, no fussing with inflections or motivations. He trusted us to *be*. Though I'm sure many of us cried for help occasionally and he would help. We were essentially more than a team.'

The ninety-three-minute *Caravaggio* opened at *The Lumière* in London's West End on 24 April 1986, followed two months later by its general cinema release. Considering the many obstacles it had overcome Derek Jarman pronounced himself pleased with the final result and critically it faired well enough. *Halliwell's Film Guide* called it, 'A classic for the gay crowd, something of a mystery for everyone else.' Whilst *Variety* praised, 'It rises above its financial restrictions to prove that less can be a lot more.'

After filming wrapped on *Caravaggio* in mid-October, Sean Bean was back recording a bit part for television. He was contracted to shoot two brief scenes in the children's adventure film *Exploits at West Poley*. Adapted by James Andrew Hall from the Thomas Hardy novel *Our Exploits at West Poley*, to be produced by Pamela Lonsdale and directed by Diarmud Lawrence the story, set in Somerset 1850, follows the tale of two boys whose antics in diverting an underground stream inadvertantly disrupt the lives of the residents of two nearby villages.

In this TV movie Sean, as Scarface, makes just two fleeting appearances. Filming took place between 7 October and 1 November 1985 at locations which ranged from the Chilterns to Mapledurham, near Reading, to Woodstock, Iver Heath and finally Elstree Film Studios at Borehamwood and Sean was needed for two and a half weeks.

Producer Pamela Lonsdale remembers, 'Sean had all of six lines to say – a tiny part – and the latter of his two scenes was when there was a confrontation at a farmhouse. Scarface was from East Poley and the people of West Poley didn't like their neighbours much but brief though his appearance was, Sean looked so right in the role. He also did a marvellous Dorset accent. He's a very good-looking young man and not pretty. His looks are incredibly strong which means, of course, that he can be perfectly cast as the nasty.'

Bean's looks also caught the eye of the scriptwriter, James Andrew Hall. He says, 'Because of his tough-guy looks, Sean is not often credited with the sensitivity he brings to a part. Although *Exploits at West Poley* was an early outing in his career it was quite obvious, even then, that he possessed that indefinable quality that would mark him out. There can be half a dozen actors jostling for attention on the screen, but one's eyes are always drawn to Sean Bean. He also has, importantly, and in my opinion it is quite rare for an actor, the added quality of stillness.'

Something that would hallmark Bean throughout his career would prove to be his accommodating spirit of uncomplaining cooperation. Pamela Lonsdale says, 'He was just poised for bigger things and yet he was very happy to take such a small role. We had such a lot to do. Time was so tight that we all worked flat out and had very little time to relax, but Sean was a delightful man to work with. All the cast and crew liked him.'

Exploits at West Poley went on to win first prize at the Portugal Film Festival and second prize at the Chicago Film Festival but Sean had a long wait to see the results of his latest, albeit brief, endeavours for the film took nearly five years to surface on British screens before it was eventually shown on ITV on 31 August 1990.

As 1985 drew to a close, having over the previous twenty-four months chalked up experience in three mediums of his craft, Sean was at something of a crossroads in his career. It was still early days and he continued to be conscious of the threatening uncertainty inherent in acting. In one sense, then, it came as a relief when, after undergoing a series of auditions, at the beginning of 1986 he landed a contract with the prestigious Royal Shakespeare Company. Stage work may not be Sean Bean's first love, but this at least was guaranteed employment; it also mapped out his next eighteen months or so.

5

NEW HORIZONS

ANOTHER ANCHOR in Sean Bean's world stemmed from his stable love life. After four years, he and Melanie Hill remained unwaveringly committed to one another; bolstered by the compatibility that came from an understanding of the nature of the business into which they were individually making inroads on a shared dream of achieving success.

In early 1986 they lived in a rented bedsit in London's Tufnell Park where Sean enjoyed reading, watching his favourite soaps on television and indulging his original love, painting. This was to be the year in which Melanie would achieve her first television exposure when, as Hazel Redfern, she joined the cast of the comedy drama series *Auf Wiedersehen, Pet*, about a squad of English builders contracted to work in Düsseldorf. As for Sean, *Caravaggio* was to be released in April, as was his television appearance in *The Practice* two months later, but before all that, his contract with the Royal Shakespeare Company commenced in March, taking him for the first time to William Shakespeare's birthplace, Stratford-Upon-Avon, where rehearsals got under way.

The three main productions in which Sean would be performing were the ever-popular standards, *Romeo and Juliet*, *A Midsummer Night's Dream* and *The Fair Maid of the West*. This was Bean's second run at *Romeo and Juliet*, only this time he was to take the lead role, partnered by Dublin-born actress Niamh Cusack.

Unlike her stage lover she came from a theatrical background; her sisters Sinead and Sorcha are actresses, while her father was the veteran stage and screen star Cyril Cusack, and in the previous year she had scored a hit in Stratford as Desdemona in *Othello*. Limbering up to take to the stage as Shakespeare's most famous young hero, though, Bean was not daunted; in fact, he and Niamh were to strike up a good working affinity.

Director Michael Bogdanov's version of *Romeo and Juliet* would be taking a contemporary approach to the story of the powerful feuding families of sixteenth-century Italy and the production included motorbikes, denim jeans, flick knives, rock music and roller skates. Bean acknowledged that such deviation from convention carried its own risks but believed that it would work as, nearing his twenty-seventh birthday, he faced the responsibility of epitomising all the adolescent anguish and mercurial passions of the tragic swashbuckling youth aged a decade younger.

For actors it is normally a relief to get through the big event of opening night not having fluffed their lines or collided with either co-stars or stage props. But nerves escaped Sean. Determined not to buckle under pressure, he stayed in command, believed he would cope and actively looked forward to the first performance.

Romeo and Juliet's opening night at the 1,500-seat Royal Shakespeare Theatre was on 8 April 1986 when Bean and Cusack were supported by actors Michael Kitchen, Robert Demeger and Richard Moore, among others. Sean already possessed an inherent ability to exhibit predatory flair and dressed in a leather jacket and sporting an earring, his fierce features and untamed look brought added spice to the oh-so familiar role.

Contrary to his expectations, Bean would enjoy portraying Romeo because it allowed him the scope to run a complete range of emotions. He had been forced, too, to review his previous perception of this character and was much happier to have discovered that Romeo – as Bean put it – had 'quite a lot of bottle'.

The nerve shown in presenting such a controversial production of this classic tragedy did not, however, find universal favour. Reviewing this opening night for the *Birmingham Post*, J.C. Trewin criticised the actors' voices as being generally unappealing. Niamh Cusack's voice he called 'intermittently shrill'. One of Michael Kitchen's speeches, he felt, was delivered at 'dictation speed'. And of Sean Bean's ability to express certain lines Trewin stated, 'At present he lacks the vocal technique.' Yet Peter McGarry for the *Coventry Evening Telegraph* would predict for the play's two young leads, 'Stardom is surely just a stone's throw away.'

The second of the three productions, *A Midsummer Night's Dream*, was also performed at the Royal Shakespeare Theatre and opened on 8 July. Directed by Bill Alexander, it was also given a contemporary handling and Sean, in the role of Robin Starveling, with his hair slicked back off his brow and behind his ears, wore a sober three piece suit, collar and tie. It was only for the third production that he donned traditional period garb.

The Fair Maid of the West had been written in two separate parts penned several years apart by one of William Shakespeare's contemporaries, dramatist Thomas Heywood. Trevor Nunn – who later directed a string of colossally successful stage musicals including *Starlight Express*, *Aspects of Love*, *Cats* and *Chess* – had the job of staging the original play together with its sequel rolled into one, and of trying to make that as seamless as possible.

The story, set in 1597, revolves around the heroine Bess Bridges, a virtuous maid who keeps a West Country tavern and who falls in love with Spencer, a wealthy young gentleman. When he is forced to flee the country and is subsequently presumed dead she sets off to bring his remains home, only to be happily reunited with him when he turns out to be still very much alive. Nunn's riotous production brimmed with zest and performing opposite actress Imelda Staunton as Bess, Sean in the role of the handsome hero was joined this time by Paul Greenwood, Joe Melia, Donald McBride and Pete Postlethwaite.

It was in this play that Sean, dressed in Elizabethan doublet and hose, was visually at his most arresting. His flattering soft feathery hairstyle was offset by his hawklike features; his prominent cheekbones etched above a strong jawline standing out in stark relief and affording him a dynamically dramatic look. *The Fair Maid of the West* was staged at The Swan, the new, much smaller theatre that stood next door to the Royal Shakespeare Theatre and which had for years been the RSC's rehearsal room. Opening night was 23 September 1986.

Sean's London performance in *The Fair Maid of the West* would impress many including Alex Norton, an actor with whom he would go on to work twice. Alex recalls, 'I had gone with some friends to the Mermaid Theatre to see this play and that turned out to be the first time I saw Sean. He was fantastic in the part. This guy suddenly just bounded on to the stage and took command. He was brilliant at all the swashbuckling stuff too and I took note of him.'

Sean performed in these three productions until January 1987 when the Stratford run came to an end. The RSC were to take the productions north to Newcastle-Upon-Tyne for one month. But before that, Sean notched up another brief television appearance when the short film *Samson and Delilah* was aired on Channel 4 on 3 January.

Made three years earlier, the mystery, based on a story by novelist D.H. Lawrence, was produced by James Scott and directed by Mark Peploe, who had also co-written the screenplay with Frederick Seidel. In twenty-four minutes it told of a stranger turning up in a Cornish coastal village during the First World War who is suspected of being the German spy then rumoured to be in the district. It starred Bernard Hill, Lindsay Duncan, Vicki Masson and Patrick Jordan. Bean's part was a character called simply Billy and *Samson and Delilah* was the second short he had appeared in.

The other was a ten-minute offering called *The Loser* in which Bean is a small-time pool shark called Rod. A Wolfpack Production, again for Channel 4, scripted by Brian Boak and filmed on location at the Edmonton Pool Hall in North London, it briefly followed the aspirations of Geoffrey, played by Phil Daniels, who hopes to break his losing streak in life by defeating Rod. In it a very young looking Sean Bean in black T-shirt and smoking a cigarette spends his time stooped over the pool table, cue in hand.

In early 1987 the RSC staged their three plays at different venues in Newcastle including the People's Theatre and the Tyne Theatre between 9 February and 14 March. The opening nights for each of the plays were: *The Fair Maid of the West* on 9 February, *Romeo and Juliet* on 17 February and *A Midsummer Night's Dream* on 3 March.

The Fair Maid of the West, in particular, went down well in Geordie land with its labyrinthine plot of intrigue, lust and adventure. The wealth of comic performances led one reviewer to hail it, 'Nothing short of a five star, 22-carat success.' And while plaudits rained down all round, Bean came in for special praise. One critic cried, 'Sean Bean carries off the role of hero with aplomb.' Whilst Newcastle's *Evening Chronicle* critic went so far as to declare, 'Sean Bean is the Errol Flynn of the piece.'

When the company left Tyneside in mid-March they headed to London for their scheduled run in the capital which commenced at the Barbican Theatre where, one year on from the first performance of Michael Bogdanov's production of *Romeo and Juliet*, the play continued to attract a mixed reception.

The Independent's theatre critic Peter Kemp illustrated this when he wrote that in many ways the play responded very well to the contemporary treatment, but that he objected to the text having been, in his view, savagely slashed. The upshot to Kemp's review was that the director had turned the tragedy into a bitter satire and of its two leads he complained, 'Cusack manages a performance of some subtlety, but is weak on passion. Bean, though, has hardly a glimmering of what the role requires.' Throughout his career, just as Sean has not let glowing praise go to his head, neither has he ever felt insecure enough to be hurt by attacks and it is doubtful if he gave critics' views more than a passing glance.

His RSC period was moving into its latter stages and it had not made a great impression on Sean. His RADA tutor Euan Smith can sympathise. He states, 'I don't think Sean felt that the RSC period had been very helpful to him, but in that he is not alone. I've known some actors to equate a stint with the RSC with doing National Service. It's also not easy to act on the Stratford stage. One actor memorably described it as being like trying to sing Mozart in a wind tunnel.'

Sean was certainly not overawed by the experience, lukewarmly he once described his time with the RSC as 'all right for a while', but he ventured to point out that the downside of this kind of institution is that it can isolate an actor. 'You begin to think you're the centre of the universe,' he said.

There are those who class stage work as touching base but Sean finds no particular draw towards treading the boards. During those

many months he had had some good times and the same isolation that
he considered to be a threat, also produced a positive benefit when the
close-knit atmosphere helped forge long-lasting friendships as Sean
found when he became mates with the accomplished actor Pete
Postlethwaite, who would later feature with Sean in *Sharpe*.

That said, over time Bean had become very alive to the tedium of
repetition. It is something that actor David Troughton, who was at the
RSC at the same time as Sean and who would also later appear in
Sharpe, understands. 'In the theatre you rehearse a lot for a particular
play, then perform it in the evening. In films, you do very little
rehearsing and are filming all day. It's totally different and it's not to
everyone's taste.'

There were occasions when Sean would cut things a bit fine, as
once when he went off during his free time to watch Sheffield United
play Leeds United at Elland Road in Leeds and he managed to get
back for that night's performance with scarcely ten minutes to spare.
The fact that it was the contemporary *Romeo and Juliet* saved his
bacon because it was easy to dress quickly. The close shave, though,
owed everything to the depth of his commitment to his favourite football team; it was not a lack of professional commitment to the play.

As summer 1987 wore on Sean chalked up another two milestones. The first of which was when he returned to Newcastle-Upon-
Tyne to make his first biggish film appearance and this time in a
mainstream movie which had been partly American financed.

The movie was the romantic thriller *Stormy Monday*, written and
directed by Mike Figgis and produced by Nigel Stafford-Clark. Born
in Kenya, Figgis had been raised from boyhood in Newcastle and after
a brief flirtation with rock music had entered the world of experimental theatre before turning to films in 1984. When the Moving
Picture Company invited him to submit feature film ideas he came up
with a tale of crooked property dealing along Newcastle's tough waterfront and the classic situation of one jazz club owner being prepared to
hold out by refusing to sell to a shady American businessman. The
romantic angle comes in when the Yank's girlfriend, a waitress, begins
an affair with a young drifter who had become embroiled in the iffy
goings-on and was on the side of the jazz club owner.

The project was funded partly by Film Four International and British Screen, but a chunk of American money came courtesy of the Atlantic Entertainment Group and when casting began for the film's four key figures, Mike Figgis made three trips to Los Angeles. The upshot was that he landed the services of Tommy Lee Jones, who would later win an Oscar for his bravura performance in *The Fugitive*, and Melanie Griffith, whose breakthrough role in *Working Girl* secured her an Oscar nomination. Figgis' elation was evident when he described this unlooked-for bonus as being like Christmas Day.

While Jones assumed the role of the gangster businessman Francis Cosmo, and Griffith that of his mistress Kate, the part of Finney, the moody owner of a murky jazz joint called The Key Club, went to rock star Sting; an appropriate choice for not only was the singer from Wallsend, just outside Newcastle but, before forming the 1970s' band Police, his first foray into music had been playing in semi-professional jazz bands.

The fourth corner of the square was the drifter, Brendan who, landing a job with Finney, ends up bedding Melanie Griffith's character and this was the role for which Sean won through in casting. Shooting started on 5 July 1987 and with a budget approaching £2 million, it was the biggest project he had yet been involved in.

It would be several years before Sean gained a reputation for screen nudity, but *Stormy Monday* marked the first time he was required to put his naked charms blithely on display. Roles that required nude scenes, however, did not faze Bean.

The aim was to create the feel and look of an American contemporary thriller and Mike Figgis felt that of all of Britain's major cities, Newcastle most resembled an American city. Filming, which took roughly eight weeks, got under way on location in Newcastle and the Tyneside area and in charge of imbuing the film with a certain stylised look was cinematographer Roger Deakins who recalls, 'We had been lucky because the Newcastle authorities let us have complete access to a place called The Side where a cobbled street runs along under the Tyne Bridge and as this gave us a big composite site, it helped to make the film very cost effective. There were a lot of night shoots required and we took almost three weeks just to rig up all the necessary lights all the way down the length of the street. It didn't have a big budget and if my memory serves me right, what helped Mike Figgis to get Tommy Lee Jones and Melanie Griffith for *Stormy Monday* was the fact that when he was casting, there had been an actors' strike going on in America.'

For the interior shots the production team moved into some empty warehouses on the waterfront, inside which they had built sets to represent the various bars and hangouts which featured in the movie. The city's actual Italian Job Restaurant – now known as '18 Dean Street' – would also feature in the film and the manager recollects, 'They took over the restaurant for six weeks and they took out our wooden balustrade and replaced it with a striking metal one, painted black.' Newcastle's distinctive bridges provided a most dramatic background.

Sean had always coveted the challenging spontaneity inherent in film work and he got his wish with his role in this intensely atmospheric movie which, besides providing him with another stepping stone in his career, also brought its perks.

Although he bared all for his intimate screen interludes with Melanie Griffith and came romantically to her rescue when she was at the mercy of the gangsters, life was not imitating art. There was no romantic off-set involvement between them, but casting an appreciative eye over his co-star he was clearly not immune to her charm. Bean found Griffith's trademark girlish breathy way of talking very sexy and he also said of her, 'She's big and buxom, which I like. I don't like skinny birds.' Cinematographer Roger Deakins recalls, 'Sean was very quiet but I got the impression that he was pretty overawed by Melanie who in those days was quite a character. She was a lively girl who knew how to enjoy herself.'

The smoky-edged *Stormy Monday* launched its director on to a hugely successful career for, on the back of this movie, Mike Figgis landed the Richard Gere Hollywood thriller *Internal Affairs* and his future credits would also include *The Browning Version* and *Leaving Las Vegas*.

And critically, the film was well received, as was the strong performance of the four main stars. Bean solidly held his own in what was dubbed an extremely stylish *film noir*, and in the process made, as one reviewer congratulated, 'an impressive star début'. One of the best scenes cited was the one in which Bean, as Brendan, arms himself to go and save Kate from a beating. Shot in slow motion against a rainy background it was symbolic of what it meant for an earnest young man to be prepared to kill for the first time, to cross the line and forever leave innocence behind. *Stormy Monday* was released in America on 6 May 1988, followed subsequently by its European release that autumn.

After shooting ended Sean made his radio debut on 6 September when, at the BBC's studios, he recorded a reading of *Romeo and Juliet* for *Woman's Hour* which was broadcast on the last day of the month. It was the first taste of what would become a regular job recording narration work for radio and television.

At home other milestones had been chalked up too; in this case major ones. Sean and Melanie moved out of their Tufnell Park bedsit and into a council house in London's Muswell Hill district and they did so just prior to the birth of their first child, a daughter whom they called Lorna.

The advent of pregnancy and the arrival of a baby had the natural effect of altering matters; the most obvious of which was the interruption of Melanie's career just after she had experienced her first television exposure. Because of the closeness of their relationship she had not been prone to insecure feelings where Sean was concerned but, maybe because her hormones were in an uproar, she – as she is later said to have told the *News of the World* – briefly felt an 'uncontrollable jealousy' before their baby was born.

Equilibrium, however, was soon restored. In their daily life Sean and Melanie had long since grown accustomed to each other's individual likes and dislikes. When it came to buying clothes, he was happy to let her select for him, confident that she knew his tastes, and he could, to some extent, be particular about his food. Because he likes plainer food there has at times been a tendency among certain sections of the Press to paint a picture of Sean almost as a chip butty bloke, when in truth his culinary tastes are not narrow but range from the type of traditional food he grew up with, to Beluga, a caviar for which he would develop a liking whilst working in Russia.

Home life with Sean had taken on a distinct shape. Bean does not see himself as being overly chauvinistic and his fondness for pub sessions and attending football matches with the lads he considers to be 'something blokes need to do'. He has openly owned up to holding the – now politically incorrect – belief that, in an ideal world, a man's role is to be the breadwinner in the family and a mother's place is in the home raising the children; a tenet imbedded in the nature of his own upbringing, but a belief which he admits had to be adjusted when his relationship with Melanie deepened.

As an actress in her own right, and a vibrant person with her own mind and ambitions, Melanie had no intention of completely sacrificing her career and Sean recognised this. He wanted her to do well, whilst admitting that had she not been in the same profession as himself, then in all likelihood he would have preferred her to stay at home.

Lorna's arrival did not mean that Melanie had to put her career on hold for too long for in time, she and Sean, whenever their work commitments clashed, simply employed a nanny. Sean is an adoring and devoted father but it became apparent that he drew certain lines. Occasionally he did change Lorna's nappies but on the whole Bean definitely did not qualify for the then trendy tag of being an 'Eighties New Man.'

Professionally, he did, however, turn into Prince Charming when in March 1988, with his RSC days at an end, he stepped into the romantic role of the prince in an episode of *Jim Henson's The Storyteller*. Directed by Peter Smith and produced by Duncan Kenworthy *The True Bride* was one of nine, thirty-minute episodes, all of them written by Anthony Minghella, and based on an old German folk tale. The damsel in distress in this family fable, Anja, with whom the prince, after many trials and tribulations, ends up living happily ever after, was played by Jane Horrocks and the story was narrated by John Hurt.

Sean got to cut a dash as a period figure on television for the first time and he measured up to the role in long cloak, tricorn hat and with his hair tied back with a black ribbon. Filmed at Elstree Studios in Borehamwood, it was also technically interesting to make as co-star

Robert Hamilton recalls, 'It was shot on 35 mm film, then transferred on to video when they could digitally add all the special effects. We worked in front of a blue screen which is not so very difficult. You're on an empty stage right enough, but you've been briefed beforehand about what's going to go in eventually, so that you hold this mental picture of what will be happening all around you.'

The True Bride was screened on Channel 4 on 23 July 1989, and on the giant American television network HBO where the series drew rave reviews with major newspapers weighing in to praise it, 'a visual stunning treat for the entire family', 'spellbinding' and 'daring'.

As May 1988 arrived, bringing with it *Stormy Monday*'s US release, Bean's diary for the rest of the year was varied enough to keep him busy. He again cropped up on British TV screens in the role of Captain Bolton in a two-part film made by London Weekend Television called *Troubles* which aired on ITV on consecutive Sunday nights on 1 and 8 May. Based on the novel by J.G. Farrell, and adapted by screenwriter Charles Sturridge, director Christopher Morahan had had the task of steering a cast which, in addition to Bean, was led by the accomplished Scots actor Ian Richardson and the late Ian Charleson. Set in 1919 in a rundown hotel on the Irish coast and taking Ireland's troubles as its axis, the story was laced with symbolism, concentrated on human elements and – unusually – the characters directly addressed the camera. Its generous budget for a television film of over £3.5 million had allowed for a sumptuous attention to detail that complemented the performances and enhanced the finished product.

Bean's next filming session after *The True Bride* was for a small appearance in the Bruce Robinson-directed Handmade Films movie *How To Get Ahead In Advertising*. From a screenplay by Robinson, produced by David Wimbury and starring Richard E. Grant, the production was a zany satire on the world of advertising in which a high-flying advertising executive gets a creative block whilst trying to develop a promotional strategy for a new pimple cream and suddenly sees the light.

The film was shot over six weeks commencing on 6 June 1988 at Shepperton Studios as well as on location. Grant turned in a blistering performance and the film's first half hour came to be classed as outrageously brilliant. As Larry Frisk, Sean's brief appearance was in the movie's opening scene. *How To Get Ahead In Advertising* was released in America in May 1989 and opened in Britain in July that year.

As summer set in Sean spent a couple of months with Melanie, helping to take care of their new little daughter. Then in September 1988 he took on his first television lead role in a BBC 1 play called *My Kingdom for a Horse* written by John Godber. Under director Barbara Rennie, Sean, supported by Andrew Livingston, Bryan Pringle, Jane Clifford and Sheila Hancock, played Steve, a history teacher, a low-key depiction of a shy young man who leads an unexciting existence except at weekends when, as a member of the Sealed Knot Society, he dresses up in period tunic, helmet and carries a pikestaff as a seventeenth-century infantryman to enact old battles.

The play is a subtle study of a man who emotionally plays possum in life, except when, as a weekend warrior, he escapes into a world where he can savour a brief but intense taste of rebellion. *My Kingdom for a Horse* brought Sean back to the bosom of the BBC for the second time, again playing a Yorkshireman. The play did not air until 12 March 1991, but when it did *Times* reviewer Lynne Truss described it as a light and lovely film adding, 'As a man of supreme inaction, Bean was great.'

Immediately after filming this and before commencing work on another BBC production, Sean was briefly reunited with director Derek Jarman who was making his new film *War Requiem* with producer Don Boyd. *Screen International* would call it, 'a thoughtful cinematic visualisation of Benjamin Britten's oratorio'. With virtually no dialogue it presented, instead, a series of tableaux depicting images of war and of the poet Wilfred Owen.

Shooting started on 17 October 1988 and its nineteen-strong cast featured the revered actor Sir Lawrence Olivier who had the distinction of having the only dialogue lines. Sean, representing the German soldier, teamed up again with the rest of *Caravaggio*'s core cast of Nigel Terry and Tilda Swinton. Nathaniel Parker played Wilfred Owen and there was also Owen Teale, with whom Bean would work closely the following year. Of the eighteen days filming, Sean was required for two.

The film's director of photography Richard Greatrex recalls, '*War Requiem* was shot in a disused mental asylum off the A2, just outside of London. Derek Jarman could see things that other people didn't. He would drive past this place on his way to his house on the coast and he just knew he could film a film about the First World War inside there. Others thought he was barmy, but he had a vision that was different to anyone else's.

'The amazing thing was that the exterior shots were actually filmed inside the building. Sean's main moment came in one particularly clever scene where people are in a snow-covered trench, but in fact we shot this in one of the asylum's attic rooms. Recent gales had blown the roof clean off and it was exposed to the sun, and the floor's insulation looked like snow.'

Richard disagrees with the later belief that the film had been intended as a metaphor for the devastation of AIDS. He states, 'Derek had been diagnosed at that stage, but it was not common knowledge. Mind you the three major protagonists connected with it were gay. We were watching some rushes one day and I remember the producer Don Boyd saying, "You know, we had better be careful. If we don't watch we'll make this into a gay film." And Derek replied, "Well, I'm gay. Benjamin Britten was gay and so was Wilfred Owen. So, I'm sorry to disappoint you, but that *is* what it's about."

'The idiosyncratic thing about a Derek Jarman film was that he treated actors like sculptures. He didn't want them to behave like film actors, no thinking, no emotion. He wanted to concentrate on their body language and, of course, looking at young men's bodies is what he preferred doing. Most of the actors he worked with were part of his circle of friends. It was always fun to work with Derek – I think people would do a film with him just because they liked to please him.'

That it was to be Lord Olivier's final screen appearance was painfully obvious. Richard recalls, 'He was very feeble. His son was looking after him the whole time. We had to shoot his scenes with him in a wheelchair because there was no way in this world that he could walk. He could just about remember his lines. It was very sad. But we were proud to have been there for his final performance.'

ABOVE   Pictured with co-star Caroline Maher, Sean played Herr Schultz in an amateur production of *Cabaret* at Rotherham Civic Theatre in September 1980. His success in this stage play spurred him on to apply to RADA.

ABOVE 1986 and starring as Romeo in a controversially contemporary version of *Romeo and Juliet*. Sean completed his period with the Royal Shakespeare Company not overly impressed by the experience but having forged some strong friendships.

ABOVE Playing a drifter in *Stormy Monday* marked Sean's first substantial mainstream film role. His screen romance with Melanie Griffith sparked the start of his reputation as a sizzling screen heart-throb.

LEFT Looking lethal, even in handcuffs, Bean's spine-chilling depiction of a manic terrorist in the Hollywood blockbuster *Patriot Games* brought his acting talents to a global audience.

BELOW In *Lady Chatterley*, Bean brought depth and vulnerability to the part of Oliver Mellors. But, he is best remembered for shocking the nation with his energetic and explicit sex scenes with the heroine, played by Joely Richardson.

LEFT A serpent in silk, Sean excelled as the sinister yet smooth aristocratic rake Robert Lovelace in the BBC period drama *Clarissa*.

Complex, even by Derek Jarman's standards, *War Requiem* had its world première in London's West End on 6 January 1989, followed weeks later by its European début at the Berlin Film Festival and would be broadcast on BBC 2 that Eastertime.

With barely a pause, Sean trained his sights on a BBC feature film called *Small Zones*. Written by Jim Hawkins from an original idea by Simon Thirsk and produced by Terry Coles, it centred on Jenny, a Hull housewife, who is living a grim existence with her abusive husband Vic. She is introduced to the writings of the Russian poet Irina Ratushinskaya who suffered the brutality of prison whilst serving seven years hard labour because in the early 1980s her poems were regarded as anti-Soviet propaganda. She was eventually freed in 1986 following a worldwide campaign for her release. Jim Hawkins drew parallels between Irina's real-life struggle against the State machine and the oppression of Jenny's domestic plight, and in *Small Zones* Irina's inspirational spirit gives Jenny the courage to finally break free of her husband's grip.

Actresses Catherine Neilson and Suzanna Hamilton played Jenny and Irina respectively. The role of Vic, however, was more complex than that of a straightforward wife-beater and waster, and director Michael Whyte recalls what he was looking for when it came to casting and why Sean Bean fitted the bill.

'Vic was a bit lost and not understanding quite what was happening in his life. He had seemed happily married but then he loses his job and cannot get work. When his wife takes the initiative to get them out of the rut he feels inadequate and reacts by becoming more withdrawn, spending long spells in the pub drinking heavily. His frustration about life and his wife getting on with things, leads him into domestic violence which escalates. And Sean was extraordinarily good at portraying someone with whom, while you can't approve of his actions, still you can sympathise. Sean doesn't alienate you. He can project a character for whom you end up having compassion and who you will not end up seeing only in black and white terms.

'We had actually brought in Melanie Hill to test for Jenny, the part that eventually went to Catherine Neilson, and it was Melanie who suggested, "Why don't you see Sean?" These were early days in Sean's career and I hadn't been aware of his work. The irony then, of course, was that we didn't end up giving the part to Melanie and yet Sean got the male lead.'

Over the one month's filming which began on 7 November on location in Humberside and at the promontory Spurn Head, Sean would earn Michael Whyte's deep respect. Says Michael, 'When the violence did come out and that side of Vic's character had to be developed, Sean was worried about being too violent. There is a particularly rough scene when he has a go at his wife when she is standing at the cooker using a frying pan, and her hand ends up in the boiling hot fat. Whilst filming the scene Sean was absolutely bone-chillingly terrifying. But afterwards he came straight up to me and said, "My God! Was that too much? Too realistic?" I'd previously done a documentary on battered wives and domestic violence and Sean had got it exactly right so I told him, "No, it wasn't too much."

'Equally there are moments when Vic is charming, a man in need of mothering and you get glimpses of the rather lovable man Jenny had married before things went wrong. Sean could switch to these moments with great effect. Sean has the wonderful ability to swing from one end of the spectrum to the other. But he was very conscious that it's difficult to find the right level at which to pitch your portrayal of someone like Vic, because you don't want to make the character so good in certain ways that people end up saying, "Nice guy. Pity he's a bit violent."

'It's a fine line. The audience has to understand where he is coming from and Sean depicted this balance beautifully. Likewise when his wife leaves him and he is left a pathetic figure who realises what he has become, again Sean's interpretation was brilliant. This was so early on in his career and yet he gave such a finely tuned performance. Really, had we known just *how* good an actor Sean is, I would go so far as to say that we would have re-written the script if we could have. But on television schedules and budgets, you just have to get on with it.'

Overall, the director enjoyed working with Bean. 'As an actor, Sean does the best drunken walk I've ever seen!' laughs Michael. 'He was always up for giving things a try and great to work with. No ego, no making strange demands. He's a quiet man who keeps to himself. But he would still socialise with the cast and crew in the evenings and I vividly remember him agonising rather sweetly over whether Sheffield United would go up or down in whichever league they were playing at the time.'

Bean also made his mark on *Small Zones'* producer Terry Coles, who believes Sean to be an extremely brave actor. 'Here was a handsome young guy taking on the kind of role that was guaranteed to repel an audience. Vic became an extremely unsympathetic character but Sean really went for it. He was quite frightening. I haven't been at all surprised to watch his subsequent rise to fame.'

A sentiment with which the director concurs, 'I've been delighted to see Sean go from strength to strength since. But you know, he has done the Hollywood villains and quite right too. He has also done them very well. But there is a *lot* more to Sean Bean than that. His full potential and the full range of his capabilities has yet to come out.' *Small Zones* was screened on BBC 2 on 4 March 1990.

The line of people within the profession with sound respect for Sean's abilities and who saw the promise he had already shown as proof that he was poised to break through to bigger things, was growing steadily. And as 1988 ended, the new year dawning would bring with it a tangible move forward in Bean's career when his roles were guaranteed to ensure him a substantially increased profile; a condition for which he was ready and raring to go.

6

BLADE RUNNER

IN SPRING **1989** Sean strengthened his burgeoning reputation for depicting ruthless hard men when, having completed his work in *Small Zones*, he walked straight into the role of Dominic O'Brien in the Tyne Tees Television adaptation of Catherine Cookson's novel *The Fifteen Streets*. Produced by Ray Marshall and directed by David Wheatley, the film's screenplay was by Rob Bettinson.

A great deal of the bedrock preparation work had also been carried out by the highly acclaimed writer Rosemary Anne Sisson, whose long list of impressive credits includes the television play *Elizabeth R*, the TV series *The Duchess of Duke Street* as well as *The Bretts*, and the mini-series *The Manions of America* which gave Bond star Pierce Brosnan his start.

As script and story consultant for *The Fifteen Streets* she was present when casting took place at Tyne Tees TV. Marilyn Johnson, who had put forward Sean for his TV film début role in *Winter Flight*, was again casting director. Bean was up for the role of the hero's violent brother and, on the day, he made an impact on Rosemary Anne Sisson that was distinctly different from the impression he usually left.

Says Rosemary, 'I met Sean Bean once, when he was briefly introduced to me at Tyne Tees Television. I say briefly because either he hadn't grasped who I was or, more likely, had no interest in wasting time on a middle-aged female writer. He was then pretty well unknown, and I might have been thought to have had some influence on the casting, but he probably didn't realise this, and wouldn't have cared if he had. Mind, if he had been up for the part of the romantic hero instead of a singularly unpleasant villain, I might have suggested that he was distinctly lacking in charm.

'To be fair, had I gone on to be involved in the production to the extent that I had expected, it would probably have been different. But *The Fifteen Streets* turned out to be one of those unhappy experiences which happen all too often to writers in film and television and I dare say the sour taste has affected my recollection of that fleeting encounter with Mr Bean!'

Having landed the part, Sean found himself heading to Newcastle for the third time, ready to start work on the TV movie. The shooting schedule which began on 22 March lasted six weeks, half of which was spent at various locations including Chillingham Road Primary School and Richardson Street in Heaton, and then the production moved to the coast at South Shields. Filming also took place at the Beamish Museum in County Durham, with its full-size recreation of a pre-First World War working colliery village and Bean joined the rest of the cast whose main members were Leslie Schofield, Anny Tobin, Billie Whitelaw, Ian Bannen, Clare Holman, Frank Windsor and Jane Horrocks, with whom a year before Sean had filmed *The True Bride*.

Owen Teale, appearing right then along with Sean in *War Requiem* which was being broadcast as part of BBC 2's Easter programmes, played the hero John O'Brien and this melodramatic Victorian tale of poverty, passion and tragedy provided Sean with his best showcase yet to display his talent for portraying a man with absolutely no redeeming features, and that to a mainstream television audience.

His flair for accents was also further cemented by his grasp of the Geordie tongue and as Dominic, a hard-drinking, aggressive dock worker he made his mark on *The Fifteen Streets* with an opening scene in which he has a violent fist fight with his father and ends up collapsing on his bed, having to be undressed by his long-suffering and perpetually pregnant mother.

The fifteen streets is the name given to the deprived working-class area in which the notorious O'Brien family scrape a living and the crux of the story revolves around the hero's love for a school teacher and the class barrier issue. Woven into this tapestry are extra trials the family suffer, usually stemming from Sean's character's unscrupulous behaviour.

Bean's penchant for portraying the villain, on the grounds that invariably these are meatier roles, was well rewarded in *The Fifteen Streets* when his no-good, bad-tempered Dominic proves to be so vivid a contrast to Owen Teale's sensitive, responsible and kind John that there were times when dull virtue seemed less appealing than rank wickedness, and the hero's charisma threatened to be diluted.

Rosemary Ann Sisson believes, 'Owen Teale had a hard job as the hero, and I thought he did it brilliantly. But Catherine Cookson had a great capacity for drawing horrible villains and Sean Bean, who has a very strong personality anyway, gave a powerful performance. He was superb in the role.'

The Fifteen Streets was transmitted on ITV on 30 August. Sean's performance in this drama, airing just weeks after the romantic *The True Bride* meant that he was beginning to appear on British television screens with growing frequency, but he was still some way yet from being a household name. The same could not be said of Melanie Hill.

Work-wise, the couple handled their professional commitments to accommodate the presence of their young daughter and Melanie was able to make her television breakthrough when she took over the part of the dizzy Aveline Boswell from actress Gilly Coman in the hit BBC 1 sitcom *Bread.* Melanie would notch up many screen appearances but she would be most associated with this comedy series, written by Carla Lane, which centred on a Liverpool family's life on the dole and starred Jean Boht, Peter Howitt and Rita Tushingham.

Overnight Melanie Hill became a known face and name and Sean was proud of this development; he was never jealous of the fact that, for some time to come, his partner was more instantly recognised in the street than he. Her reign in *Bread* lasted until 1991 and as his workload increased significantly with each passing year, they continued to juggle work commitments with their home life success-fully.

While Melanie enjoyed this exposure and UK television audiences were watching Bean act the brute in *The Fifteen Streets*, Sean embarked on the first film to take him overseas. This was *Windprints*, written and directed by David Wicht, in which Sean had the lead role of news cameraman Anton van Heerden. White South African Wicht's début feature film, though reflecting many of his own life's experiences, also took on board thorny aspects of his country's apartheid policies.

Anton van Heerden lands in hot water over contentious footage he filmed in Soweto and because it is politic for him to vanish from Johannesburg for a time, his boss sends him on an assignment to Namibia. He teams up with British journalist Charles Rutherford, played by John Hurt, to trace the whereabouts of an outlaw called Nhadiep who is murdering members of his own Nama tribe, thereby spreading fear and causing homesteaders to vacate their farm lands. Nhadiep's Houdini-like ability to escape justice has gained him mythical status locally but van Heerden scents a mystery and wonders if Nhadiep is committing these crimes on someone else's behalf.

With his blond hair lapping his collar and the requisite distinctive South African accent, Sean depicted the liberal van Heerden as a successful urban white Afrikaner who, challenged by a friend to actively get involved in his country's politics, finds a conflict between being an objective observer of Afrikaners' racist treatment of the Nama people and reporting the truth. Along the way, van Heerden's emotive response to events is offset by Rutherford's ingrained cynicism and he also cops flak from the local Afrikaners for not behaving like one of them.

David Wicht had ploughed a great deal of time into *Windprints* and considered it to be far removed from being a formula film. He described the script as very dense but rich in characterisation and atmosphere, which meant it had not been an easy transition from script to screen. Producer Michael Games, also making his feature film début, felt that the movie was not taking an overtly political stance; rather he considered it to be a complex human drama.

In order to imbue *Windprints* with Africa's rhythms, texture and colour, with the exception of Bean, Hurt and Marius Weyers as Henning, a ruthless Afrikaner, the remainder of the cast were white and black South Africans, and the art house film was shot in the arid landscape of Namibia.

At least it had been arid until the film unit arrived to commence work around Keetmanshoop and Berseba. The moment the cameras began rolling, the heaviest rain the region had experienced in fifty years fell. Floods hit the location site just as a vital indoor scene was being shot. While those on set had to ignore their anxieties and get to work, outside the assistant director rounded up every available pair of hands and all were frantically attempting to divert the course of the raging torrent.

When filming ended and Sean and the others looked out, they were met by an astonishingly chaotic scene. The wild waters were visibly rising and people were desperately trying to retrieve vehicles and equipment, some of which eluded them and were swept away. No help could be forthcoming from the region's officials as they were at full stretch trying to save the lives of the local farmers. Michael Games put it succinctly, 'People out there were drowning.'

Fortunately, when the crisis passed, nothing had been damaged that the crew could not repair or replace and everyone understood that isolated location shoots brought their hazards and inconveniences. The receding waters left a coating of mud and stinking filth everywhere and the irony was that the sun had shone throughout; the torrent had come from upstream. Just as the flood had plagued them, so the scorching heat of over 40 degrees with no natural shade, brought the threat of heatstroke and meant that copious supplies of drinking water had to be brought in.

The cast and crew, after their flight to Cape Town, then to Luderitz, had faced a long drive to Keetmanshoop and once there had been virtually marooned. It was a daunting seven-hour round trip between location and Luderitz if they fancied a meal in a restaurant so they had to amuse themselves when off duty as best they could. With Bean's penchant for football it's hardly surprising that one of those pastimes was to form the Windprints United football team, whose amateur matches drew hundreds of locals to the touchlines as curious but enthusiastic spectators.

Windprints opened in Britain on 29 June 1990. Filming had provided Sean with an extra special delight for he had particularly enjoyed working with John Hurt. Indeed, Sean credits the accomplished star of such movies as *The Elephant Man, Scandal* and television's *The Naked Civil Servant* with being his biggest inspiration; the actor who taught him a valuable lesson in the need to adopt a disciplined way of working.

It could only have been a source of deep pleasure, therefore, when hard on the heels of filming *Windprints*, Sean stepped straight into making his first substantial co-starring feature film appearance in *The Field* in which John Hurt also co-starred along with Brenda Fricker and Richard Harris.

With the movie *My Left Foot*, and its *tour-de-force* Oscar-winning performance by Daniel Day-Lewis as Christy Brown, already to their credit, the dream team of Dublin-born director Jim Sheridan and producer Noel Pearson had turned their attention to another intense drama set in rural Ireland in 1939. Sheridan had written a screenplay for *The Field* based upon the acclaimed sixties play of the same name, by writer John B. Keane. Sheridan wanted to depict the story of one man's vehement obsession in a film that he would describe as being about evil and madness, as well as one which dealt with some profound spiritual issues.

Veteran star Richard Harris, making his first movie appearance for nearly ten years, put in a towering lead performance as The Bull McCabe, a big built, white-bearded, strong-willed, tenant farmer. His inherited manic devotion to the land, and one field in particular, puts him on a disastrous collision course with a wealthy Irish-American played by Tom Berenger who rolls into town and becomes a rival bidder for the field in which generations of McCabes had invested years of back-breaking toil to farm; a field that the Yank intends to cover with concrete and build a road over. It is a gripping and powerful piece of cinema, with outstanding performances from, in addition to Harris, John Hurt as 'Bird' O'Donnell, a ferrety figure, almost the village idiot, and Sean Bean as McCabe's son Tadgh.

Working with a modest budget of £5 million, six-weeks' filming began on 2 October 1989 on location in the village of Leenane, Connemara and then moved to the Ardmore Studios in Dublin for a further two weeks. Remote and almost untouched in the intervening half century, Leenane became, for the duration, the fictional town of Carraigthomond and the surrounding stony, dramatically desolate terrain visually matched the movie's bleak themes.

The schedule was punishing enough, with some extra specially long days required and even an all-nighter, without the production being plagued with relentless rain. And this cheerless existence was hardly alleviated when one local onlooker helpfully volunteered that he could well remember the previous summer – it had been on a Friday! Richard Harris would receive an Oscar nomination and, to some, it would not have been out of place for Sean Bean to have been similarly honoured for his supporting role.

Sean does not adopt the Method style of acting favoured by the likes of Day-Lewis, but as Tadgh he assumed completely the skin and identity of a clearly mentally disturbed young man. Riddled with confusing unexpressed emotions and prone to violent outbursts, he was also relentlessly cowed by the expectations of a powerful father. The role was a total departure from anything Sean Bean had under-taken so far and director Jim Sheridan drew an extraordinary perform-ance from him; a view that is wholly endorsed by the original playwright.

John B. Keane says, 'I was mightily impressed. It was a most refreshing representation of the character and this fine actor showed a rare understanding of Tadgh's frustrations. A film actor depends a great deal on facial expressions and it was here that Sean excelled. He brought the true torment to the surface, and he showed – as I have never seen it before or since – the mental collapse of a young man, of all the young men from whom fathers expect too much. His overall performance was outstanding.' He adds, 'Sean and I had a brief chat on the night the film was premiered in Dublin and he proved himself to be a kind, gentle and compassionate man.'

After *The Field* opened in Dublin on 21 September 1990 it did outstanding business in Ireland. *Screen International* speculated that internationally it might prove to be a harder sell. In fact, it opened in America on 1 March 1991 and went on to take its place as one of the year's most powerful and critically acclaimed films.

An awareness of having been part of something a bit special must have stayed with Sean when filming wrapped at the end of November 1989 and contentment in his career was complemented by personal happiness at home. According to Sean, after nearly eight years together, there had never been a doubt that they would wed, it had purely been a question of when. With Lorna at the toddler stage they had also decided to increase their family and so stapled to this, came the added thought that it might be good for the kids if their parents' relationship was put on a more formal footing.

Watching television together one night at their Muswell Hill home a programme about marriage came on and Sean suddenly asked Melanie if she 'fancied a bit of that, then'? It was not perhaps moonlight, roses and a hopeful suitor on bended knee, but she readily accepted his characteristically unfussy proposal.

Sean and Melanie married in February 1990. The groom in a suit and collar and tie, sported a small gold earring in his left ear, the bride was radiant in white with a delicate floral headdress and Lorna was their dainty bridesmaid. It was made a glittering occasion when the ranks of their family and hometown friends were swelled by dozens of showbusiness acquaintances. The reception was held in a nearby Muswell Hill hotel.

Whether or not it is true, it has repeatedly been reported that their honeymoon had been arranged to accommodate Sheffield United's fixtures. Certainly, Sean's commitment to the club remained staunch and would find expression in a couple of ways in early 1990. On 27 January he had recorded the narration for a BBC 2 series called *United*, about Sheffield United, that would be screened in five consecutive episodes over April and May.

Bean concedes that the depth of his devotion to football, and to one team in particular, is difficult for some people to get their head around. But he simply describes it as 'a genuine love affair'. That his support for Sheffield United was a serious business was not in doubt, but a momentary spasm of elation led him to nail his colours permanently to the wall, so to speak, by having a tattoo emblazoned on his flesh; a tattoo that now ranks among the most mentioned in showbusiness.

The date was 5 May 1990 and in the 1989/90 season, when Sheffield United played Leicester City at Filbert Street, they needed to win the game to secure promotion. The Blades not only won, they scored five goals against their opposition's two and sent their delirious fans clean into orbit. On a gigantic high Bean, with a mate called Farquhar, bowled out of the stadium and headed into town where, at a cost of £2 each, they got themselves appropriately branded for life. Farquhar opted for the words 'Sheffield United' while Sean chose '100% Blade', which he had etched into the skin high on his left arm.

The tattoo, of which he was so proud, could on occasions present a challenge for filmmakers to conceal whenever Sean was required to shed his clothes. But for his next role, the start of what would be a busy period, there were no such worries.

Of Berkshire-born writer R.D. Blackmore's fifteen novels, *Lorna Doone*, published in 1869, is considered to be his masterpiece. Set in the seventeenth century, this classic tale of romance and revenge had been given the big screen treatment before, and now Working Title Films and Thames Television were to bring it alive again.

The adventure turns on the thirst of young West Country yeoman John Ridd for vengeance against the Doones, an aristocratic clan of outlaws from the neighbouring valley, for having killed his father in front of his eyes when he was a child. His dreams of revenge, though, become complicated when he accidentally meets and falls in love with Lorna Doone.

This colourful television production lay in the hands of director Andrew Grieve and producers Anthony Root and Alan Horrox, working from a screenplay adapted from Blackmore's novel by Matthew Jacobs. Although set on bleak Exmoor, it would be filmed around spring on the outskirts of Glasgow where the undulating moorlands, bubbling streams and hidden waterfalls more than met their location requirements.

The choice of location provoked an outcry as the film's cinematographer Paul Wheeler recalls, 'Some people in the West Country complained bitterly that it was not true to the novel, and the film's publicity ran into quite a few problems over it. Frankly we were taken aback by the fuss. But we needed an authentic barn church and a rugged countryside that wasn't dotted with electricity pylons. From my point of view, therefore, Scotland was an excellent decision.

'Fourteen of us went up from London and we worked with an entire Scottish crew, who were great. It was a fascinating shoot, but absolutely freezing. There was a horse-drawn carriage which, for authenticity, had no glass in the windows and the snow one day went literally in one side and clean out of the other, proving that the wind was actually horizontal. One actress's cheeks were so frozen once, that she couldn't speak her lines.'

Supported by a cast which boasted Hugh Fraser, Billie Whitelaw, Robert Stephens and Kenneth Haig, were the four central figures – the heroine Lorna Doone played by Polly Walker, the hero John Ridd which fell to Clive Owen, the colourful highwayman cousin of the Ridds, Tom Faggus, whom Miles Anderson portrayed and Sean's character, the hot and savage Carver Doone.

Period roles do not suit every actor but Bean, over time, has amassed a string of them, spanning several eras and achieving authenticity in them all. Here, in seventeenth-century costume with lanky shoulder-length hair, and in the opening scene wearing a dazzling pearl drop earring, he brought a piratical air to the murdering marauding character. But his success in the role was not down to window-dressing. His evocation of savagery communicated itself clearly and the single most illuminating moment of the depth of his immersion in the role came in one scene.

It was during a shoot-out between the Doones who had surrounded a house in which the Ridds were cornered, and a one-eye close-up on Bean, in the heat of battle, allowed the camera to pick up the glittering hatred burning realistically in its depths. Paul Wheeler confirms, 'Sean is an actor who goes right through. When he walked on set he was Carver Doone in his every fibre. You could've cut Sean open and you'd have found the character inside, which means the camera can interrogate him severely with safety. You won't find a chink. And you rarely meet such integrity. He's an extraordinary actor.'

That Bean was equally capable of snapping back out of being Carver off set made for a good rapport with the crew. Paul explains, 'He likes people and therefore is approachable. Some actors you have to leave alone, they need their space and you can respect that. But it makes it easier to work with actors like Sean because the friendliness that develops from having a common purpose makes it all so much easier.'

For Wheeler the most memorable moment of working on this film came on set when Sean got closer to him than he was comfortable with. Paul recalls, 'There's a big fight which starts with guns and muskets and we all know about special-effects men. They tell you that it's perfectly safe to get in there with your hand-held camera, which means you stand at least ten feet further back, or preferably shoot it from the next county!

'Anyway, it then develops into a sword fight. I was in the middle of the fight. Now Sean is an exceptional swordsman, but he was so close that as the tip of his sword in the heat of the action came lunging over me, I literally felt my hair blow. It was heart-stopping and it was not an accident! When the take was over, one of the grips told me that there had been about one inch to spare. Well, I turned on Sean hurling a volley of expletives at him and he replied calmly, "But that's what you do. I'd never have touched you!" ' Unable just yet to respond to Bean's mollifying tone Paul was still intractable. He goes on, 'I yelled, "That's all very well, but you might have bloody well told me what you were going to do!"

'We did that hair-raising take a few times because each time something would go wrong in the background action, but it got a little easier because I could have confidence in Sean. In fact, he's a very repeatable actor. When an actor has to do the same thing time and again some become wooden and end up doing it by rote. But Sean, in the like of this scene, lost his temper all over again and is again, going all out to try and kill you with frightening ferocity and yet the tip of his blade every time without fail ended up right where it should be. His precision is astonishing. It can be hairy, but it's also exciting. Sean has the physicality of an American actor and the training of an English one. His is solid talent.'

This exciting new version of *Lorna Doone* featured as part of ITV's Christmas highlights when it was broadcast on Boxing Day 1990.

From mid-1990 the pace of Sean's workload again perceptibly moved up a gear; the first half of this period reuniting him with the worlds of the short, and of stage work. Over three days, commencing on 14 July, he recorded *Wedded*, a twenty-five-minute play by Jim Cartwright, about a couple whose marriage is on the rocks. As they drive through the night the husband concentrates on the road, while the wife reflects on the path of their troubles. Shown on BBC 2 on 29 August, Bean's co-star was Lesley Sharpe, with whom he had worked five years earlier in the triple bill at the Royal Court Theatre Upstairs.

And it was to the stage of the Theatre Upstairs that Bean made a surprise return when the Royal Court started its season in August. He began rehearsals for The Soho Theatre Company's production of a new David Spencer play, *Killing the Cat* – a play which secured its writer his second Verity Bargate Award, and was to mark Sean's return to the London stage after a two and a half year break.

The director was Sue Dunderdale and Sean had the starring role of Danny, the son of working-class Irish parents who, on a visit home from London, lets a family skeleton out of the cupboard by remembering the sexual abuse that his sister had suffered at the hands of their father. Possessing his own violent traits, Danny tries to confront and untangle the dark issue of incest. For this production Sean was joined by Kate McLoughlin, Sally Rogers, Henry Stamper, Valerie Lilley and Dominic Kinnaird.

It would have taken much to tempt Bean back to theatre work, but in addition to admiring the young playwright's style, Danny's troubled vulnerability intrigued Sean and such a complex play, dealing with a deeply taboo topic, provided him with a challenge; not least the challenge of trying to place himself comfortably in his character's situation and the dilemma that this represented. Speaking of the play at the time Sean opined, 'You don't want to recognise yourself in it. Yet you have to relate to them [the characters] without justifying the father's behaviour.'

Watching how Bean approached this testing role, it became clear to David Spencer that it was vital to Sean to believe in everything as it unfolded. The playwright found it fascinating to follow the process whereby, having assumed the role, Bean then set about carefully crafting it.

Sean's role as Danny was well received and it was the interaction between the father (Sam, played by Henry Stamper) and son that would draw particular praise from Nicholas de Jongh of *The Guardian* who pronounced, 'Henry Stamper's pugnaciousness is matched by

Sean Bean's impressive Danny, haggard, brooding and wracked.' *Killing the Cat* had its first performance on 23 August and ran until 15 September and would signify Sean Bean's final stage appearance.

In the coming years Bean would not desert television to concentrate purely on theatrically released feature films and he has become one of a handful of British actors who successfully maintain a unique balance between working in both mediums; a tricky achievement but a shrewd one. Major motion pictures bring an actor's abilities to a global audience. But by not neglecting the television set in homes throughout the land, an actor is also able to impinge on the nation's consciousness.

The first television drama which Sean settled into was his role as Gabriel Lewis in the TV movie *Tell Me That You Love Me*, directed for the BBC by Bruce MacDonald, with producer Sara Curtis which, from a screenplay by Adrian Hodges, wove a story around the editor of a glossy magazine who has reached a certain age, has a useless ex-boyfriend whom she continues to see, but who feels that there must be something better to life. Then, out of nowhere, appears Gabriel a mystery man and, in theory, epitomising everything that is pure romance.

Filming for this many-layered, cleverly scripted drama stretched between 8 October and 4 November and brought Bean back into contact with a RADA contemporary, James Wilby, who portrayed the useless boyfriend Michael, while Judith Scott took on the mantle of the heroine, Laura Simms.

Screenwriter Adrian Hodges recalls, 'We already had Judith Scott and James Wilby and Sean was the last of the three principals to be cast. The role of Gabriel Lewis was quite difficult. We wanted someone who was a dreamboat, but who could convey sensitivity. One of the things that is true about leading, handsome men is that they can have the looks, but are not necessarily able to deliver a convincing depth.

'There was not a single doubt that he [Sean] was the perfect candidate. As soon as he walked in, he had the air of a warm and loving man, but someone with hidden qualities. He is very male, but also very sensitive. It was a straightforward piece of casting and from the moment he was available, we wanted him.'

Tell Me That You Love Me was Adrian's second screenplay and the first to make it to the screen. He says, 'The story pre-dated the now popular sub-genre of the romantic stalker. I have always been interested in the confusion that can arise between what someone imagines to be the perfect romance, and the reality of it. Women's glossy magazines, pre-lads mags, were more innocent in those days. The character Laura Simms has daily contact with questions like how many orgasms can you have in one night, what makes the perfect body or the perfect partner and the tragic thing is, the magazine is put together by a dysfunctional band of women. When Gabriel appears in her life he is entirely concerned with anticipating her every desire and making sure he gives it to her. But what seems so wonderful, begins to pall and she discovers him to be oppressive and intolerant of her friends. She comes back to reality, but he can never move beyond being a fantasy figure.'

He goes on, 'Gabriel is a man who you might feel is building up to be dangerous but, in fact, he isn't at all. Rather, he is a very unhappy man who ends up not hurting her, but killing himself. And one of the best aspects of Sean's performance was that he really caught the intrinsically sad quality of the character in a way that not every actor could have done. He perfectly captured that pain.'

That Bean dislikes, even mistrusts, too much character analysis and prefers to concentrate on becoming the role as it is happening became obvious to the writer. Adrian says, 'I didn't go to the rehearsals but I spoke with the producer and the director and they both said that Sean didn't like talking about the role. He likes to go on and do it. It may be that he is not someone who feels the need to talk about a role. In this case, he certainly understood it anyway.

'This was a particularly hard lead role because as Gabriel, Sean couldn't give anything of himself to it – I mean, that he could not latch on to anything, because it was all about a hidden personality. Therefore he could not reveal anything. When Sean went on to portray Richard Sharpe, I thought that he played him as an interesting package. Sharpe is always hopping into bed with a leading lady but beneath all that he seems to be a tormented character and Sean is so effective at conveying the feeling that there is a lot going on at a deeper level.

'*Tell Me That You Love Me* had a couple of public screenings at the National Film Theatre, during the London Television Festival and it was marvellous to see it shown as a feature film. It got a very good audience reaction too,' adds Hodges. Following these screenings, the drama transmitted on BBC 1 on 8 September 1991 when it pulled in an impressive six and a half million viewers.

Once filming wrapped, Sean promptly headed back to Ireland where he joined rehearsals which were under way near Dublin for another, but very different, TV movie. This time Bean was charged with portraying a commanding British army figure who becomes involved in the complexities of the political situation in contemporary Ireland and the border activities of the Republican movement, which were echoed by a feud between neighbouring families.

In The Border Country, written by Daniel Mornin, was A Little Bird production for Channel 4 Television and Sean starred with Juliet Stevenson, Sean McGinley, Saskia Reeves, Ian McGihinney and John Kavanagh. It was a short shoot, only three weeks, commencing on 19 November and director Thaddeus O'Sullivan recalls Bean's involvement.

'Sean plays an SAS type who gets involved with the wife of one of the Republican guys. Although Sean became famous for playing these kinds of roles very effectively, I didn't cast him because of seeing anything like that in him. He came across to me as soft and sweet mannered, which was perfect because I didn't want a heavy. At least, I didn't want him to *appear* like a heavy. Smith is sweet on the surface and that's what attracts this woman because he is the opposite of her intense Republican husband. Or so she thinks. Of course, the irony of it is that she falls for the guy who appears to be mild mannered but who is, in fact, there to kill her husband.'

In The Border Country was a low budget film and as such all their filming needs required to be concentrated on one spot. Thaddeus recalls, 'It was shot at a village called Howth, on the outskirts of Dublin. Howth was partly State-owned which meant it was preserved. Fires had cleared the gorse away, so we had the perfect dramatically dark landscape in which to film before the ground could reconstitute itself. The cottage was there too.

'The drama was more like a theatre piece, in that it was highly stylised and melodramatic – the characters were less naturalised and more symbolic and although this meant it was a difficult thing to act in, Sean took it easily in his stride, despite the fact that it was not the usual thing that he had done before.

'Most actors find it hard when there is no back story. Smith represented the oppressiveness of the English security service existing in Northern Ireland and Sean played him simply and without side, so that the audience could react to him instead of playing a character who expresses everything in detail, which wouldn't have worked. It puts audiences off if they are expected to get too involved with a character's background and Sean was excellent at keeping that distance.'

The director enjoyed working with Bean. Thaddeus explains, 'I was surprised that he took the role, because he was becoming well known then in the business and this was just a small part in a simple film. But there's no grandness about Sean. He is a very down-to-earth man.'

Of making the movie, he states, 'I loved it. Actors cannot hammer too much at this kind of drama or they will kill it stone dead. You've got to have some fun with it. It was only a fifty-minute drama and was seen by the people at Channel 4 as being somewhat experimental. So there was no obligation on me, as director, to be a good boy, to watch the political situation and to explain things too much. Personally, I enjoyed the drama of it all.' Channel 4 screened *In The Border Country* on 2 March 1991.

Returning home, Bean had the Christmas break with his family before beginning work on his last lower-key appearance, which involved him taking the lead role in another BBC film, for the Screen One series, called *Prince*. Produced by Ruth Baumgarten, *Prince* reunited Sean with *The Fifteen Streets'* director, David Wheatley.

For the most part, casting directors and others involved in such selection, were quick to spot the extra something that would draw them to single out Bean for a part. But there can also be a deceptive air about him. Off set he never puts himself on display, with the result that sometimes it was not instantly obvious that he was suited to a particular role and this happened initially when he went up for the part as Jack Morgan.

The screenplay was written by Julie Burchill and Morgan was based on her own father. At the audition, because Burchill's father and Sean Bean were totally different in physique and background, she could not immediately see him as the character she had scripted until Sean began to read for the part. She described his transformation as eerie.

For the depiction of a man's single-minded devotion to his pet Alsatian dog and how this had affected the individual lives of his family, Sean's supporting cast included Celia Montague, Janet McTeer, Jackie McGuire and William Armstrong. Shooting took about four weeks over January and February and *Prince* was screened in the autumn, on 6 October.

The wrap on *Prince* closed a chapter in Bean's career, and by spring 1991 he was about to embark on a new and exciting phase, starting with the male lead role in a lavish period TV production of a literary classic that would see him performing at his scheming, wicked and thoroughly amoral best.

7

HEROES AND VILLAINS

SEAN BEAN'S STRIKING performance as the eighteenth-century aristocratic rake, Robert Lovelace, in the BBC television adaptation of novelist Samuel Richardson's *Clarissa* was destined to linger on in the minds of many.

To condense the longest novel in the English language [at over one million words] and described as one of the most powerful fictional explorations of sexual politics, to a three-part mini-series had proved to be a Herculean task for co-screenwriters David Nokes and Janet Barron.

Set in Georgian England, the narrative revolves around the central drama of a beautiful and virtuous heiress, Clarissa Harlowe, who escapes the clutches of her loathsome family, only naively to fall prey to the evil designs of the elegant and handsome Lovelace, a treacherous libertine. He cons her into believing his protestations that in her love lies his redemption, but he is, in fact, meticulously plotting her downfall and goes to extraordinary lengths to achieve his goal, which is to seduce a virgin renowned for her piety. Following what he calls 'The Rake's Creed' he cunningly tricks her into travelling with him to London under his 'protection', where he goes through an elaborate charade before, ultimately, he drugs and rapes her.

Directed by Robert Bierman and produced by Kevin Loader, the assembled cast included Jeffry Wickham, Jonathan Phillips, Lynsey Baxter, Sean Pertwee, Cathryn Harrison and Diana Quick; the role of the eponymous heroine went to Saskia Wickham and was to be the twenty-four-year-old's screen début.

Shooting which began on 29 April 1991 would stretch into mid-July and Robert Bierman vividly recalls casting Bean.

'Sean wasn't the only person I looked at. I screen tested him with three or four others, one of whom was Chris Eccleston. I had looked to see who I thought were the up-and-coming top actors. I wanted Sean to be the best and when he did the screen test, he was clearly miles better. Sean also very much wanted the role. A lot of young actors can be cocky and so self-assured, but his spirit at the interview was very genuine. Initially, *he* wasn't sure that he was right for the part but soon realised it would be great for him especially because, to date, he hadn't had the chance to truly show that side of himself.

'I then put Sean with each of the four girls who were up for the part because I wanted to see how they would pair. There was Jennifer Ehle and Saskia Wickham, plus another couple. At one point we had paired Jennifer with Chris – two good actors – but the dynamics didn't work as well as they did when we put Sean with Saskia. In a screen test you cannot make actors better than they are. And when we saw Sean and Saskia together, they were streets ahead.'

Just how seriously Sean took the screen test became obvious to the director only later. Says Robert, 'I discovered that he had been very nervous during the test. There was a moment when they had to hold one another and Saskia told me some time after that Sean had been shaking. Yet he looked so confident. He had done a lot of preparation. He knew who he was. He knew how to play Lovelace.'

Nerves also understandably afflicted Saskia Wickham as she explains, 'I'd never done a screen test before. Since leaving drama school I'd appeared twice in theatre and this was only my third job. I did the interview and had met with Bob Bierman and everything had gone well, I thought. Two weeks passed and nothing happened, so I rang and they said that they were going to offer the part to someone else. But then they phoned back and said she didn't want to do it and would I come in for a screen test.

'I was very nervous anyway, then I got there and discovered it was with Sean Bean, who even then was pretty well known. It was in a tiny room in Limegrove and I was shaking all over. But there was something with Sean, some kind of spark between us, that worked. I felt very lucky to be doing the screen test with him. Because it's not just about your own performance, casting the right couple was important.

'When it was over and we went outside, I said to Sean, "You'll definitely get it because you were great." And he said the same to me. But I went home and cried all afternoon because I was sure that I hadn't got it. The next day though they rang to say that I had. If I hadn't been paired with Sean, it wouldn't have happened for me.'

The director was thrilled with his two leads. He recalls, 'The budget was over £3 million – an enormous amount of money in TV terms – and a lot was riding on it. That meant a lot was riding on Sean. The drama was called *Clarissa* but the focus was mainly on the male lead. A weak Lovelace would have sunk it and one of the reasons we chose Sean was because he has so many layers. Sean Bean is not a cuddly bloke and Lovelace was just perfect for him. There is a dark side and a charismatic side. Sean's a good-looking guy, but he can project a sinister quality.

'I had seen all his work before and had been impressed by some of the things he had done, like *Caravaggio*. In that he had been this beautiful bisexual boy who could not have been more diametrically the opposite of Sean Bean and yet he was incredibly believable in the role. In the case of Lovelace, he's a charming devil and the calculating part of the character required an actor with the mental dexterity of Sean Bean. Lovelace was a part that could have been written for Sean Bean in 1748 and had been waiting for him for nearly 250 years.'

Clarissa came about almost by chance. Bierman states, 'The BBC had *The Buddha of Suburbia* coming, but the script was not ready so they looked around and found *Clarissa*. Although the BBC had been the best at producing period dramas they had not made a costume piece for years, because that genre had dropped out of fashion. So with this we wanted it to be different and exciting. We also wanted to bring young blood to the lead roles. Sean was in his early thirties and Saskia in her early twenties.'

Throughout his career Sean would often consciously draw on his working-class roots to give a role added authenticity. But he was just as adept at shedding them like a snake its skin to become the complete embodiment of an aristocrat. And Lovelace's lethal attraction for the viewer was something akin to the fascination of watching a deadly snake.

For Sean, the key factor in being able to engender such an appeal lay in making particular aspects of his bold, cunning character as wickedly enticing as possible, without ever dropping his sinister qualities.

Robert Bierman says, 'The big job in a sense for Sean was over once he got the part. The pressure was off. And working as Lovelace, he knew then he was right in the role, which is very important. He likes the challenge of complexities in a character; one dimensional roles are not enough for Sean. He made Lovelace so alluring that even when his wickedness culminates with the rape, people still felt sorry for him afterwards.'

The rape scene in *Clarissa* was shocking and memorable in television terms. It takes place in the brothel into which Lovelace has tricked Clarissa, now drugged, and two of the prostitutes service the rape by holding the heroine down for him. The director recalls, 'Normally I spend a lot of time with actors on these scenes but for some reason this time I didn't. I plotted it out as we got to it. It was simple to do. We discussed it and I said this is what I want. The really shocking bit hits home when Lovelace slaps Clarissa and I felt that it really had to be a slap. It doesn't work the same if it's faked and after two and three quarter hours of this drama, this is the bit everyone was waiting for. If it didn't come off, it was all wasted.

'We discussed various ways of doing it but in the end Saskia said to Sean, "Just slap me, hard," and he really did! It was a simple scene, but we had to get it exactly right so it took a few takes and that was hard on them both. It was the physicality of it that was shocking. Rape scenes are hard to film at the best of times and not have them come across as grubby.'

For Saskia it was quite a challenge. She recalls, 'We filmed the rape scene in the first month and I was absolutely terrified. There I was, just fresh from drama school really, starring in this period drama and faced with a scene like this! But Sean was fantastic about the whole thing. He is always very professional, but he was extremely caring too.

'Bob Bierman came to me and said, "I want to try something that is a bit near the knuckle, and if you don't want to do it then just say so." And I thought, "Oh my God! He's going to ask me to take my clothes off!" When he said, "I want Sean to hit you and for real." I was so relieved I cried, "Oh fine! No problem!" I thought, I'd rather be hit by Sean Bean than take my clothes off! Then when Sean clattered me round the face, I burst into tears! It was really sore, but it was also the complete shock of it because I had never in my life been hit. Mind you, I remember thinking as I was crying that this will look good. Bob said, "Cut," then said we had to do it again and told me not to cry so much next time, not realising that the tears had been real!'

There had to be three more takes of that slap and each time Saskia had to have a wet cloth pressed to her cheek to stop it from swelling. She says, 'Poor Sean. He was really sweet but on a film set you can't keeping asking if someone is all right. You just have to get on with it. Then the next day he arrived for work and handed me a little package. Inside was a beautiful glass box with flowers etched on it. He said quietly, "Well done for yesterday." He also felt bad about having had to hit me.'

Someone else who vividly recalls this particular scene is *Clarissa's* director of photography John McGlashan who would be BAFTA nominated for his work on this drama. Says John, 'Whenever I read in a script the words, "And then they make love", I confess my heart sinks. I immediately conjure up having to cope with this controlled balletic piece, all nipples and knickers, and it is frankly a real pain trying to film that kind of thing tastefully. But with *Clarissa's* rape scene there was so much clothing in evidence, no bare flesh at all, that it was a technical exercise. But, of course, the effect of that was to show the calculated brutality of it all. What horrified me most, though, was the look on Lovelace's face – the sheer cruelty that crept in. Sean scared me then, I must say.'

For all the grim drama of the scene Saskia remembers one light-hearted moment whilst filming. She says, 'When Lovelace has to have his orgasm Bob told Sean, "Just do two or three thrusts and that will do." Sean replied, "But it's not going to seem like I can't make it last, will it?" Bob laughed, "Don't worry, Sean, I'll have it going on for ever." '

The working relationship between the two leads was a very happy one. Saskia says, 'I never found it difficult with Sean. We shared the same make-up and hair caravan and, with the exception of one day, we worked every day together. He is such an easy going guy and fabulous to get along with. Sean has no ego or vanity. Or if he has, he is honest about it. He will ask straight out, "Do you think I look better in this, or this?"

'He is an astounding actor and incredible to work with. We didn't really talk that much about our scenes and sometimes I would have liked to, if there was something that was worrying me a little. But whenever we stepped on set Sean went straight into it, which spurred me into it as well. He was equally capable of snapping right out of being Lovelace as soon as a scene ended. One minute he was up to all sorts of devious tricks with my character then the next thing he's asking, "Fancy coming for a lager afterwards?" '

John McGlashan noted this too. He recalls, 'He was very good on the English accent but whenever a take was over he would instantly revert to his Northern accent and sometimes he would come up to me quietly and ask, "Was I all right then? Was it okay?" He was very humble and an extremely professional actor on set.'

That Sean should seek a word with him did not surprise McGlashan. He says, 'Directors of Photography often establish a good rapport with actors. We are on the floor with them, and they'll often seek help, or affirmation of their acting from us because we see how they look through the lens.'

John McGlashan noticed a rare moment when Sean was taken unawares. He recalls, 'It was when he is provoked into a blazing sword fight in an alley with Jonathan Phillips who played Clarissa's brother, James. Sean is a very disciplined actor but I felt that enthusiasm had momentarily got the better of Jonathan a bit, because although it was meant to be a spectacular fight, Sean, I could see, was certainly surprised by the ferocity of Phillips' attack.'

According to Saskia, the director was also in for a surprise. 'The scene with Jonathan Phillips ended up with an accident. Jonathan was supposed to really boot this log out of the way. Bob was watching the action on the monitor and as the log went out of shot he had just asked, "Where did that log go?" when it landed on his head and knocked him out!'

Bean looked striking in the exquisite satin clothes and powdered wigs but he also managed a complete transformation into a lowly country yokel in order to exchange notes secretly with Clarissa. It was during one such scene that Sean came a cropper.

Dressed in rustic clothes, a battered hat crammed over a bushy hairstyle and with blacked-out teeth, Lovelace has just collected Clarissa's note. Smug that his scheme is working, he whistles jauntily as he approaches a five-bar country gate which he vaults over only to vanish ignominiously from sight of the camera to the accompanying screech of outraged scattering hens. Seconds later came a low-pitched, 'Oh fuck it!' from Sean before he reappears, dishevelled, but ready to do the scene again. And this wasn't the only laugh on set.

The end scene of the first episode when Lovelace manipulates Clarissa into running off with him in the night involved a manservant from the Harlowe house hunting the fleeing heroine through the grounds with a snarling hound and Saskia recalls, 'That dog just would not chase a flea. It was a great big dog and the soppiest, loveliest animal you have ever seen. It refused to chase us and in the end I think they had to get a bloke to drag a bit of beef on the end of a chain or something to get it to run towards the camera.'

Clarissa featured nearly 1,500 different costumes. The ladies were laced into corsets and stomachers over panniered skirts which restricted free movement but helped concentrate the mind, while the men favoured satin breeches, wide-sleeved shirts and square-cut elaborate coats. One particularly stunning dark green velvet coat that Sean wore was so richly embroidered with silver and gold that it weighed nearly as much as a suit of armour.

It had a generous timescale too. John McGlashan says, 'In those days you were allowed very good schedules for drama and we had about sixteen weeks to shoot this.'

He continues, 'We filmed at a couple of big country houses; one was a private property up North which had a wonderful staircase with a wavy hand rail which turned out to be carved like a serpent. There was another big house near Stratford and one in Hampstead. Exterior and street scenes with coaches and horses were filmed outside The Inns of Court in London but mostly it was studio based. It was almost like doing a feature film with the huge cranes, plenty of extras and fantastic settings.'

Among the sets built was a three-storey Georgian house, a coaching inn and one spectacular street scene which took three weeks to construct, including laying a 'floor' consisting of four tons of cobbles and pebbles set in concrete. McGlashan recalls, 'This was on the stage at Ealing studio and with the narrow alley and high gabled houses overhanging, it was really magnificent.'

The long schedule, away on location, brought its moments. Robert Bierman says, 'Sean and I had nothing in common off set. He adores football and The Blades and I don't like football. He's a beer drinker and I don't like beer. But we got along fantastically well. We had a good laugh, which was important when working on something for so long and something that could seem to be a dry subject. But Sean likes pub time. So when some of us would go out for an evening dolled up in our sharp suits, he preferred a more casual way of relaxing and would go out with the prop boys, the crew, rather than come with us.'

Not every evening, however, was spent socialising in the pub. Bierman reveals, 'One morning I turned up to find some very sorry looking people standing before me. The night before the producers, Sean and some others had tried to wreck one of the hotel rooms. But it had been in a childish way. They had been ringing round the hotel guests and giving them early morning 4.00 a.m. calls that they had never asked for. They'd taken drink and drunk it and they did a little bit of damage but nothing remotely serious.

'In the end it was a rather pathetic attempt to do a rock star trashing the room routine which ended up being like a naughty school-boy prank that left them very shame-faced the next day. They ended up making abject apologies all round and handing over a cheque to the management. They'd just been letting loose a little and everything was all right, which was just as well because we had to stay there for a bit longer yet.'

Over the weeks Saskia Wickham had enjoyed so much about working with Sean and certain scenes would stand out. She says, 'I remember when I was supposed to kiss Lovelace. Usually it was Sean seizing me and kissing me, which was great – I had no problem with that at all. But then when we come home from the ball I had to kiss him. And suddenly I discovered I was nervous so I ended up giving him this rather hasty peck and dashing off up the stairs. Bob shouted, "Hey Saskia! You might look like you enjoyed it!" Maybe I didn't want to show just how much I would have enjoyed kissing Sean Bean.

'In the eighteenth century life was always so close to death and you had to have an edge to survive. And that is one of the great things about Sean. He has that danger in him, an exciting edge. He gives off a kind of tingly sensation. You never know what he is going to do next. It's marvellous.'

By the time shooting ended on 19 July, Sean had also made a deep impression on the director. He states, 'Sean is easy to direct because he is so good. He doesn't need things greatly explained – he gets it right away. I describe some actors as being like thoroughbred horses – the really brilliant ones respond to the lightest touch – and Sean is on that level. The incredible sensitivity you can get out of him when developing a character is amazing. Likewise, the amount of subtle adjustments that Sean can make are limitless. And it's these delicate touches that you build on which are the touches that let an actor bring depth to a character.'

Clarissa screened later that year between 27 November and 11 December and, prior to transmission, as Robert Bierman explains, something of a splash occurred. 'Over the course of filming a number of journalists came to the set. They were given access to what was going on, as well as to the cast and crew, who gave their time to talk to them. Well, there was a big exposé just before the drama screened and it caused a huge fuss because it was a story saying how the BBC had destroyed this famous novel.

'What happened was a journalist who had claimed to be from *Vogue* had, in fact, been freelance and had proceeded to sell a story to one of the national newspapers in which everything anyone had said had been twisted around so that it bad-mouthed everyone. It was looked into and dealt with, but someone hadn't done the vetting properly and it caused a big scandal.'

Clarissa, nevertheless, proved to be hugely popular, with Bean's performance of what one critic called 'a chauvinistic sexual psychopath' being acclaimed and, furthermore, provided a showcase for Saskia Wickham's talents with her portrayal of a dutiful but deceptively strong-minded heroine. It also marked the first time that Sean became front cover material when he and Saskia featured on the cover of the *Radio Times*.

Just weeks after shooting on *Clarissa* ended, Sean moved on to his next role and discovered that one of the period drama's co-stars, Diana Quick, also had a guest role in the same *Inspector Morse* episode *Absolute Conviction* for which filming was under way in August.

This was the fourth episode of the sixth series of the award-winning detective drama starring John Thaw and Kevin Whately, and, produced by Deirdre Keir based on a screenplay by John Brown, *Absolute Conviction* was directed by Antonia Bird. Bean played Alex Bailey, one of three former 1980s' entrepreneurs in luxury real estate who had been jailed for swindling millions from their investors. All three are inmates in the same prison and when one of them dies, Morse investigates.

As the coldly cynical Bailey, Sean's involvement in this episode was not large, but it added yet another television appearance to his growing list of credits. *Absolute Conviction* was aired the following year, on 8 April 1992.

Sean's and Melanie's desire to have another child resulted in the birth that year of a second daughter, Molly. Thrilled, Sean does, however, also crave a son. He once described the prospect of someday carrying on the Bean family tradition of father taking son to watch Sheffield United play as being 'close to bliss on earth'.

While Melanie had chosen again to disrupt her career to have their second baby, Sean's career was set to zoom when he landed the coveted major supporting role of the villain in the American blockbuster movie *Patriot Games*, opposite superstar Harrison Ford. This high-profile part would provide Bean with his first taste of filming in Hollywood and the three-month shoot would necessitate his longest absence so far from his home and family.

He had a close shave before he even left British soil when, whilst attending a football match in London, he got carried along with the enthusiasm of his fellow spectators and spontaneously joined in a pitch invasion at the end of the game. Caught up in the good-natured euphoria, it only dawned on Sean once he was on the turf that he had to fly to America the next day and that if he got arrested he would miss his flight. As the cops were busy trying to round up the invading revellers, he made a beeline across the pitch and out to the tube station and home.

From a screenplay by Peter Iliff and Donald Stewart based on the bestselling novel by Tom Clancy, *Patriot Games* was the sequel to *The Hunt for Red October* and with Ford assuming the role of Jack Ryan, an ex-CIA analyst, from actor Alec Baldwin, this Paramount Pictures movie lay in the hands of producers Mace Neufeld and Robert Rehme, under the stewardship of director Phillip Noyce.

American star Anne Archer played Ryan's wife, while Patrick Bergin headed up a small fictional splinter faction of the IRA. Sean was cast as terrorist Sean Miller who ends up waging a rabid personal vendetta against the film's hero because, while in London, Jack Ryan foils an attempt by the terrorists to abduct Lord Holmes, a relative of the British Queen, and in the process shoots dead Miller's younger brother.

Patriot Games reunited Bean with Polly Walker, here playing one of the terrorists, with whom he had worked in *Lorna Doone*, and also Richard Harris from *The Field* whose cameo role in *Patriot Games* was as Paddy O'Neil, a fictitious Republican figure in America. Along with actors James Fox, Samuel L. Jackson, James Earl Jones and Alex Norton among others, shooting commenced mid-October 1991.

For this $42.5 million budget blockbuster Bean adopted a pronounced Irish accent to became a menacing madman who looked lethal even when in handcuffs and under heavy guard at his arrest early in the film. The electric charge he unremittingly radiated throughout the movie was heightened by an aggressive-looking crew-cut. Easy with an Uzi, Sean's capacity for depicting cold-blooded murder was unnerving. Miller's single-minded quest for revenge was an integral cog in the wheel that drove the film and would lead up to a thrilling climactic clash between himself and the hero, Jack Ryan.

Sean found no problem in assuming the cloak of the psycho, in part because he does not see such screen characters as being all bad. Instead, he prefers to believe that there is good in them too, and it's more the case that it is the darker side of their personality which proves to be the dominant force. Nevertheless, the energy of vibrant anger required to portray a hate-filled figure meant digging deep within himself. Sean has explained, 'You can't put things on. You've got to *feel* them.' He also added, 'You have to have it inside you before you can bring it out and show it on screen.'

Reserving these darker emotions for his screen performance, Sean was delighted at the prospect of sampling the new experiences that securing this part brought. One of these memorable moments occurred when, arriving in Los Angeles, he was swept by stretch-limousine to Paramount Studios to meet Harrison Ford. The smooth ride cushioned amid impeccable and pampered luxury was Bean's first taste of celebrity high-life and he intended to relax and enjoy it.

Ford is said to generally prefer to keep a courteous, but distinct, distance from people, and Bean's nature is the opposite of pushy, yet these two naturally reserved men clicked. Sean liked Harrison's unstarry style and was not in awe of the Hollywood giant. That Ford's entire attitude was to get the job done and go home to his family, also neatly dovetailed with Bean's.

Some filming would take place in England, including the shooting of the movie's explosive opening – the terrorist attempt to abduct Lord Holmes, played by James Fox, as the car in which he is travelling supposedly leaves Buckingham Palace. This scene was actually shot at the Royal Naval College in Greenwich and Malcolm Godfrey of the Royal Naval College recalls, 'Most of the action was filmed in the Grand Square. Ironically it was filmed on Remembrance Sunday! There was a chapel at the college where a Remembrance Service was in progress so the film crew were under threat to shoot no scenes of a violent nature – they were not allowed to fire a single shot – before 12 noon, when the service would be over.'

James Fox recollects, 'It was a very powerful way to open a movie and Sean was terrific as Miller. It was clear he had tremendous screen presence. I feel that he showed a lot of hurt and powerful anger in what was a *very* strong performance.'

Sharpe as a Blade! As the romantically dashing nineteenth century rifleman Richard Sharpe, Sean perfectly embodied one of the best ever television heroes which for years stirred the imagination of millions.

ABOVE After his separation from Melanie, Sean and actress Abigail Cruttenden began a romance on the set of *Sharpe* which led to their real-life marriage in November 1997. They have a daughter, Evie, but reports that the marriage had foundered surfaced in July 2000.

ABOVE Having met as drama students, Sean and actress Melanie Hill remained together for 15 years, and have two daughters, Lorna and Molly. One of the most stable relationships in showbusiness, however, ended in divorce in August 1997.

BELOW Whatever the ups-and-downs of his love life, Sean is the proud father of three girls. He is pictured here with Molly when he opened the 1994 Christmas Fair at Athelstan Primary School in Sheffield.

Another scene shot in England included the moment when Miller is sprung from police custody by his friends, after an astonishing ambush on the armoured van taking him to prison. This was filmed at London's Canary Wharf. But most of the time was spent in the US, working in the epicentre of the film world.

A hungry and competitive city whose citizens are consumed by filmmaking and where ferocious networking goes on round the clock amid wall-to-wall glitz and glamour, Tinsel Town is also a place of huge temptations with perfumed predators constantly on the prowl. Workwise, Bean found the sheer dynamism of the movie industry there intensely invigorating, but the high-powered social scene, with all its effusive sham, held no appeal for him. At the end of a day's filming he preferred to switch off, wind down and conserve his energies for the next day's work.

Living quietly, he avoided parties and was content in his hotel room, after having had a meal, to settle down alone before the television in between phoning home. He missed his family so much that half way through his long spell away, Melanie and the girls flew out to join him for a visit, during which time they enjoyed a family outing to Disneyland.

That brief break apart, it was all work which could fall prey to the usual delays. In the movie, the terrorists' London contact was Dennis Cooley, a dealer in antiquarian books who, discovering himself to be under police surveillance, gives the law the slip to join his comrades at their training camp in the Libyan desert. Alex Norton who played the part recalls, 'They flew us down to shoot these desert scenes to an area just south of Los Angeles, near to the Mexican border, that's well known for its incredible sand dunes. I was only supposed to be needed there for one day as Sean's character kills me, but it rained so the one day turned into almost a week.

'*Patriot Games* went through daily rewrites and when we were there the director Phillip Noyce and the producers were having a disagreement over my character. In the script Cooley is shot but for some reason the producers didn't want that. They wanted me to be left in the desert. In the end we shot two endings for me, one when Sean Miller guns me down, and one when I am left blinking into the sun as the terrorists drive off and leave me stranded. But the only thing is, for the scene when Sean shoots me, because the producers hadn't intended this to happen, they hadn't brought any bloody explosives for the bullets. So that's why it ends up with Sean pointing the gun at me, you see my face registering what he's going to do, and that's it.'

Patriot Games' seventy-five-day shoot was completed around the end of 1991, but then the filmmakers hit a snag. In early 1992, when the film underwent test screenings, the all-important final fight scene produced a negative audience reaction that was strong enough to necessitate an expensive re-shoot.

The climactic clash between Miller, who is by now so consumed with killing Ryan that he murders his two fellow terrorists who try to get in his way, and Ryan who is just as desperate to save his family, takes place in a storm on board a racing speed boat, bouncing crazily over choppy seas in the dark. The two end up in a to-the-death struggle under water and this was the mistake.

After a build-up of such heart-pounding intensity, the crunch came almost in slow motion and the necessary energy simply evaporated. Harrison Ford later described it as, 'all very balletic' and apparently everyone knew immediately that it had not worked.

Bean rejoined Ford and the crew at the gigantic tank built on the backlot of Paramount Pictures studio complex – a half-acre site encircled by eight feet high walls and filled with a million gallons of water. At 1.00 a.m. they got to work under high lights, amid wind simulators, wave-making machines and torrential rain courtesy of giant sprinklers positioned on top of a series of telegraph poles. Only this time, when the two men fought to the death they remained on board one of the speed boats.

When the filmmakers' hitch over the movie's original ending had made the American Press, Harrison Ford had had to correct some lurid claims that he had suffered a Near Death experience whilst filming the underwater scene. He had, he revealed, no more than bumped his head and the small cut he had received had not even needed a sticking plaster. During the re-shot ending it was Sean's turn to be injured, when a boat hook caught him just under one eyebrow and cut open his eye, necessitating eight stitches.

This hiccup aside, filming *Patriot Games* – a movie for which the producers had been afforded unprecedented access to the CIA's headquarters at Langley in Virginia – had been an exciting experience for Bean. He enjoyed working with Harrison Ford, who reciprocated respect for Sean's acting abilities. Ford's superstar status afforded him a significant say in the movie's editing and all of Sean's explosively acted scenes had been left intact. And as the movie's UK casting director John Hubbard of Hubbard Casting affirms, 'Sean's performance in all of his scenes was highly praised indeed by the people at Paramount.'

Patriot Games went on general release in America on 5 June 1992, followed by its UK release on 25 September. Some reviewers were wary that it might glamorise terrorism, although that had not been the filmmakers' intention, and *Variety* indeed called it 'morally repugnant'. But the movie was a box-office smash hit. For Harrison Ford it was another triumph. For Sean Bean it brought his talents to a global audience and catapulted him firmly into the league of being a top-notch screen villain.

When filming on *Patriot Games* had originally wrapped Sean had returned home from Hollywood in early 1992 eager to repeat the experience. He had appreciated the gutsy role and by spring, it was to be four-in-a-row when Sean went from international terrorist, to South London hood for his starring role in the British television film *Fool's Gold*, which – in its own way – proved to be another startling experience.

At dawn on 26 November 1983 a gang of robbers, three of them armed with revolvers, and with the help of an inside man, launched a daring raid on a security warehouse near London's Heathrow Airport. They had expected to find close on £2 million in cash. Instead, they made off with three tons of gold bullion, worth £26 million. It was a brutal blag, in which one of the six security guards was doused in petrol and threatened with being set alight, whilst another guard was pistol-whipped.

The Brinks-Mat bullion raid was Britain's biggest ever robbery and as such it brought Scotland Yard's Flying Squad down on the villains' trail. They were caught within three weeks and £20 million in cash and goods was recovered. But of the 6,800 gold ingots stolen, only 11 were ever found and mythology has it that anyone sporting gold jewellery in Britain post-1984 is likely to be wearing part of the melted down spoils.

Nine years later London Weekend Television decided to make a film of this notorious heist. The filmmakers were aware that the full truth would ultimately prove elusive, but *Fool's Gold* was to be based on a combination of official data and information gleaned from talking to some people connected to the crime. And what particularly intrigued director Terry Winsor and producer Jeff Pope, who also co-scripted the movie, was the human story of double-crossing among friends.

The gritty drama did not aim for gratuitous violence, but neither would it shrink from realistically depicting violent men committing a brutal crime. On a budget of under £500,000 the cameras were ready to roll on 23 March 1992 with Sean Bean in the lead role of the terri-fyingly aggressive gang ringleader Micky McAvoy. Co-stars included Trevor Byfield, John Labanowski, Brian Croucher, Larry Lamb, David Cardy and Sharon Maiden and the one-month's filming would take the cast and crew to locations in London's East End, Kent and Spain.

For Sean, it was a complete whirlwind because he learned that he had the role only one week prior to shooting commencing. Terry Winsor explains, 'We had looked and looked and couldn't find the right actor to play McAvoy and then Sean literally walked into the room and we could tell at once that the camera would love his face.'

With very little preparation time Sean was pitched into under-going a crash course on the robbery and the figures behind it. The lack of time would have precluded it anyway, but he preferred not to visit the real Micky McAvoy who was serving twenty-five years' imprison-ment, and instead concentrated wholly on the script.

Winsor goes on, 'It was a pretty tough film. McAvoy was trying to branch out from being the strong arm man in other gangs, and this time he was the architect of the robbery. As McAvoy, Sean had to go through this whole interesting process from being a real hard man, to being quite a sympathetic character who in the end gets stitched up by his mates. We had a tussle about whether people should feel sorry for him, or not. And we decided, not.

'But there's just something in Sean that he elicits a kind of sympathy, even for such a ferociously tough man. It's a fantastic quality and is quite unique to him. What Sean also has is the ability to make the person he is playing come alive. He lifts the written character clean off the page and that doesn't just happen. He really works at it.'

Sean saw Micky McAvoy as a hard man, who loved his family and who was so determined an individual, that once all the planning had been done, there could be no turning back. It was a role which he embraced with gusto and fresh from portraying Sean Miller, he effort-lessly conveyed ruthlessness as the gangster capable of jabbing the muzzle of his gun menacingly into the neck of a petrified security guard. In fact, so immersed did he become in the role, that he managed to give himself a jolt; he has described as 'chilling' the first moment he caught sight of himself wearing a stocking mask.

The director certainly remembers the depth of the star's immersion in the part. He states, 'Sean was incredibly locked in. One particular day he had just filmed a scene during the robbery which is particularly violent. A lot of hard stuff is going on and there's a great deal of shouting and noise and when it was over Sean discovered that he had run out of cigarettes. He went out to a nearby off-licence to buy a packet and when they didn't have his brand, he went completely berserk. That's a measure of how mentally involved in the role he still was. Sean actually had to catch himself up and realise just what he was doing.'

For the first time, too, Sean found his work spilling over into his home life when unconsciously he retained his Cockney accent after hours. Terry says, 'Sean's accent in the film was terrific and it would have been hard to jump in and out of it, because for a South Yorkshire tongue to make the transition to South London isn't easy.'

Bean had had help in mastering this accent from co-star Brian Croucher who portrayed one of McAvoy's accomplices, Brian Robinson. Brian said, 'Sean struggled a bit with the Cockney accent early on, so the producer told me to help him with his vowels at times, mainly because I was with him a lot on set. But he's a very talented actor. He worked extremely hard, always, and I could easily see that he was a guy who'd have strong appeal to the ladies – he can exude that rough trade type appeal.'

Brian has most effectively portrayed many screen hard men and he reveals part of the key to achieving this authenticity. 'It's an understanding of selfishness, of greed and of sheer ruthlessness. Playing these roles can be great therapy for an actor. You can get rid of angst and frustration and all that crap on set, then you can go home and kiss the wife and play with the kids happily. Our job is to tell stories. Sometimes in doing that, you come a bit near to the edge and you can get strung out for a while, but that's the deal. I've never met Mick McAvoy but I believe him to have been a dangerous man, and Sean very clearly brought that real element of danger to his portrayal.'

Trevor Byfield who played Jimmy Kimpton, a fictional character based upon a real person, was also on familiar screen territory with this role and he reckons he knows the secret of Bean's adeptness at playing the villain. Says Trevor, 'It's got to be that chin of his. He has such a strong face. Sean really enjoyed the role and even though he was just on the cusp of big things right then, he was an easy guy to work with, with a good sense of humour. I remember us all larking around and having a giggle.'

Terry Winsor agrees, 'Everyone gelled while making that film. As a director, what I do tends to be pretty intense with not much relief, but there were moments when something would go wrong which was funny. I remember one scene when this bloke had to burst aggressively into a room and when he did, he came through the door with his gun backwards and pointing at himself.

'On small films the relationship between the actor, director and camera is such that a very strong link develops and the contributions become much greater for it. Sean is the sort of person I can really invest in. He is very keen to take direction. But we also talked at great length about the role and he would come up with ideas of his own. As we went along, we discovered a pattern developing. That kind of collaboration is very invigorating and it takes on a life of its own, which adds an extra exciting dimension. The script, then, becomes just the starting point and it produces a far better and more enjoyable end product.

'We were incredibly ambitious in what we aimed to achieve and certainly for me, it pushed what I wanted to do on a bit further. We made what was essentially a feature film on a minuscule budget and *Fool's Gold* went on to win the Best TV Movie Award at the New York Film Festival.' Shooting ended on 23 April but because the drama could not be screened until all court trials connected with the real life robbery were over, it was not transmitted until 14 November 1992.

Summer 1992 was a hectic time. It was after filming *Fool's Gold* that Bean was recalled to Los Angeles to re-shoot *Patriot Games'* ending. And it was on his return from America that he embarked on the role that would kickstart his reputation for sizzling screen nudity, and his legendary status as a hot screen lover, when he took on the role of Oliver Mellors, Lady Chatterley's lusty, forthright gamekeeper.

Although Sean's good and bad guy roles would begin to alternate, still the recent emphasis had remained on the latter and so it was quite a switch, after portraying a succession of villains, to jump now into the part of the romantic hero – albeit, a laconic, moody and scowling one.

Based on the novel *Lady Chatterley's Lover* by D.H. Lawrence – which had been banned in Britain for 30 years and only published in unexpurgated form after it was the subject of a sensational Obscenity trial in 1960 – *Lady Chatterley* was a screen adaptation by screen-writer/producer Michael Haggiag and director Ken Russell. With a budget of £4 million, this four-part serial was produced by London Films/Global Arts Productions for the BBC.

It was not going unnoticed that Sean Bean was fast cornering the market in playing leading figures from literary classics, and this was one of English literature's sexiest roles. Bean read this controversial novel for the first time when he got the part as Mellors and his own view of the story was, that it was not so much scandalous, as about a release of passion and love. He also felt that Lawrence had grasped completely the tensions inherent in a relationship between two people of differing class. Sean responds best to complex characters and because to him Mellors had interesting layers and undertones which as an actor he could explore and gradually reveal, he therefore posed a sufficiently satisfying emotional challenge.

To Michael Haggiag, Sean seemed the natural choice for Mellors.

He says, 'As soon as Sean was available, we wanted him. As I recall, we didn't even screen test him. We chose him because he was from the right area and had the right look. For me, Sean was perfect because he has a certain vulnerability mixed in with the strength, and in a nice balance. He's capable of being both brutish and tender and that was what we were looking for. He also expressed perfectly, the class rage. And not just rage, a sense that the reality of their different stations in life also hurt. Yet, at the same time, you felt that Mellors was okay in his own skin and that element is very true of Sean himself. He also has charisma. People are interested in watching him on screen, in seeing what his reaction to something will be.'

The task of scripting Lawrence's most famous novel for television had not been easy. Michael reveals, 'When you start to do an adaptation, you want to be true to the spirit of the original book. Only in this case, I found that there was more than one original! Plus, it was a complex theme that was very close to Lawrence's heart. I discovered, in fact, that he had re-worked each of the three versions about ten times.

'It was a controversial story, but Lawrence was trying to make it into a cause – his notion being that sexuality was a revolutionary statement. There was a counter-enlightenment notion that, through the body, people learned about life. I thought the first novel was the most accomplished but it had developed more into a political book and those politics no longer held any interest now. So I ended up plumbing the books for the dialogue, which is where I felt I could find the spirit of it.'

When it came to tailoring the sex scenes to an acceptable form for prime time television Michael Haggiag concentrated on a specific approach. He says, 'Again I felt that a lot of it was in the words. For example, D.H. Lawrence's use of certain words like "fucking", to describe having sex, was scandalous then. But although there were tough scenes, I also wanted to concentrate on the tender, romantic side.'

To portray the racy post-First World War story of a beautiful young aristocratic lady who is married to the wheelchair-bound Sir Clifford and who embarks on a steamy affair with their brusque game-keeper, with whom she ultimately falls in love, director Ken Russell operated with a small cast that featured, in the other two key roles; James Wilby as Sir Clifford, and the part of Constance Chatterley was played by Joely Richardson. Internationally acclaimed, award-winning cinematographer Robin Vidgeon was to handle *Lady Chatterley's* photography.

The eleven-week shoot was due to begin on 11 May 1992 and Sean was still finishing off his work on *Patriot Games* in Los Angeles. Initially, concern had arisen over the fact that, for continuity, he would need Sean Miller's crew-cut again, which for Mellors would have been a major snag. However, when Bean rang *Lady Chatterley's* producers it was to report that he had good news and bad news.

The good news was that he had managed to keep his hair from being shorn. The bad news was the acquisition of that great big gash over one eye. Some serious make-up camouflaged the injury when work on *Lady Chatterley* got under way.

It proved to be a lively experience as Michael Haggiag explains, 'Ken loves to outrage. People expect it of him and if he didn't give it to them, they'd be profoundly disappointed. I didn't write some of the scenes in the way they ended up. For instance, I didn't write the scene when Mellors takes Lady Chatterley from behind and it's a difficult experience for her. That was very much Ken's idea, and it's a question of sensibilities. I'm not saying Ken was wrong or right. Personally, I felt we could have exploited the erotic side a bit more through the awkwardness in the tender moments, rather than by just being brutish. But I chose him as director and there has to be a necessary passing of the baton.

'Our working relationship was sensitive and difficult. Ken can be very mercurial. He was amenable all through the pre-production stage, but then when it came to the actual shoot and he got the bit between his teeth, he was a terror. He stormed off and created little dramas and it was all a show, all a performance. It makes for an absolutely thrilling experience working with him, but one that's also sometimes akin to being on a huge roller coaster.

'My own personal view, too, is that Ken did certain things that were wrong for *Lady Chatterley*. For instance, when he cast himself as Connie's father. And I felt that the actress Natasha Richardson, Joely

Richardson's real sister, would have been a better choice for Connie's sister.'

Visually *Lady Chatterley* proved to be a treat, with exquisite costumes and settings. Standing in for the Chatterleys' grand country residence was Wrotham Park in Hertfordshire which is an extremely popular filming location that has been used in countless productions; its popularity is due partly to its proximity to London which allows a cast and crew to travel to and from the set daily.

The production then transferred to woods in Oxfordshire and on to Pinewood Studios, where the scenes inside and outside Mellors' hut were filmed, before they ended up on the Isle of Wight to capture the family get-together at Lady Chatterley's father's seaside home. It was during the crossing from Southampton to the Isle of Wight in atrocious weather, that the final scenes were filmed when Lady Chatterley and Mellors end up together on board ship heading for a new life in Canada. Robin Vidgeon recalls, 'We ran into the blackest clouds imaginable. It was mid-afternoon and yet it was pitch black.'

When *Lady Chatterley* wrapped on 25 July it was on schedule, on budget and on course to become the serial that contained some of the most explicit and raunchiest sex scenes ever seen on British television; it would be trailered as *the* TV event of the summer of 1993.

Nude love scenes were not new to Sean, but his responsibilities on this production would test him to the extreme. As the smouldering Mellors, Bean exudes a threatening sexuality which Connie finds invigoratingly tantalising. Once their mutual lust is unleashed, his ardent desire verges on the violent, as with rough urgency they greedily consummate their affair.

Mellors' first caveman-like approach leads to a soulless quickie inside his hut. With even less finesse he later rips off the heroine's knickers for more grunting, forceful vertical sex against a tree, and again over sacking on his hut floor in a series of frank, panting, prolonged expressions of sweaty, uncontrollable lust. Not until half way through the series did it become clear that Mellors' tough exterior protected, almost impenetrably, a vulnerable and complex inner self at which point explicit sex developed into heartfelt passion.

Such graphic scenes left no scope for actors' inhibitions and it was fortunate that both Sean and Joely were relaxed about them, although initially Richardson's views on how to handle them had not exactly matched Bean's – she had contemplated a more controlled approach. Bean admits that, though he does not know why, the love scenes with Joely Richardson had been particularly easy for him. Perhaps it lay partly in a mutual professional respect and that Sean's wry sense of humour appealed to his leading lady. Robin Vidgeon confirms, 'Sean and Joely were very comfortable together both on set and off it. She is very gentle by nature and so is he. Sean is not an Ollie Reed. He's not flamboyant.'

One scene, however, did give Joely pause as Michael Haggiag recalls, 'It was, naturally, a closed set when the love scenes were being shot but I was told that Joely initially raised an objection to the scene when Mellors takes Connie from behind. At this point Ken Russell supposedly looked around at the few people present and asked, "Well? How would you do it? Does nobody do it like that?" People sort of mumbled, "Well, yes . . . I suppose . . . maybe." "Okay," said Ken, "So we do it this way." '

Cinematographer Robin Vidgeon reveals, 'Ken always wants a bit more. But in the end there were no real problems and we managed to get things done by mutual agreement. I think Sean and Joely discussed between themselves what they would, and would not, do. They too wanted to deliver what they felt was right for the story. It's what you *don't* see that's sexy and I think that Sean and Joely brought an eroticism to their love scenes.

'Joely had not long had her baby and when we came to do the first full-frontal nude scene when she comes into her husband's bedroom, I remember that she was very conscious about that and yet she looked so beautiful. There were no full frontals with Sean, which I thought was unfair. What's good for the goose, should be good for the gander.'

Sean himself believes that if an actress is expected to be naked for a scene, then there is no reason why the actor should not have to be, too, and *Lady Chatterley*, in the flamboyant care of director Ken Russell, provided ample scope to put this belief into practice. Any shred of embarrassment had had to be quashed as Bean later explained, 'You have to commit yourself 100 per cent. If you don't, it looks tentative and self-conscious.' Although he did readily concede, 'Lying with your pants

down, surrounded by dozens of people is not exactly an everyday situation. It's not very nice having a camera up yer bum.'

The scene in which Joely Richardson and Sean had to run round
in the rain naked proved to be memorable, in more ways than one. In
part it felt exciting and the rain machine was spewing warmish water
over them, which was not unpleasant. But on the other hand, there
were gigantic speakers dotted around the wood blasting out classical
music and the sheer absurdity of it all struck Joely forcibly to the point
where she felt there was nothing for it; she and Sean *had* to have a
laugh with the scene.

Some people who may not have shared the amusement were the
passengers on the top floor of a passing double-decker bus who, Sean
felt, got a bit too close when their route took them past the set just as
Connie and Oliver were experiencing their ultimate expression of
freedom. Michael Haggiag believes the road was sufficiently far away
but he sympathises, 'I guess if you are running around naked in the
open, any passer-by would appear to be too close for comfort!'

Robin Vidgeon recalls this particular scene well. He laughs, 'I had
quite a hard job strategically placing plants and ferns and things in the
foreground to cover up Sean's naughty bits for the viewer. I did it as a
long track shot which means that when I was filming I wasn't watching
the frame, I was watching Sean's dangly bits which, of course, had to
be edited out. Who knows, the out-takes might end up one day on
Denis Norden's show!'

With two relaxed actors handling such provocative material there
had to be several such funny moments and one which appealed most to
Joely was when Sean had to rip Connie's knickers off; not her actual
undergarment but a pair conveniently attached lightly to the inside of
her dress. Joely later recalled, 'We ended up trying not to giggle because
Sean was pulling them for ages, and they seemed to go on *forever!*'

In the end, to Michael Haggiag it was certain subtle touches that
Sean brought to his performance that stood out. He explains, 'What
struck me was his awkwardness after he had taken Lady Chatterley up
against the tree then walks her through the woods and he is trying to
be protective of her. They are walking almost hip to hip and there is
that kind of Sunday-promenade-with-your-girlfriend feel to it which

was perfect. Sean was wonderful at showing that. I liked many of the qualities he showed on set and off. Sean is very real. He doesn't put on any airs which is extremely refreshing.'

Robin Vidgeon feels, 'Sean's performance was nicely understated. He's a real joy to work with – a true professional. He was always on time and helpful to other actors. You get some who concentrate solely on their own performance and that's it. They don't give their co-stars something to spin off of, but Sean does. He is a hands-on, on the set all the time, thinking actor. He's got such a dry sense of humour and likes a joke. Everyone, the crew, the lighting people, the lot, all liked him very much.'

When *Lady Chatterley* was screened, after the 9.00 p.m. watershed between 6 and 27 June 1993, it came in for much criticism and the most frequent tag attached to it in reviews was 'erotic'. The Broadcasting Standards Council, after receiving around twenty complaints, criticised the series for showing sex scenes that went on far too long and were too rough, and pointed out that sex had taken place no less than three times in one episode. But the programme pulled in an average weekly audience of around twelve million. The *Evening Standard* hailed it as, 'A triumph of style over stuffiness' and the *Daily Star* reported, 'The sex scenes are amazingly graphic, particularly where Mellors makes brutish love to the lusting aristocrat.'

An indication of the rousing effect that the sight of Sean Bean butt-naked was to have came when *Lady Chatterley*'s screening sent many female journalists into raptures over him; even one of their male colleagues wrote of Sean, 'He can touch the wanton in the most demure of women.'

Early proof that the journalist was right came when, in the teeth of the Press attacks on the series, one intrepid lady from Burnham-on-Sea wrote to a national newspaper to declare that personally she would suffer bark-burn any day to find herself sandwiched between a tree and an ardent Sean Bean!

Sean's rampant sex symbol status, confirmed by his role as Mellors, is something that he takes with a liberal pinch of salt and he treated with nonchalant amusement being called 'the middle-class woman's bit of rough'. His image would, however, let him in for some bald ribbing from his hometown mates. Notably, when Sean was once voted 'Rear of the Year', in their roughly affectionate way they apparently re-christened it, 'Asshole of the Year'. And his former Brook Comprehensive teacher Ian Footitt declares, 'When I saw him in *Lady Chatterley*, I thought, "Well we certainly never taught him to do *that*!"'

That Sean will modestly respond to talk of his potent sex appeal with remarks like, 'At least they don't say I'm an ugly twat,' is in keeping with his general attitude to stardom. For no matter how loud a fanfare is blowing around him he holds fast to the belief that the most important thing for an actor is getting the work in and doing it well. He calls it a great leveller, aware that fame can be an ephemeral thing.

It's a reality of the business that projects can also flare and die and over the years Bean would experience his fair share of projects that failed to come to fruition. He had been involved with a potentially very interesting project at the start of 1992 called *Inside the Wolf's Lair*. Director Paul Street recalls, 'It was shot on spec as a development for a pilot intended as a television series and it was set in Hitler's bunker in the last days of the Third Reich. Miles Anderson played Adolf Hitler, Ian Bartholomew was Joseph Goebbels and Sean was cast as Rudolf Hess.

'Sean had literally just got off the plane from LA where he had been filming *Patriot Games* and he came straight to Bray Studios where we filmed it over three days. He looked incredible as Hess and was incredible in the role. He arrived, I briefed him and gave him his speech which was a copy from an old news report, and he got it right away. It was a tough subject that raised a lot of issues because it was a psychological study into the Third Reich and it reached the point where the network was pushing for a franchise but unfortunately, it didn't make it.'

Sean's profile, however, was inexorably rising and the fact that in the light of this he and his family continued to live in their three-bedroomed home in Muswell Hill began to draw comment from journalists. But Bean did not wear living in a council house as some sort of working-class badge. He just failed to see why it should matter. He liked the neighbourhood and it was quiet.

However, by the autumn he did have one outward sign of extravagance – a sleek light green Jaguar Sovereign parked outside. As a kid he had always coveted that type of car and as well as providing a comfortable family vehicle, it made journeys up the motorway to Sheffield to see United play a lot smoother and quicker.

1992 had already proved to be a benchmark year in which his career blasted off. Undoubtedly the biggest event was the summer release of *Patriot Games*, which had lifted Bean atop a tidal wave of lavish praise and left him inundated with offers from an eager Hollywood film world.

In television terms he had filmed starring roles in two major programmes and he was already one of Britain's busiest actors when in October, Fate offered him his most famous TV role as the heroic and dashing Richard Sharpe; a starring role that he would very much make his own and, in the process, would stir the imagination of millions.

8

THE DASHING RICHARD SHARPE

THE SECRET OF *Sharpe*'s phenomenal success was a combination of elements that began with a hard core of individuals whose dogged determination never waned, despite many obstacles, in order to bring the colourful action-adventure stories set during the Napoleonic Wars to life on the small screen.

When their vision was then interpreted and enhanced by a team that brought together a marvellous blend of experience in screenwriting, directing, producing and filming, it left only the inspired casting of the central fictional figure, the fearless renegade rifleman Richard Sharpe, to launch a hit historical drama that has, to date, run for five series over as many years, and to create one of the very best heroes ever seen on TV.

The first series appeared on British screens in 1993, but its origins go back seven years earlier to when Andy Allan, an executive with Central Television, suggested to Muir Sutherland, formerly director of programmes at Thames Television, that he should read Bernard Cornwell's book *Sharpe's Eagle*.

Says Muir Sutherland, 'Bernard had at one time been news editor at Thames Television where Andy had been his boss and when I left Thames in 1986 to start my own company Andy said to me, "Look, you should read these books. They would make very good films." My wife is Spanish and I spend quite a bit of time in Madrid, so I have a strong connection to Spain where these adventures are set. When I read *Sharpe's Eagle* I loved it and wanted to buy the rights to it and all the *Sharpe* books. But I said to Bernard, "You know, the story doesn't really begin with *Eagle*. So he wrote *Sharpe's Rifles* for me to precede it.

It was then that I took the idea to Central Television. This was 1987/88.'

Central Television's head of drama Ted Childs was enthusiastic, but top quality television drama is costly and, in addition, to do proper justice to stories involving hundreds of extras, extravagant battle scenes and hair-raising adventures virtually means making feature films on TV budgets. But the three men kept alive their passionate belief that it would happen.

Muir goes on, 'Central TV said that they would fund us, but it was too expensive to make it in Spain. My partner and long-standing friend, Malcolm Craddock and I set out to recce possible alternative locations. We looked at Yugoslavia and the Czech Republic, but nothing was ideal.'

Then in 1991 Ted Childs came up with a solution, 'Central TV began developing a co-venture in which we were dealing with the Soviet Union and it occurred to me that the way to make *Sharpe* cost effective, would be to film it in the Ukraine, which was then part of the Soviet Union. It had the Mediterranean climate, the architecture was not dissimilar and the mountains looked close enough to be in Spain. So we based the series in and around the coastal resort of Yalta and Simferopol. By television standards it was much cheaper to film there, than to attempt it in Spain where, for example, to get one trained horseman, dressed in French Hussar costume, would have cost in the region of £275 per day, and we needed countless numbers of them, over an extended period of time.'

Muir Sutherland recalls, 'Malcolm and I went out to Moscow to meet with a Russian producer and were shown videos of various parts of Russia. We decided that the hilly terrain in the Crimea looked most like Spain and this time when we looked at the cost, we knew we could do it.' Ted Childs adds, 'For the like of scenes in palaces, we filmed in Portugal. It worked out better to just pay to film there, than to build sets elsewhere.'

The *Sharpe* novels were based on the Duke of Wellington fighting Napoleon and mostly centred on the struggle for the Iberian Peninsula. Against this bloody backdrop runs Richard Sharpe's exploits as a maverick British soldier. The son of a whore brought up in a brothel he had escaped life on the streets by joining the army, where his fortunes change when he saves the life of Lord Wellesley (the future Duke of Wellington) from a scouting band of French Hussars. Wellesley's reward is to raise Sharpe from the ranks to Lieutenant in the 95th Rifles, which is when Sharpe's troubles begin.

His regiment would go on to be the South Essex but his first command is taking charge of a surly ragbag of soldiers who are, in fact, all crack riflemen. This group called 'The Chosen Men' form a specialised unit and are sent on various missions during Wellington's Spanish campaign at the beginning of the nineteenth century.

A ruthless fighter, fearless in the face of the enemy, Sharpe not only has to battle with the French, he finds himself fighting prejudice on all fronts: the men under him are initially distrustful and disrespectful as they do not consider him to be a proper officer, and the officers mock and reject Sharpe as one of theirs, because he is not a gentleman. When a stream of buxom beauties from all stations in life, who are ready and willing to melt into the hero's arms, is added to this spicy brew, the recipe is set for a series of rattling good yarns.

All involved knew intrinsically that it should have the feel and scale of a big screen production and screenwriter Eoghan Harris translated this into his adaptations of the Cornwell novels with consummate flair; in addition, each two-hour film would be shot in wide screen format. With director Jim Goddard now in place, the crews were under way with preparation work in the Ukraine, while in Britain thoughts turned to casting.

Bernard Cornwell calls Richard Sharpe, 'A man of principles, with no ideals.' and when the search began in summer 1992 for the actor to personify the dark-haired, blue-eyed Cockney character of the novels, the writer's personal preference was for a rough diamond, although he was not involved in the selection. A shortlist of likely young British talent was drawn up for this plum part and in the end it was Paul McGann, star of *Withnail & I* and *The Monocled Mutineer*, who won through. In August he headed to Russia to begin filming but disaster quickly struck.

Muir Sutherland states, 'When we went to Russia, at first it was difficult because Russians were not accustomed to taking instructions from more than one person. Then about three days in, on a day off, Paul was playing football down on the beach when he twisted his knee.'

Paul received medical treatment and went back to work, but with restrictions on the type of scenes he could film to give him a chance to recover. Richard Sharpe is such an action hero, though, that soon there were no scenes left in which Paul did not have to be physically active and he was still in pain. By late September it became clear that the future of the production was in jeopardy.

Muir continues, 'We had had the insurance doctor out from London and we had tried to work around it, but after five weeks it was obvious that it was not going to work out. The Central TV management team also came to Russia at one point and could see the position. They said that the insurance would take care of it and assured us that they were still prepared to back *Sharpe*. Still, we all returned to London, wondering what on earth we were going to do.'

So, following a series of highly-charged meetings and discussions, after six years and millions of pounds invested, it was announced that production would be halted. Tim Bentinck, who played Captain Murray in the first film, recalls, 'We were all shipped off home. I was on a weekly salary and put on stand-by.'

As the crisis had been unfolding, the producers had alerted John Hubbard, the series casting director in London, to find a new lead actor. John Hubbard recalls, 'When I had originally gone along to a meeting with Malcolm Craddock, Jim Goddard and a few others, Sean had been at the top of the list for the part of Richard Sharpe and I said, "It's Sean Bean, isn't it?" Jim Goddard didn't know Sean's work, someone else wasn't sure and there was a generally lukewarm response. I went back to my office and said to Ros, my wife and partner, "I don't know what I'm doing here. I must've completely lost it! The guy I felt should definitely get it, didn't get a vote!"

'Rufus Sewell was screen tested, as was Paul McGann and a few others and Paul got it. Everyone was very happy about that. I felt that Paul was great. He played a different hero to the one Sean eventually portrayed, in that Paul's Richard Sharpe took a more romantic approach. Then came the accident and the insurance people said, "We can't have a full crew on full fee while we wait for Paul to mend." And that's when Malcolm Craddock came back to me. When Malcolm and I spoke this time, I remember clearly voicing my own personal feelings about it. My exact words were, "Let's not fuck about. Offer it to Sean Bean."

'Malcolm said to give him a few moments and he would get back to me and he did. He said, "Let's go for it." I closed the deal with Sean's agent then, Michael Foster, in less than forty-eight hours and Sean was immediately on his way. Now, of course, everyone says how tailor-made he was for the role. *Sharpe* became a classic for five years because of Sean Bean.'

As whirlwind, career-changing moments go, this one rated the tops for Bean. An unlucky break for one actor had just handed him, on a platter, the part that would become not only his most famous television role, but also his favourite one. And in October 1992 Sean was bound for the Ukraine.

Bean liked the refreshing zest of Bernard Cornwell's stories that unashamedly provided a feel-good diet of high adventure and romance. The forthright, passionate Richard Sharpe was a complex character who possessed the kind of qualities that Sean personally admires because Sharpe had come up the tough way and because, as a man of integrity, he was a hero who could be relied upon to fight for what was right. 'He's a bit of a hard bastard,' said Sean. 'But though on the battlefield he's full of confidence, off it he's shy and ill at ease.'

Bernard Cornwell only discovered that the project had run into difficulty after the event. He says, 'Muir Sutherland and Malcolm Craddock were having too frantic a time to tell me I think. The first I heard of the crisis was a week after they had gone back to Yalta with Sean Bean now in the role. Casting Sean was an act of desperation on the producers' part, and what a great thing that turned out to be! And there had been other changes made. There was to be a new leading lady and a new director.'

The outgoing Jim Goddard's place was taken over by veteran director Tom Clegg. Actor Tim Bentinck recalls Jim Goddard's views on this period of his working life. Says Tim, 'I later worked with Jim in Lithuania on *The New Adventures of Robin Hood* and he remembered *Sharpe* as having been a logistical nightmare, and that it had just been one constant uphill struggle.'

Like Sean, Tom Clegg was thrown in at the deep end with just one week's notice but he would become the tireless dynamo at the centre of all five series of *Sharpe*. Says Tom, 'It was a little tricky not having been involved in any pre-production and having had so little time with the cast. Plus, in taking over from someone else, you are not sure if the characters have developed and so on. But at least I had four days, Sean had two! It meant that you had to be pretty sure that the characters would work.'

Sean Bean was just the raffish, rough diamond that was right for the role and everyone knew it. On set he cut a long, lean, unshaven hawklike figure in a dusty green uniform, with his blond hair straggling over his collar and a cavalry sword clattering at his side. He *looked* a leader of men who, with his own natural brand of authority, exuded a tantalising blend of bruising masculinity and touching chivalry.

Bernard Cornwell says, 'I take nothing away from Paul McGann, because we will never know what kind of Sharpe he would have made. But there is a self-contained independence to Sean, which is just right for Richard Sharpe. Sean plays an excellent villain. In *Patriot Games* I personally believe that he acted Harrison Ford off the screen, which isn't an easy thing to do. And part of what Sean brings to Sharpe is this stunning presence of being a villain, but a villain who fortunately is on your side. There is an understated violence about him and yet he is morally the good guy. Sean was terrific in the role.'

Director Tom Clegg declares, 'On the very first morning Sean walked out on set in his uniform, ready to start, and I knew in that instant that I was not going to have any problems. I just knew it was all going to work out well. You could not get more ideal casting than Sean as Sharpe – a guy coming up from the bottom to achieve success, a guy who finds difficulty communicating with women and who is awkward in the presence of officers. And also someone who has that street aggro.'

Certain aspects of Bean's portrayal would be different from the hero of the books. Sean was blond, where Sharpe had been dark-haired. But one of the most noticeable departures was that instead of playing him as a Cockney, Bean would be using his own soft, deep, Sheffield tones. Tom Clegg explains why. He says, 'It was my opinion that Sean should stay with his own accent. He really had enough to do, without having to sustain an accent in such a long running series. I had heard his London accent in *Fool's Gold* and it was okay, but I thought that the earthy quality of Richard Sharpe would be better served by Sean's natural accent. I spoke to Sean about this. We discussed it with the producers too and we all decided that this was best.'

The director and producers out in the Ukraine also had their own distinct ideas when it came to depicting Richard Sharpe. Says Tom, 'We wanted a hero that would be accepted in contemporary terms and not someone who would get bogged down with sticking to historical detail. Sean doesn't like hats and he wanted to wear the shako as little as possible. We also didn't want him to be shaven. We wanted the stubble when he went to see Wellington. We wanted his uniform to be patched and him to be wearing boots stolen from the French, and for him not to wear his collar buttoned up.

'Well very soon we started getting snowed under with memos from London saying we must have him wearing his shako, and he must be buttoned up at all times and when he went into battle he must do this and that. And we ignored them all. We didn't want some chocolate-box pristine soldier. We wanted someone who looked like he had been through the wars and that image also suited Richard Sharpe's rebel qualities.'

The third change from the original cast was that of the female lead. Some would come to regard the many leading ladies over the *Sharpe* series as being marginalised but this certainly did not apply to Sharpe's first love interest. She was Comandante Teresa Moreno, nick-named 'The Needle', the partisan leader of a band of Spanish guerrillas that Sharpe and his men are assigned by Lord Wellesley to daringly escort behind enemy lines. She is more than a match for Richard who falls deeply in love with her. The actress originally cast to play this feisty role opposite Paul McGann had been Diana Penalver but the part was now taken over by the sultry beauty Assumpta Serna.

Tom Clegg recalls, 'I watched the rushes of what had been already filmed and I didn't like the first actress as Teresa. Muir Sutherland agreed with me. I said, I think if we don't recast, it will be a mistake. I didn't see her as the right woman for Richard. I said, "As Sharpe, Sean will walk all over her." '

The Spanish actress's call-up was startling. Assumpta says, 'I was in Switzerland finishing a movie when on a Saturday I got a call from my agent to say that on Monday I have to meet with the producers of *Sharpe* and that the next week I was to go to Russia. This began a two-year period of my life. I arrived in Russia with no appropriate clothes. It was my secretary in Spain who packed things for me and a suitcase arrived from Madrid after me. I was shooting by the Tuesday; it was kind of traumatic.'

There would be plenty that was traumatic about the working and living conditions in the Ukraine. All cast and crew had been given, for health and safety's sake, specific recommendations to take with them stocks of food and bottled water, and to make arrangements to keep repleting these; Melanie would send Sean a constant stream of food parcels from home.

Tim Bentinck says that the first foray into Yalta had been dire. 'The Russians were supplying the food and some people came down with dysentery.' And David Troughton who played Lord Wellesley in the first series concurs, 'I was very ill for nine months afterwards, which is why I wouldn't go back. For me it blighted the whole thing.'

Assumpta Serna relates, 'I had been told that there would be no water and very little food and so my big suitcase arrived filled with all sorts of cans and bottles. The cooks there were so bad. They were all Russian. The Mafia had not yet moved in, though, and you could hire a taxi for one dollar a day, so a few of us would go to the local market on a day off and carefully buy food. The make-up artiste, who was from Portugal, and myself cooked some nice lunches for the cast. Yes, they were extreme conditions but I think that helped people to get together and it created a common bond.

'What was hard was the weather. We were shooting in October and November and it was always so cold. All the time we were in places where there was a lot of wind and which were completely open to the elements. Being on location was like camping in the wilderness really. You couldn't find silk underwear, of course, and I found that newspapers were great for boots and also for the chest. I would pack newspapers under my clothes to block out the wind and the cold.'

For actor Michael Cochrane, who portrayed Sir Henry Simmerson over three series, it was the accommodation that stood out. He says, 'It was unbelievable. We were all being put up in an ex-KGB sanatorium. There was a strange basement there which I ventured into once and never ventured into again. In later *Sharpes* we moved to somewhere a little better, but there was nothing ever grand about our living quarters.'

And Julian Fellowes, who played Major Dunnett and had filmed originally with Paul McGann as Richard Sharpe, has vivid memories that survive to this day. '*Sharpe's Rifles* had come to a grinding halt and there was a general sense of lassitude among the cast, induced by eating minced cat with hedgehog sauce night after night which was, more or less, all that was on offer. The truth is, Simferopol is *not* a must for the traveller, no matter how intrepid.

'The televisions in our rooms had no plugs and their wires were simply stapled to the skirting boards, as apparently the all-important status derives from having a television in your room, not from whether it works! In fact, we did not actually complain much, especially for a Grumble of Actors, but we did put up with quite a lot. I remember that my bathroom had no lavatory seat, as well as no waste pipe beneath the basin which meant that if you brushed your teeth and then pulled out the plug, a basin-full of toothpasty water was thrown against your crotch. After a bit, I got the hang of it, of course, and learned to dodge the flow but it was all a bit draining.

'The Russian period was tough. For my role of Major Dunnett I would fly off and come back for another scene or two after a gap of several days or weeks. Every time I returned, I saw that the morale of the unit was under an increasingly severe threat. Apart from anything else, as I have said, the food on that first film was simply *incroyable*. There was one really bleak moment when we queued up for our nightly plate of grey slime. The girls who served it were not generally to blame for the stuff, so we bore them no grudge. Their English was imperfect, but much better than our Russian and, as a rule, we gave them an easy time of it. But on this particular evening, one fearless actor could not resist asking what this mess actually was. "Cottages pie," replied one of them brightly. There was a silence until Sean spoke, his voice weary, "And doesn't it bloody taste like it." '

Not everyone, looking back on the experience, can bravely muster a humorous approach, however, and this is certainly true of Brian Cox, an actor of over thirty years' experience. He played the fascinating figure of Hogan, a wily fox who is Richard Sharpe's earliest ally, and he is blunt about the entire experience.

'I couldn't stand doing *Sharpe* and have no fond memories. During the first time out there a lot of people ended up physically sick. We had a kind of infection that is carried in the water – one actor took years to get rid of an amoeba in his liver. Then Paul was injured and it folded and we came back to London to this hiatus, during which we all gathered for talks about the situation that involved Equity. It meant that when Sean took over, everyone was at a pretty low ebb. And it was a strain having to reshoot all the same scenes again. It was nothing to do with Sean. He is a pretty sanguine fellow and took it all in his stride.'

Of Bean, Cox says, 'He's a nice guy, open enough but also with a guarded quality at the same time. He would go off on his own sometimes. Yes, Sean likes his football and is a lad. But there is also a quiet, private inner self at work there.' He adds, 'But the experience as a whole was fairly traumatic, so much so that I didn't want anything more to do with it after it was over.'

Central roles in every *Sharpe* series would be those of 'The Chosen Men' played by John Tams, Jason Salkey, Lyndon Davies, Paul Trussell, Michael Mears and Daragh O'Malley whose character Sergeant Pat Harper becomes Richard Sharpe's closest friend. The on-screen dedicated loyalty between this group of men, and the male bond between Harper and Sharpe in particular, created a strong anchor and added much to the intrinsic appeal of the films.

Daragh O'Malley recalls, 'When we had gone out to the Ukraine the first time with Paul McGann we had filmed about 80 per cent of the first film, *Sharpe's Rifles*, before it had to be aborted. So when Sean came into it we returned to shoot, all over again, the same film that we had almost finished the first time. It was strange, and probably unique, to film the same film twice.

'Sean was remarkable and to come right into it with like one week's notice in a difficult situation – I have the highest admiration that he was able to do that. And right from the start he made that part his own. Harper is this very strong Irish character who has taken the King's shilling but, with no prospect of promotion, really, he dedicates his life to minding his friend Richard Sharpe and sort of lives promotion through him. Sean and I became friends off set in the sense that the central cast working so closely together became friends. I enjoyed all my work with Sean. We had a good relationship, we trusted each other.'

For Daragh, one of his most abiding memories of shooting *Sharpe* in the Crimea was the extreme cold. He reveals, 'The cold was absolutely frightful and relentless. In winter we were working in temperatures of minus 20 to 30 degrees. The only heat was the heat off the engines of the Russian army vehicles. The sanatorium had been a KGB holiday home where if you had been a good KGB officer, your reward was two weeks in this place near the Black Sea. We had masseuses there and they were built like Russian tanks. Altogether we put up with conditions that were quite untenable though. We were all very committed to the work so we battled on, but we had to dig pretty deep.'

With collective and admirable resilience everyone did make the best they could of things and all concentrated on meeting the very demanding schedule. Due to the time lost originally, winter was closing in which meant only two films could be made for this series (one less than would be normal) and, as would be crucial to every series, the key to keeping on track was the meticulous planning that went into every stage.

If Sean had any nerves he had no time to acknowledge them. Director Tom Clegg explains, 'There was a major battle scene to be filmed but since Sean and I had had such short notice I said to those involved with setting out the shooting schedule that I thought it would be easier if we started with a few simpler scenes, to get the feel of the role first, and it was agreed. Then when the schedule came through, there it was, the battle of Talavera straight away. So Sean was really flung in at the deep end. But in hindsight, it was a very good decision because Sean loves all the action stuff. He's very athletic and is quick on his feet and quick with his hands. In rehearsal he needs telling only once.

'He also enjoyed all the stuff he had to do. And he did 99.9 per cent of everything himself. We used no doubles, apart from when there was an occasional far-off shot of him riding away into the distance. He's excellent, too, with a sword. This was not a foil or an épée, but a huge cavalry sword and his fighting as Sharpe is one of savagery, not slick skill. Sharpe's personality comes through in the savagery he shows to his opponents and Sean's intensity was extremely focused. He has such a presence on the screen – the camera just loves him. It's very reassuring to work with Sean.'

On the acting side, Sean's workload was the most demanding and the depth of his commitment would impress many of his co-stars. David Troughton recalls, 'It was exhausting work at the best of times, but Sean had a schedule out of hell. He was on set every day, all day and he coped brilliantly.' And Michael Cochrane declares, 'He set a really good example for the rest of us by not complaining and just getting on with the job, even after some very late nights when we had to get up at 4.00 a.m. next day to be taken out to the wilds of the Crimea to start shooting.'

Sean slipped seamlessly into being Sharpe and those who had originally filmed with Paul McGann recognised that Bean brought a different interpretation to the character. Says Julian Fellowes, 'It was immediately clear that Sean was perfect for the part. Sharpe is a character who finds himself in a society that is constrained by a rigid class system and yet he, while making no bones about his own background – indeed, while being rightly proud of it – is so manifestly a figure of authority that he is accepted as having the right to office by virtue of his own qualities. Much the same could be said of Sean.

'Paul McGann is an excellent actor. But his screen image is essentially built on being a kind of victim ranged against authority. Sean, on the other hand, is a screen presence of authority. His performance, or rather this quality in him, instantly made more sense of story lines that had Sharpe operating as a man in control and not as a figure attempting to gain control.

'Also, physically, while they are both well favoured by nature, Paul had then a certain delicacy of feature that unavoidably gave him a Dandini-esque quality when he was in the uniform. Sean is what used to be called "a real man" in the sense that his camera presence cannot be softened, no matter how much gold braid or lace he is loaded with. In other words, once Sean had arrived, Sharpe was guaranteed a kind of unforced, relaxed stature. He was a man at ease with his own strength, unthreatened by rank or authority in others. I would say it was very directly because of all this that *Sharpe* was as big a hit as it was. I have often heard it said that *Sharpe* was Sean's lucky break. I have no hesitation in saying that it was a lucky break for *Sharpe* when Sean arrived to play him.'

David Troughton feels, 'Paul and Sean had different approaches. Paul's was more a romantic hero, whereas Sean gave Richard Sharpe a Northern hard edge.' And it was this edge that particularly appealed to executive producer Ted Childs who declares, 'Sean is able to convey an evil strength which is why, of course, he has turned in so many bravura performances as the villain. But he also has the capacity to convey a dogged courage which was essential for Richard Sharpe and he was manifestly credible in depicting the rugged working class. I think, too, that it gave the character an extra dimension that Sean was a Yorkshireman.

'I was at a dinner once for the Green Jackets and they were explaining how they saw themselves as Artful Dodger types, bright lads who are capable of operating on their own. That 95th regiment in a way was an early SAS outfit and Sean conveys those roles extraordinarily well. He's very good at handling being from humble origins and is intrinsically a brave actor. He also photographs very well in uniform, which was vital, and is entirely believable as someone for whom all these high-born ladies would fall.'

Sean Bean's reputation as a screen lover would grow over the years and over the span of five series of *Sharpe* he would rescue damsels in distress, tumble into bed, enjoy intimate encounters with a host of beauties and even, with breathtaking ardour, kick down bedroom doors in the heat of passion. But in real life Sean, away from his wife often and for long stretches at a time, did not cheat on Melanie.

Bernard Cornwell says of the many love interests written into the various *Sharpe* stories, 'I wanted to reward Richard for all his hard work. It wouldn't have worked without the women, and it wouldn't have worked if he had been married all the way through. And this is another part of the appeal of Richard Sharpe, I think: the fact that nothing frightens him on the battlefield, but he is unsure of himself with women. It's probably the most important role that women play in *Sharpe*, that they drag this daring hero down to show that he can have feet of clay, in a way.

'As for Sean. He has a reputation for not misbehaving. There was an actress once who went about complaining that Sean wouldn't go to bed with her. She complained that he was more interested in football! I think it had more to do with the fact that Sean was faithful to his wife.'

Director Tom Clegg also reveals, 'Sean never messed about and he had plenty of chances. He would never be rude to anyone, but it just became obvious to any woman with designs on him that he was not interested. And he's very much a man's man. In the evening, in the bar, he wouldn't go over and talk to the actresses. He'd stay at the bar counter with the lads.

'As for the many love scenes. Well, he had mixed reactions to those. Some he was comfortable with and some he was not. He either clicked with an actress or he didn't and when I was casting the various leading ladies, I would consciously wonder, "Will Sean get along with this woman?" He did not go out of his way either to make actresses feel particularly comfortable around him.'

Sean's first *Sharpe* leading lady, Assumpta Serna, remembers her own experience. 'To me, Sean Bean was a mystery when I arrived at the set. I had seen him in *Patriot Games* in which he was very scary and here he was to play the romantic hero. It was very hard at first. His accent was a problem for me and my English was not so good then, so I had to concentrate really hard. I wanted to get very close to him, because I felt that I needed to for the sake of the role, and I found it hard to understand why he didn't talk much. We would be sharing a car and he would be reading the newspaper. I tried to bring up subjects, but he was not communicative. Still, I perservered.

'Then one day, I saw him on set laughing with the boys and I thought, "Wow! Sean Bean laughs!" He walked away and I immediately went over to the boys and asked, "What were you laughing about?" I wanted to find out what I could use to get Sean to talk to me because so far nothing had worked. They told me that they had been talking about football and they showed me newspaper stories of Sheffield United. So, okay, I knew what to talk to him about. And from that moment whenever I mentioned Sheffield United, his whole face lit up and he was animated. It was my breakthrough.'

Comandante Teresa was *Sharpe's* strongest leading lady and Assumpta was incredibly dynamic in the role. She based her performance on a real figure in history, Agustina de Aragon who had fought the French in the Napoleonic Wars. Assumpta says, 'I saw Teresa as a fighter, more than as a woman. Yes, she was Richard's love interest and yes, she offered herself to him in the intimate scenes but she was not submissive or passive when they were making love. I had to fight with the producers to get this strength into the character. And the interesting thing is, because Teresa is a match for Richard, the off-screen tension between myself and Sean helped when it came to filming our scenes as these two characters who need very much to be together, but who can only be so for a very short time. We took advantage of the tension to help create that on screen.

'For me, one particular moment stands out. There was to be a scene in the forest when we see each other and a lot is going on in our heads and in our hearts. It was important to convey that, and both Sean and I wanted it to be right. The writer was on set that day so we sat down and helped to construct the dialogue for these two characters who were confused. I end up saying simply to Richard, "I want to be next to you," and this was a reflection of what was going on.'

When it came to shooting their love scenes Assumpta made a few discoveries about the star. She reveals, 'We didn't rehearse much, there wasn't the time, but Sean was extremely attentive during these intimate moments, always making sure that I was physically comfortable with the way we were lying, bringing this kind of thoughtful touches. And there were little surprises I discovered then. A real emotion can be translated to a similar emotion in these kinds of scenes and he would give me a real smile, a very deep look; there were intuitive moments.

'Because we did not know each other out of the set, these real emotions were an unexpected discovery. It was the tenderness of the moment that I remember, and the care that I could see when he passed this through his character to me. Sean and I did not have lunches together, we did not go out together. It was a working relationship and after the first awkward period, we developed a good professional respect for one another.'

Whilst in Russia Sean greatly missed Melanie and the girls and he would telephone them every night. But it helped that a strong camaraderie developed out in the Ukraine and in a sense the whole film unit became a surrogate family. So although the conditions were trying, they had a lot of fun off set; sometimes on it as Michael Cochrane can vouch for.

Bernard Cornwell drew some astoundingly good villains over the years and Michael's Sir Henry Simmerson ranks high among them. Some of the best scenes overall would be those between Simmerson and Richard Sharpe. Michael recalls, 'Sharpe loathes my character but it was sometimes very hard for us to keep a straight face. I had some wonderfully preposterous stuff to do – all that harrumphing and so on, which Sean found hugely amusing.

'We enjoyed our scenes together, I suppose because they were very ballsy scenes but one or two of them took a bit of time to do because I am a bit of a giggler. Once you've found amusement in something you have to say which shouldn't be at all funny, it is death. It grows inside you and it's the sweetest agony known to an actor – trying to contain laughter. Of course, Sean then found it very hard to keep a straight face himself, which in turn made me worse.'

Off-set the good humour could find more unrestrained release. Executive producer Ted Childs relates, 'We had what became famously known as "The Bacon Riots". It's a tradition that any British film crew and cast working abroad, makes certain that they have bacon brought in for a bacon roll at 10.00 a.m. every morning without fail. Once or twice the people were late in coming and if that happened there would be a riot. It was all good natured though – it became something of a standing joke.'

Sean personally came in for some bantering because of his passionate devotion to Sheffield United as Tim Bentinck recalls, 'Out in Yalta, people could hardly get the chance to ring home. There was always such a bloody queue for the phone. The sanatorium was run by armed guards who were at our beck and call, which was pretty weird. But anyway I'd go down to phone home and have to take my place in the line. That was par for the course.

'But then sometimes we'd all be standing there as usual, only the queue would never be moving. After a time somebody would pipe up, "So who's holding us up then?" and there'd be a collective groan, "Oh, you might know. Sean!" What he would do is he would ring his mum when Sheffield United were playing at home and she'd prop the telephone receiver next to the radio, because the local radio station was covering the game, and miles away in Russia Sean would be listening to the whole bloody match! When he'd come off the phone and walk past this great big line of us we would rib him shouting, "Oh yeah, yeah. You're the star. You're earning the money! You bastard!" '

Tim goes on, 'Sean is good fun and a bit of a joker. He's exceptionally good at accents and he'd go around trying to catch us out in any way he could. On bus journeys to and from the locations he would fool around too. He'd grab hold of the bus microphone and would go into the tour guide routine, making up these hilarious quick-fire announcements that had us all in stitches.'

Just as Sean was a natural at rallying the troops' spirits on and off the set, his character of Richard Sharpe could, on occasions, fuse with his real self. Bernard Cornwell occasionally visited the *Sharpe* location and he was with them for a time when they had been filming in Portugal. Says Bernard, 'Sean and I got on very well. He's confident on screen but quite shy off of it. He plainly likes his privacy. He's not offensive about guarding it, but quite rightly he values it. Anyway, this one night a few of us had gone to hear some old traditional singing that was considered to be very special, but it was in an unsavoury part of town, one definitely not high on the cultural list for tourists let's say.

LEFT Sean and Pierce
Brosnan made for a
dynamic pairing in the 1995
Bond movie, *GoldenEye*.
Pierce says, 'What Sean
especially brought to Alec
Trevelyan was a deep-
seated pain and anger.
I couldn't have had a better
actor to act opposite me in
GoldenEye.'

BELOW Rogues gallery:
Sean, as mastermind villain
Trevelyan, lines up with his
GoldenEye cohorts, played
(from left to right) by Alan
Cumming, Gottfried John
and Robbie Coltrane, for a
photocall at Leavesden
Studios, Hertfordshire.

ABOVE   It was a dream come true for Sean to run on to the hallowed turf at Sheffield United's football ground at Bramall Lane, for his starring role as Jimmy Muir in the movie *When Saturday Comes*, which premiered at the Warner Village cinema, Meadowhall, Sheffield on 27 February 1996.

ABOVE A passion for football has been an intrinsic part of Sean Bean's make up all his life. He describes it as 'a genuine love affair' and a memorable win for his team in 1990 led Sean to have his left arm tattooed '100% Blade'.

LEFT   Sean formed part of an international core cast headed up by Hollywood superstar Robert De Niro for the 1998 complex suspense thriller *Ronin*, directed by John Frankenheimer.

'It was after midnight and we were heading out of the restaurant when some locals thought that they would pick a fight with these British people. Well, by the time I myself got out of the restaurant Sean and some of the guys who play "The Chosen Men" were seeing these locals off. Sean's men in *Sharpe* had naturally gathered around him now and in this skirmish they scored an instant victory. It was extraordinary. It was like Sean Bean in real life became Richard Sharpe before my eyes.'

Filming on the first series of *Sharpe* wrapped in December and the unit scattered. It had been a remarkable experience and at this point Bean could have no way of knowing that it marked the start of what would form a major chunk of his career for the next four years.

Daragh O'Malley, for his part, was sure that that was it at an end. He says, 'I didn't think it would take off and I lost a substantial amount of money to the other actors in bets that there would not be a second series. I lost a small fortune to Jason Salkey alone, who plays Harris. I moved to Los Angeles after the first series and it was always a complete surprise to me when I got the call about a new series. Each year that I returned to the set practically the first thing I had to do was clear off my debts from the previous year's bets!'

Returning home from the Ukraine, after the long haul in such arduous conditions, Sean spent the first quarter of 1993 resting and becoming reunited with his family. More than ever he had to start making the best use of his free time as his work commitments would inevitably cut deep into his ability to devote attention to Melanie and their daughters; he liked spending time with little Molly, and with Lorna whom he would soon start taking to watch football matches. Though proud of his involvement with *Sharpe*, he disliked the fact that such long overseas work meant that he missed important developments in his family's life, such as when Molly took her first steps; that she had grown from a baby into a toddler in his absence was difficult for him, and Lorna had now started school.

Likewise, he would be disappointed whenever he missed progress in Melanie's career. Her television appearances had continued with a guest role in a 1992 episode of the series *Spender*, starring Jimmy Nail as a Tyneside undercover cop. But Sean would miss seeing Melanie make her feature film debut when *The Hawk*, a British thriller starring Helen Mirren and George Costigan about a serial killer on the loose, was released.

The weeks flew by, then, come summer his low-profile relaxation ended with a bang with the screening of the first series of *Sharpe*, followed quickly by *Lady Chatterley*, as well as his filming another romantic role in a new television series to be aired in the autumn, and a small appearance in each of two feature films; the first of which was called *Shopping*.

Written and directed by Paul Anderson and produced by Jeremy Bolt, this Channel Four Films movie provided Jude Law with his film début in a tale of ram-raiding, joy-riding and rival gangs. The eight-week shoot commenced on 13 April, of which Sean was required for two days. Experienced cinematographer Tony Imi was credited with creating the film's atmospheric quality and Bean's two scenes were shot in an underground car park at the Isle of Dogs, and at a set built in a disused warehouse in London's East End.

In *Shopping* Sean was cast as local gangster, Venning. Paul Anderson recollects, 'Venning was a small role, but an important one, and we needed someone who could bring real weight to it. Originally we saw it as a part for a much older actor and when we wondered who we could try for, we drew up a long list of names which included the likes of Alan Rickman – the kind of actor you might expect to see in this role.

'I had the same agent then as Sean, Michael Foster, and it was Michael who suggested that we approach Sean. Sean had the sexuality, the darkness and the energy that you would not normally associate with such a part and it was so right. It was also very believable that he could run a gang.

'*Shopping* was my début as director and since then I have come to appreciate just how vital it is to get the casting right. If you cast wrongly, it doesn't matter what else you do right, it will never be right. The film had Sean Pertwee and Jonathan Pryce, but Jude Law and Sadie Frost were names that meant nothing to anyone then. And it was a big deal for us that Sean Bean agreed to take such a small cameo. Michael Foster, I think, helped by prevailing a little upon him to do it.'

Short-lived though it was, Paul has happy memories of working with Sean. 'We were due to start shooting on a Monday and on the Friday before, Jeremy Bolt and I invited everyone to the office for a drink. The first day of principal photography is pretty tough. No one knows anyone else and we thought a little drinks get-together would be a good idea to break people in. And what stands out for me was that when Sean arrived, he had with him a carrier bag full of beer. He was surprised that we were supplying the booze because he knew that we had such a tight budget so he thought he would take along some beer. And here he was going about giving people beer out of his carrier bag, which I thought was really sweet. You don't get many stars who would do that.'

Once shooting commenced Anderson states, 'Sean made it very easy for me directing my first film. He was not intimidating to work with and that's another quality that's rare. If you get an actor who is at least twenty times better than you, as a director, it's easy for them to give you a hard time. But Sean always took my direction. Even when he felt that I was wrong, he would try to make it work my way first, really try. And if it didn't, then we did it his way.'

After the Crimea, shooting in London was positively luxurious to Bean but Anderson was conscious of the conditions for Sean's scenes, particularly the one in the underground car park. Says Paul, 'That was a right rat-infested shithole and that was after we had cleaned it out. But Sean was extremely good natured and no matter how appalling the surroundings, he never complained.'

Of the scene when Sean Pertwee, playing the role of rival gang leader Tommy, nervously reports to Venning, the director recalls, 'I hadn't known that the two Seans had worked together before and the chemistry was very good between them. As Tommy, Sean Pertwee just crumbled in front of Sean.

'Venning's two scenes make a strong impact on *Shopping*. Sometimes you have to save an actor's performance by cutting it to ribbons in the editing room. But I tell you, we used every goddam piece of footage that we had of Sean Bean. He's a real movie star and was fantastic to work with. We had a lot of fun and it was a happy experience. He had fallen in love with the pinstripe suit that we had

had hand-tailored for him as Venning and we gave it to Sean after-wards.'

Released on 24 June 1994, *Shopping* also marked one of the few occasions on which Sean and Melanie worked on the same film; hers was also a fleeting appearance as Sarah, the live-in lover of the father of Jude Law's character Billy.

It was just weeks after shooting this cameo appearance that Sean Bean's name was once again thrust firmly into the spotlight. On 5 and 12 May 1993, ITV screened the two films, *Sharpe's Rifles* and *Sharpe's Eagle*, and pictures of Sean as the sword-wielding Richard Sharpe in striking regimental uniform, were extensively plastered across the newspapers; a heroic figure, the likes of which had been absent from the screens for years. The shows pulled in twelve million viewers each week, and the enthusiastic response made it clear that he had a hit on his hands, and the ball had but started rolling.

Suddenly everything was happening breathtakingly fast, for it was hard on the heels of *Sharpe* that the screening of the four-part *Lady Chatterley* came, which precipitated an avalanche of exposure. It was practically impossible not to see and read about Sean Bean. He was everywhere, and simultaneously in one week he dominated the covers of both the *Radio Times* and *TV Quick*, as a bare-chested, stubbly-chinned chunk of earthy manhood who oozed raw masculinity straight off the page.

But despite the collective orgasm that some sections of the Press seemed to feel Bean capable of inducing among the nation's female population, Sean personally had no desire to road test his sudden elevation to being the hottest star around, and had no intention of starting to hang out in trendy bars, or to in any way deliberately court the attention of swooning fans.

His lusty screen reputation, however, did spark one unwelcome side to his fame when, amongst his fan mail, he began to receive some dodgy letters in which women graphically detailed their fantasies about him; on extreme occasions some even enclosed Polaroids.

Behind the publicity hype, on the question of screen nudity itself, Bean had set views. While it was hardly enjoyable having to strip in front of strangers, he admitted that when it came to having to grapple naked with a beautiful woman, he could think of worse ways of earning a living. However, this thinking had decided parameters.

Melanie understood that his on-screen displays of impressive sexual prowess were just part of his job, which made for a quiet home life. But it raised an interesting point in that Sean felt unable to take a similarly sanguine attitude should the situation be reversed and it was Melanie who was cavorting naked with hunky screen lovers. When once asked his views on such a prospect he stated, 'She's my wife, and I wouldn't like it if I saw her stripped off on TV.' To the obvious accusation of applying double standards on this issue, Sean offered no defence and simply stated that that was just the way he felt.

An illustration of how shy he was of all the fuss, showed when he was too embarrassed to go to a newsagent's counter at Bristol railway station to buy a newspaper because his own face was staring off the front covers of the *Radio Times* and *TV Quick* on display nearby.

Sean was in Bristol to shoot his part in *A Woman's Guide to Adultery,* an ensemble piece about four women each involved in an adulterous affair, and which explored the consequences, tensions and moral implications of this kind of betrayal, as well as examining loyalties among women.

For the Hartswood Films production for Carlton Television, Frank Cottrell Boyce had adapted the screenplay from Carol Clewlow's novel into a three-part television drama which, produced by Beryl Vertue, starred Theresa Russell and Sean Bean, Amanda Donohoe and Ian McElhinney, Ingrid Lacey and Danny Webb, and Fiona Gillies and Neil Morrissey, as the four sets of lovers.

Rose (Theresa Russell) is a lady of principle, who believes not just that adultery is wrong, but that it is an extra crime to move in on another woman's husband, and she abides by what she calls the Eleventh Commandment, Thou shalt not hurt another woman. All this changes when she falls for Sean's character, Paul, a long-haired, softly spoken photography lecturer in whose class she enrols.

Paul firstly appears to Rose as very macho but that soon fades when he talks passionately about the art of photography. And although married he challenges her directly, accusing her of having puritanical views and talking provocatively to her of appreciating the thrill of sin and the heady heedlessness of love, which by the end of the first episode has Rose agreeing to join him on a trip to Paris.

Beryl Vertue once likened her task of casting the various screen couples to being a matchmaker and that in looking for the ideal Paul she had to have someone with a very high fanciability factor. In that respect, she commented, women went quite silly at the mere mention of Sean Bean's name.

A Woman's Guide to Adultery was to be shot between 27 May and 17 July 1993 and in addition to filming in Bristol, they would go on location to Paris. Bean had reportedly turned down the offer of a role in an American Disney movie to make this drama because it would afford him the chance to work with director David Hayman, whose work as an actor and director he admired. Unfortunately Sean would ultimately count his role as a flop.

Early on, Sean had reservations about the script, and particularly with his character, and he later revealed that some steps were taken to improve Paul in the piece. Sean's role was to embody an especially interesting man, someone so convincing that Rose would be prepared to overturn her long-held principles for him. He also had to exude predatory sex appeal, as well as being capable of conveying the anxiety which creeps in over the risk of his wife discovering the affair and the power his mistress could have to shatter his marriage.

It was a role that was well within Sean's capabilities, but it turned out to be the one occasion when he did not feel at ease and, as a result, his performance in the mini-series suffered and would end up displeasing him so much that he once baldly described himself as 'crap' in it. And he added that he agreed with those critics who called his performance weak.

Made amid the ballyhoo surrounding his role as Mellors, for Paul, Sean again had to bare all, being photographed by his lover unbeknown to him as he lay sprawled face-down and naked across a bed fast asleep. He did not object, as it was relevant to the plot, and inevitably when *A Woman's Guide to Adultery* was later screened between 29 November and 13 December it further stoked his steamy screen lover reputation.

On the whole this was fine by Bean, but one off-shoot was to make him wonder briefly if people would start to think of him only as an actor who strips off. He once, in fact, made the point that, for a certain span of time, if an alien had read his reviews it would have been easy to assume that he was a porn star. Pragmatically, though, Sean took the overall view that he would rather be an employed sex symbol, than an out-of-work actor.

In the evenings director David Hayman and Sean had great fun together, enjoying a few beers in the local pubs. But on set, it was just one of those things. With his enormous respect for Sean as an actor and a friend, David remains unfazed by the experience and hopes to have the chance of working with Bean another time, when he is sure that things would be entirely different.

Still expanding his repertoire, in the first week of August 1993 Sean moved straight from this TV drama, back into film work when he joined the cast of a new Warner Brothers production of *Black Beauty*.

This would be the fifth time that the timeless children's classic by Norfolk-born nineteenth-century novelist Anna Sewell, would be given the big screen treatment. Caroline Thompson, an already successful screenwriter, with *Edward Scissorhands* and *The Secret Garden* to her credit, had written the screenplay and would also be making her directorial début on *Black Beauty*. And, together with producers Peter MacGregor-Scott and Robert Shapiro, she adopted the device of having an actor voice the black stallion who narrates this famous story of a horse's life and experiences at the hands of a succession of very different owners. Sean played one of those owners, Farmer Grey, and his scenes were completed within the first fortnight of the movie's three-month schedule.

The cast which included David Thewlis, Jim Carter, Peter Davison, Peter Cook, Eleanor Bron and John McEnery worked at various locations around Hampshire, Buckinghamshire, Sussex and Oxfordshire; the courtyard of the magnificent Blenheim Palace provided the setting for the bustling street scenes of Victorian London. And filming this family favourite meant sometimes falling prey to the two hazards of being at the mercy of the weather and of working with animals.

David Thewlis recalls, 'We were plagued with rain which caused so many cancellations and made it very difficult. Consequently it took a long time to shoot and working with horses made it even harder.' This sentiment was endorsed by cinematographer Alex Thomson who took over filming *Black Beauty* after Sean had shot his scenes in Buckinghamshire. Shooting also took place at Pinewood Studios but for the outdoor locations the unseasonably bad weather tested Thomson's resourcefulness.

Says Alex, 'The lack of light made it hard to match pick-up shots and of course working with animals? Well horses naturally don't know what a mark is, so you can have it all planned out and they go and move, and that's it. I had to wing it a bit at times. It was pretty routine to work on and it ended up not an incredible picture, but it seemed to strike a chord with teenage girls who were mad on horses.'

Filming ended in October and *Black Beauty* was to go on general release in America on 29 July 1994, with its UK release on the following 17 February. Some critics felt that having the horse narrate the tale surrendered any dramatic quality but *Eyepiece* would hail it, 'a triumph of British film making'.

Black Beauty was still in production when Sean had to gear himself up for the wrench of leaving his family once more. Following on the success of the first *Sharpe*, a second series had been commissioned and this time there would be three films to shoot. The schedule would be a gruelling eighteen weeks which, although he was eager to step back into Sharpe's boots, at the same time would necessitate a length of separation that would be hard on him and on his family.

With *A Woman's Guide to Adultery* screening in his absence abroad, this hat-trick of major television appearances meant that he had dominated the small screen all year in either romantic or lusty roles. And by the time 1993 ended, Sean Bean enjoyed a rock-solid three-pronged professional reputation as a sizzling sex symbol, a rugged action hero and a chillingly lethal villain.

9

BALANCING ACT

FAME CAN BE a fickle mistress and Sean Bean was not swept away by the tide of the publicity surrounding him. His focus remained on doing the job and right now his ambition was to have his work reach the widest possible audience. He wanted to act in international movies, but he also did not underestimate the power of television and in September 1993, professionally speaking he was happy to return to the role of Richard Sharpe.

From a personal point of view, however, this time was harder because the cannonball-like nature in which he had been catapulted into the lead in *Sharpe* in 1992 had left no time to do anything but get on with it. Plus, he had had no idea of what working in the Ukraine would be like. Now he did. Also, he and Melanie were not looking forward to being parted again, and for so long. Towards the end of filming last time, she had managed to come to Portugal to spend some time with Sean, but the conditions in Yalta, coupled with the break-neck schedule that had to be met, made it impossible for Sean's family to visit him on location.

Lorna and Molly were too young to grasp any true concept of time and when their father told them that he had to go away for a while, it was difficult for them to understand that it was not like when he went off to see Sheffield United play, in that he would not be there again when they awoke next morning. The girls missed him terribly and Sean later discovered that his elder daughter's way of coping with his absence this time around, was to watch videos of the first series of *Sharpe* every night.

It was no easier for Sean to leave his family, than it was for them to see him go and he would recall occasions when it was tough waving back at them through the rear window of the car that was taking him off on the first leg of his journey. It was his job, however, and he coped with that. Perhaps on this occasion, though, it took him longer to conquer those feelings because when he arrived in the Ukraine to start work on the second series it was in a slightly distracted manner.

Sean closely identified with Richard Sharpe, but having let go of him for nine months and having played dramatically different roles in between, he found that he could not automatically slip back into character. This surprised and frustrated him and in the initial period of filming he got very uptight about it.

Director Tom Clegg confirms, 'Sean found it hard to just step back in at first, but it's always difficult coming back after a break. It was easy for me. I'd been in post-production for series one and went straight into pre-production for this series, so I was constantly living *Sharpe*. But after a couple of days he got it back.'

It helped that there was a familiarity to it all. Assumpta Serna as Teresa was again Richard Sharpe's leading lady, this time for two of the three films and she recalls, 'It was like being in a family and this time, because Sean and I had come to creatively respect one another, I knew right away that he was not going to be a problem.'

Teresa had not lost any of her strength, but this time around her femininity would come more to the fore, especially around Richard. But Assumpta recalls the moment she surprised the male cast in general. She says, 'There was one day I had to put myself in a beautiful dress which was funny because seeing me as a woman caused a sensation on the set. The men were like, "Wow!" Oh yes, I had them at my feet then.'

The three new films would operate on the same basic premise that Sharpe would distinguish himself in some heroic way or be sent out on a dangerous or secret mission on behalf of the Duke of Wellington, (who from now on would be played by Hugh Fraser) and each would be a stirring adventure, which chronologically moved on from the last. By now Richard was a captain, soon to be a major, his men would follow him to the ends of the earth and the officers' resentment had deepened because Sharpe's promotion was based on merit.

Each lavish £2 million budgeted two-hour film had a tight thirty-day schedule, and for the director the biggest danger was letting inertia set in. It was crucial that everyone who came on set each morning knew exactly what they had to do and again the production team and director had done an enormous amount of preparation. Sean holds the greatest respect for Tom Clegg whom he has described as 'a battler, who never gives in'.

Daragh O'Malley concurs, 'For Sean and I it was key to see the commitment that Tom gave to the films. The work load was heavy and there was never much rehearsal time. The camera kept moving which meant that we would usually only get one take, as a favour occasionally you might get two. But Tom got us through it all. Any weariness on our part was removed because he gave us a lift and we fed off of his enthusiasm.'

One of the toughest aspects of keeping to this demanding schedule lay in the fact that the stories were packed with battles, combat, explosions and action, all of which gave rise to problems like firearms that occasionally did not work, horses being difficult to manage, and because there were people from several nationalities milling about, interpreters were sometimes needed to elucidate a point. Sean did most of his own stunts, but every *Sharpe* film required a huge amount of such work and the Russian stuntmen employed earned the admiration of all.

Michael Cochrane declares, 'These guys were astonishing. They do everything our stunt guys do, but without any padding. They just strap a bit of tape on and go for it. There was one guy called Slava who was in charge of the horses and he would gallop full tilt straight at the camera and yank the horse up and over and then he'd come crashing off. It was breathtaking, extreme stuff.'

It was their indomitable spirit that impressed Ted Childs too. Says Ted, 'In the UK, stuntmen will do their stuff with explosives going off all around and so on and once a take is over that is it. But then, if you look to the cameraman and he is shaking his head, that immediately means getting into negotiation with the stuntmen to do the sequence again.

'In *Sharpe* they were using black powder, I mean old fashioned explosives. There was one stunt I watched when there was an enormous bang, followed by a rock fall. When it was over, out of the gloom and debris emerged the Russian stunt arranger. He saw the expressions and immediately said, "You don't like? Okay, we do it again." Now in Britain in that situation, you're talking of fistfuls of notes. But the Ukrainian stunt people will do it over again, no problem. They will do anything.

'The Ukrainian horsemen were tough too. Ukranian soldiers made up the extras and the only problem we really had was in getting enough uniforms. Yalta was a spartan world and it was particularly tough on the British and the West European people, but they did enjoy the adventure of it in many ways. Although, as in any situation in which people are working long hours and living in each others' pockets for long stretches at a time, there would be occasions when people got on each other's nerves a little.'

This time Sean's workload amounted to eighteen-hour days, six days a week, for the four and a half months. And again his uncomplaining professionalism drew admiration from those around him. Scott Cleverdon, who played Price, in *Sharpe's Company*, states frankly, 'Basically, Sean had no time to be alive. He was either working, or learning his lines, or getting up at 4.00 a.m. It's stressful and tiring. I was surprised he didn't have a breakdown between that and the conditions. But I think, if nothing else, there was literally no time to crack up.'

Teresa was Sharpe's great love, but the real life love match occurred between Assumpta Serna and Scott Cleverdon and they later married. Scott goes on, 'Assumpta had a stove in her room and she hung pictures on the wall and tried to make it like home a little. Whereas Sean practically had no time to unpack.

'One of the things though that you see in Richard Sharpe is the directness of the guy and a grim determination, and that's what Sean particularly brought to the role. One day I was sitting around with some of "The Chosen Men," or The Frozen Men as they were most of the time, and both Lyndon Davies and Jason Salkey said to me, "Sean is 100 per cent Richard Sharpe."

'Sean is the last man that you would expect to be an actor. He's so down to earth. In fact, his straightforwardness is beguiling to the point that it ends up being mysterious. You wonder what else is going on there at a deeper level.' Another cast member in *Sharpe's Company*, Clive Francis, who played a commanding officer called Windham, recalls, 'Sean was very courteous, charming and rather shy, and he was never off the set. I admired his unstinting patience.'

Over the course of the shoot, stretching from summer into winter, they worked in temperatures which ranged from being in excess of 100 degrees to sub-zero, and off duty – although they created a makeshift bar for themselves – Bean admitted, there were times when he was climbing the walls with boredom. He also described it as akin to being in a war situation for real, but once again a sense of camaraderie prevailed.

Daragh O'Malley recalls, 'There was nothing to do there. Some people began to bring their lives with them. They would bring out stereos and televisions and videos and have their families send out hours on end of video-taped English programmes. We had the makeshift bar but we could only get Israeli beer which was not very inviting.

'What got me through was huddling in bed and listening for hours on end to the BBC World Service, including all the sports coverage on a Saturday afternoon. I became the unit bookmaker. They called me William O'Hill and over the course of the five series I took several thousands of pounds off people in bets.'

Sean has a reputation in the business for being a trooper but that did not guarantee that his patience was infinite. Producer Muir Sutherland remembered that in the Ukraine Bean blew his top only once, but as he put it, 'When he did, we knew about it.' It happened towards the end of the shoot when everyone was drained, and he felt that for days on end particular scenes were being filmed that clearly would not match in because the weather had dramatically changed, so eventually he erupted. Both Muir and Malcolm Craddock were listening producers, however. Says Muir, 'Sean was our star. So naturally if he was upset about something he would make it known to us.'

The location site itself was very much a tent city where rudimentary clothes lines, strung between the tents, were draped with serried rows of pegged washing. Says Scott Cleverdon, 'It was all tents – make-up tents, wardrobe tents, we ate in tents, we rested on camp beds in tents with dirt just inches below you. Let me tell you, if you decided it wasn't fun, you were in big trouble.

'But if you leave aside all that, what Sean and the rest of us got to do was not only walk a mile in someone else's shoes, but in a different time. And as actors, the whole thing is that you get to play again. When you're lying in a ditch and castles are blowing up around you, you remember watching these things on telly as a kid. And especially being in uniform on horseback – you just feel, "This is it!"

'It was the lot of the Russian soldiers who made up the ranks that I felt for. They were living pretty hard lives. They'd sold all the things they could, including bits off their uniforms to be able to enjoy a few extra perks while at the same time they were freezing their arses off.'

If Sean had any 'complaint' about the *Sharpe* stories that he relished getting his teeth into, it was that although there was a lot of gutsy action, due to the mid-evening time slot in which they were shown, a fair degree of restriction was placed on just how gory the battle scenes could be depicted. And, as an experienced hand at the steamy screen clinches, he also felt that the love scenes, of necessity, were a bit tame.

This second series did have a stronger romantic theme, however. Teresa tells Richard that she has borne him a child and he wants to marry her. At one point he leads the storming of a French-held fortress city in which his lover and his daughter are among those under siege. And finally, tragedy strikes when Teresa is murdered by Sharpe's great nemesis, Sergeant Hakeswill, and dies in Richard's arms, leaving the hero in tears.

Killing off Teresa was in line with Bernard Cornwell's belief that the stories would not work so well if the same love interest ran throughout, but director Tom Clegg also explains, 'Assumpta wanted her character to develop, but the show was not about that.'

Assumpta Serna exiting in *Sharpe's Enemy* paved the way for a bevy of beauties to appear over the years, starting now with actress/model Elizabeth Hurley who in *Enemy*, as Lady Farthingdale, gets up close and personal in a brief scene where she has to reveal her charms to the hero. And she was followed in this series by Alice Krige, the delicately beautiful actress who portrays La Marquesa, a spy for Napoleon, in the third film, *Sharpe's Honour*.

Just as the love interests had their place, so too did the villains against whom Sharpe constantly battled, and undoubtedly the most outstanding bad guy was the odious and repulsive, shaven-headed Obediah Hakeswill. Bad blood already exists between Sharpe and Hakeswill dating back to Richard's time in India when Hakeswill, a rapist who cheated the hangman's rope, had had Sharpe flogged for something he did not do. Now Sharpe holds a higher rank and the scenes between these two would rank among the most popular.

For Bean there was the added delight that the flesh-creeping, head-twitching Hakeswill was played by his close friend from his stage days, Pete Postlethwaite who, Oscar-nominated for his performance opposite Daniel Day-Lewis in the film *In The Name of the Father*, is one of Britain's finest and most respected actors.

Scott Cleverdon was thrilled to meet Postlethwaite. 'Pete was the first person I saw when I arrived at the place we were staying. He's an extremely funny guy, a real party animal. He can party a helluva lot harder than I can and he was a sweetheart to everyone.' Pete Postlethwaite, who appeared in the first two films of this series, was also the favourite of *Sharpe*'s creator. Says Bernard Cornwell, 'Of all the villains, Hakeswill was the best. The stupidest thing I ever did was to kill him off.'

By the time filming drew to a close in December Sean felt that *Sharpe's Company* in particular was so good that it could have stood on its own as a feature film. As it was, between 25 May and 8 June 1994 *Sharpe's Company*, *Sharpe's Enemy* and *Sharpe's Honour* were screened on ITV, and in doing so, served up another helping of *Boy's Own* style adventure.

Bean was captivatingly magnetic all over again as Richard Sharpe and, once more, each weekly show averaged twelve million viewers proving that, despite the supposed growing sophistication in viewing tastes, men were still drawn to stirring derring-do bravery and undermining the claim that modern woman no longer found this kind of raw masculinity hugely attractive.

When Sean returned home his next joy, after reuniting with his family, was to go to the pub, where his first decent pint of lager in months tasted like nectar. The snowball success of *Sharpe* meant that the last third of 1994 was already spoken for; but before that he could look forward to two new and very different roles, as well as to appreciating the fruits of Melanie's increased professional profile.

In television terms, 1994 would be her busiest year yet, with appearances in three mainstream series. She played a hard character as Lena in *Finney*, Emma Shepherd in *Crocodile Shoes* and, in spring, became familiar to British viewers as Sister Pamela Lockley in the popular BBC 1 medical drama *Cardiac Arrest*. His wife's vivid portrayal of a tough nut in *Finney* came as a revelation to Sean, who jokingly commented that he considered himself well warned of what Melanie might be capable of, the next time he rolled home late from the pub.

Few, however, were surprised at the effectiveness of Bean's performances in his next two roles as once again, executing a neat turnaround, he went from embodying the very figure of honour, integrity and romance, to assuming the cloak of two separate sinister, sadistic and thoroughly amoral characters; the first was as the villain in the romantic drama *Scarlett*.

The story of two of cinema's greatest fictional lovers, Scarlett O'Hara and Rhett Butler, was to be resurrected with a six-hour TV mini-series based on Alexandra Ripley's bestselling novel *Scarlett*, the long-awaited sequel to Margaret Mitchell's blockbuster *Gone With the Wind*. The rights to Ripley's book reportedly cost a staggering $9 million and with a £27 million budget, *Scarlett*, adapted by William Hanley, would be produced by Robert Halmi and directed by John Erman. For months there was newspaper speculation surrounding the central casting.

Producer David O. Selznick's epic search for the right pairing of the two leads for the 1939 multi Oscar-winning *Gone With the Wind* was legendary. Decades later, Robert Halmi is said to have interviewed a thousand hopeful actresses over a six-month span, screen testing eighteen of them, before spotting Joanne Whalley-Kilmer whilst watching the 1989 film *Scandal* on late-night television. He thought her incandescently mesmerising and knew that he had found the British actress to take on Vivien Leigh's role.

The part of Rhett Butler in *Gone With the Wind* had originally been turned down by Hollywood screen idol Clark Gable and although at one point American actor Tom Selleck is said to have been approached this time around for *Scarlett*, it was Britain's Timothy Dalton, star of two James Bond movies, who was offered the role of the handsome hero, and Dalton is likewise said to have initially turned it down. He reconsidered, however, feeling that if he passed up the chance to play such a legendary cinematic figure, he may regret it.

The lavish period piece takes the drama on from post Civil War America to Victorian London and Ireland as the minx-like Scarlett schemes to rebuild the beloved Southern family home Tara, find her Irish roots and somehow win her way back into Rhett's heart. Along the way, she falls into the arms and the clutches of an English lord, The Earl of Fenton and this was the role filled by Sean Bean.

Looking suave and debonair, with wealth, position and respect in society Fenton is, in fact, a cold-blooded ruthless aristocratic rake who is capable of committing rape and murder and who, whilst skilfully romancing the headstrong heroine, subjects the chamber maids in his household to a series of degrading sexual acts, even stubbing out a lit cigar on one servant's bare flesh.

Too late, Scarlett discovers his true nature and their relationship reaches a dramatic crescendo when overpowering her, Fenton rapes her before ultimately rendering her unconscious. When she awakens, he is dead on the bed from a stab wound and she becomes the focus of a scandalous high society murder trial in London.

Although there were parallels between the characters of The Earl of Fenton and *Clarissa's* Robert Lovelace, Sean's performance in *Scarlett* was completely fresh as he crafted the part of two essentially different men occupying the one skin and whose public face so cleverly belies his private one. It was an evil and manipulative role that interested Bean.

Commencing in Britain on 9 January 1994, the six-month shoot spread over fifty locations, moving to America at the end of March until late April, after which it resumed in mid-May in Ireland where it eventually finished on 23 June. Sean filmed his scenes first in Britain, then re-joined the cast in Ireland and the mini-series' cinematographer Tony Imi, with whom Sean had already, very briefly, worked on *Shopping*, remembers his work on *Scarlett*.

'When Sean came on set he *was* Fenton instantly. He exuded exactly the degree of menace and ruthlessness that we wanted. He is a consummate professional who knows his job but he also listens and will do whatever is expected of him. Some actors come in and they are very quickly ranting and raving. American directors and producers really like working with someone like Sean, someone disciplined and very willing. If a scene needs doing again, he just gets on with it and doesn't give anyone any nonsense.'

For *Scarlett* Sean had the requisite bedroom nudity to handle and his scenes with the chamber maid, over whom he exercises almost a *droit de seigneur*, contained deliberately unsettlingly acts of contemptuous cruelty. Says Tony, 'Bedroom scenes can be difficult. When it came to that one in particular with the Irish maid, I suggested to the director and to Sean about doing it with Sean naked and the girl behind him, and Sean had no problem with that at all. We didn't show anything, of course. We came in on his bare leg, then up to his naked buttocks and really I shot it all from the side angle. The only problem we had was hiding his '100% Blade' tattoo, but loads of make-up did the job.

'What's remarkable about Sean is that he is believable in any part and when it comes to this type of role, he has a very period face. He also moves so well, has great coordination and he carries period costume well.'

On this shoot it was noticed that Bean had become slightly distant. Tony Imi states, 'Sean prepares well and he is friendly, but in *Scarlett* he very much came in in character, did his thing and would go. He wasn't one to ingratiate himself with the crew.'

Tony continues, 'The mini-series was shot in England, Ireland and South Carolina and it was totally organised. Joanne and the key cast went from country to country which anchored everything nicely. The big court scenes when Scarlett stands trial for Lord Fenton's murder were shot at Shepperton Studios and the dramatic boat scene when

Rhett and Scarlett capsize and are battling in rough seas before being washed ashore off the American coast, was filmed in the tank at Pinewood Studios.'

Scarlett, which was released worldwide, first aired in America on 13 November and drew an average 18.5 per cent share of a very fragmented viewership. Tony Imi says, 'Personally speaking, I didn't think it quite worked with Timothy Dalton as Rhett Butler, but then Clark Gable was a very tough act for any actor to follow.' Some of the mini-series' critics held the same view.

Scarlett was an American, German and Italian co-production, and so was Bean's other film role that spring. Called *Jacob* and based on a screenplay by Lionel Chetwynd, it was directed by the renowned British theatre and film director Sir Peter Hall. It was a working of the biblical tale of double-crossing between Jacob and Esau, the sons of Isaac and Rebekah, and Sean, adopting an American accent, played the elder nasty, philandering brother Esau opposite American actor Matthew Modine in the title role. Alongside them the co-stars included Joss Ackland, Irene Papas, Juliet Aubrey and Lara Flynn Boyle.

The roughly four-week shoot (fitted in in Sean's case just before he went to Ireland to wrap up his scenes for *Scarlett*) took him this time to the Atlas Mountains in Morocco and for his role – 'a camel and loin cloth sort of thing' as Bean put it – he had to endure having large areas of his body covered in glue so that fake hair could be applied. This unpleasant process took three hours in make-up every morning and Sean later declared, 'I know that Esau was described as hairy in the Bible, but I didn't realise how hairy!' The TV movie was screened in Britain on 4 December.

Before that, Sean spent from June to early August at home, when the only work commitment to cut into his free time was to carry out two narration jobs. The fruits of the first one transmitted from 8 July 1994 when a five-part BBC 1 documentary series began called *The Contenders*, which featured the athletes' preparation for the upcoming Commonwealth Games.

The second was for a documentary on soccer violence in Britain called *Trouble on the Terraces* which went out in a ninety-minute video that proved to be contentious. It followed a discussion format in which psychologists and others analysed the social causes behind such mind-less mayhem and the show included clips of some of the worst examples of soccer hooliganism captured on film. The documentary courted controversy when certain authorities in Yorkshire claimed that it risked glorifying soccer violence and some people queried the wisdom of such a well-known football supporter lending his voice to it.

To Sean it had just been another job and when the video's release in mid-September brought some Press attention, in her son's defence, Rita Bean denounced as daft the merest suggestion that because Sean had recorded the voice-over for it, that that in any shape or form added up to him endorsing soccer violence. It was a storm in a tea cup, which Sean missed for in August he left for the Ukraine, and was already back in harness as Richard Sharpe for the third time, to shoot the latest series of adventures.

By now it was a familiar journey as producer Muir Sutherland recalls, 'We used to go via Moscow, but then we found ourselves a route that went from London to Istanbul where we stayed overnight, then flew directly on to the Crimea.'

The overnight stay in Istanbul did not allow much time to sample the exoticism of this Turkish city and anyway, Sean seemed scarcely in the mood to be enamoured of either the ornate architecture or the local cuisine. Muir remembers, 'Once when we were there we had to be at the airport at 11.30 a.m. so I arranged that we should all meet at 9.30 a.m. as that would give us an hour to be able to see the Blue Mosque. But I stressed to everyone to have already had their breakfast by 9.30 a.m. and be ready.

'Come nine o'clock there was no sign of Sean so I called his room and he said he wasn't ready yet. I asked him to make it down in the next half hour and he said, "Okay." 9.30 a.m. arrives and so does Sean only he says, "I haven't 'ad me breakfast yet." I told him we were all going to see the Blue Mosque and he replied, "I'm not interested in the Blue Mosque. I want me bacon and eggs." The man at the hotel bustled about saying, "Sir! It's kebabs we have here. We can give you kebabs and chips." Sean growled, "You are jokin'!" At which point I steered Sean away, assuring him that we'd be bound to find him something better than kebabs and chips for his breakfast.'

Once in the Crimea, again it was the same deal. Three feature-length action-packed films to be made to a tight schedule and in conditions which – even by the standards to which everyone had grown accustomed – were especially bleak this time. A drought in the Crimea brought a chronic water shortage which necessitated getting increased stocks of drinking water in from other Eastern European countries. And cholera had broken out in nearby villages – close enough to cause anxiety.

Says Muir Sutherland, 'Sean didn't care much for the cholera epidemic in the Ukraine. None of us did. And the water shortage in Yalta was a chronic problem. For a while we had to ration it so that people only got water every fourth day. We tried to alleviate it in any way we could and because the ex-KGB sanitorium had had wells, we put out quite a bit of money to have these reworked.'

Actor John Kavanagh, who played Father Curtis in the third of the three new films *Sharpe's Sword*, recalls, 'You had to be extremely careful because of the cholera and the TB. You couldn't drink the water. You had to have bottled water and you also had to watch not to swallow any water in the shower or when you were getting washed.'

Daragh O'Malley graphically describes conditions this time around, 'Yalta became a quarantine zone. Road blocks were set up all around and no one could get in, or out, and we were in there filming. The water shortage was diabolical. Try imagining this. We were in a building with something like 150 people and nobody could flush their toilet. We had to collect buckets of water – we were allowed two bucketfuls each – from this thirty year-old Moldovan petrol tanker and had to lug it up several flights of stairs so that we could flush a toilet that hadn't been flushed for four days. There was one particular prominent actor who felt very indignant that an actor of his standing should have to do that. One morning I saw an actor coming out of his room and he was washing his teeth with the remains of the contents of a beer can.'

As if this was not enough, in the intervening months since filming series two, the Russian Mafia had gained a strong foothold. Ted Childs recalls, 'After the end of the Soviet Union régime it became dangerous. We had to have people driven to locations under armed escort. The breakdown in law and order was rife.'

Daragh goes on, 'The local Mafia held the production to ransom once for water and the producers had to pay them. And there were dangers around every corner away from the set, off duty. Sometimes Sean, like many others there, was very concerned about getting out of the Crimea alive. One night out socially, Sean had a gun pulled on him. It was dangerous out and about there. I went to a casino once but it was run by the Mafia. You couldn't help feeling that someone could get killed.'

Amid these testing conditions Sean and the others worked at a relentless pace. To shoot two hours of screen time in thirty days, as Chris O'Dell, cinematographer for this and the next two series, recalled meant having to achieve a rate of completing an incredible twenty-five to thirty-five set-ups a day. Sean's leading ladies this time were Jayne Ashbourne in *Sharpe's Gold*, Allie Byrne in *Sharpe's Battle* and Emily Mortimer whose role in *Sharpe's Sword* was distinguished by the fact that she had very few lines of dialogue since her character was rendered mute early on by witnessing an horrific attack, and only regains her voice near the end.

Sharpe's Sword brought back the character of Sir Henry Simmerson at his most wicked, nastiest best and Michael Cochrane says, 'Yes it was arduous, but filming a *Sharpe* is also great fun – all that shouting and behaving completely outrageously and acting big, which in film you very rarely get the chance to do. We all found it very liberating!

'And Sean has a great sense of humour. He's good company and a very generous actor. There's no bullshit about him at all. He knows he's a good actor and everyone around him knows it too. He's got a lot of self-confidence but it doesn't translate into ego. There was never a single occasion when he was in any way arrogant. I enjoyed it immensely when the director said that Sean and I had scenes together, because we had such a bloody good time shooting them.'

For James Purefoy, who plays Sharpe's friend Jack Spears in *Sword*, Sean stood out in a particular way. 'Sean is a natural leader and by that I mean that he looked after the acting company. Whenever he realised that someone was experiencing some kind of problem he would have a word with the producers and the next thing it was dealt with. It was done quietly and not in a flash way, but people gradually twigged how these things were getting sorted out for them.

'What I particularly liked about Sean as Sharpe was the simplicity with which he did it. There can sometimes be a tendency to try to over complicate a character but this wasn't appropriate with Richard Sharpe and Sean's simplicity and clarity was so effective. We would see some Press articles in which the journalist would be busy analysing *Sharpe* and its popularity and Sean would jokingly dismiss it saying, "It's a rock and a fuck."

'Sean is an extremely private person but he's also a warm guy whose sense of humour is often self-deprecating. He is also really funny about his own success – he has this air of total astonishment about it all. I've worked with Mel Gibson and in some ways Mel and Sean are the same, naturally unassuming.'

James describes Sean as 'relentlessly honest', but is more tight-lipped about the ways in which some of the other members of the large cast of the *Sharpe* adventures occupied their time. 'People drank a lot of vodka and pretty much hung out in bars. So many things went on during those long months out there, though, that it came to be that everyone ended up sworn to absolute secrecy. It was an unspoken thing, but everyone knew. Suffice to say, that people entertained themselves as best they could.'

Julian Fellowes says, 'Sean took quite a tough stand about the living conditions of the actors. Thereafter, the food *et alia* improved. In this, I believe, Sean was using his "power" – if actors ever have any real power – absolutely correctly. One thing I did disagree over. By the second shoot Sean had been determined that they should bring out a driver for him from England. This struck me as madness since the motorists of Yalta clearly belonged on some kind of kamikaze mission and it seemed to me that the only reasonable chance of survival would depend on being driven by a native member of this Suicide Club.'

For all the privations suffered in the Crimea it was possible to feel a sense of the place. Studios do not have ghosts. Whereas working on location can engender a feeling of involvement with the place, its past as well as the present day. And this was true for John Kavanagh.

'There was a magical sense of history and make-believe merging. It was the whole thing. Sean brought a tremendous authenticity to this leader of men and the sight of all the uniforms and the location added to it. We filmed just seven kilometres from Balaklava and when the piper played in the film, it was probably the first time the pipes had sounded there since the Crimean War.'

John had an intriguing role as Father Curtis, a priest who was also a spy for Wellington, code named El Mirador, as well as an expert swordsman. Says John, 'I loved the whole thing and especially because Father Curtis really did exist. He had first fought against the English at Trafalgar. But when Napoleon crowned himself Emperor that was too much for him and he switched sides to become one of the Duke of Wellington's greatest assets.'

He goes on, 'Sean was very easy to get on with. Mad about football, of course. I'd first met him briefly when we worked in *In The Border Country* and both times he was good company. He's a team player and that was badly needed in a place like the Crimea.'

While out there this time Sean had decided to video tape as much of the experience as he could. It would not only serve as a memento and record for himself, but it was a way of showing his family what his life and work had been like over those four and a half months.

When filming wrapped in early December Sean surprised John Kavanagh. Says John, 'When the shoot ended and we were on the way to Portugal, Sean decided to take the train, even though this entailed a twenty-seven hour journey! I discovered he was frightened of flying. Mind you, I don't blame him. If we had known how dodgy the Ukrainian planes were, I would have thought twice about it myself.'

It was, though, much more deeply rooted than that as director Tom Clegg reveals, 'Sean is a very bad flyer. On one flight he had been up in Club class while I was in economy class but he had come back to sit beside me and to have a cigarette just when we hit turbulence. That in itself wasn't especially relevant. Sean hates flying, full stop. Anyway he got very upset – I mean, had a real panic attack. I thought at one point that I would have to ask the stewardess to get oxygen but Sean recovered. After a little while, once he had calmed down, I suggested he should go back to Club class and order himself a big brandy or a whisky. He began to go then looked back and asked, "Is it free?" '

This third series of *Sharpe* was the last to be filmed in the Ukraine. Tom Clegg explains, 'It was a combination of reasons. Certainly, we had exhausted the locations in Russia but also some of the actors didn't want to go back to the Ukraine, including Sean. He likes relatively simple food and the food was often not to his liking. He missed Melanie and his children. He missed his mates and a good pint. He missed his life back home basically. He had always had mixed feelings about the Ukraine and in the end he just would not go back.'

And Muir Sutherland confirms, 'Sean came to Malcolm [Craddock] and myself and said, "I've had enough of the Ukraine. I love doin' *Sharpe* an' all, but we must go somewhere else from now on." So I went off to look at Turkey. The first Turkish connection I met there, turned out to be no good but someone put another connection our way who was excellent.'

Between 12 and 26 April 1995 *Sharpe's Gold, Sharpe's Battle* and *Sharpe's Sword* were aired on the ITV network to the delight of its by now faithful following. Among the cast and crew no one was sorry to see the last of the Crimea and all looked forward to the next *Sharpe* series being filmed in Turkey.

After his return to Britain Sean travelled to Sheffield on 10 December to open a Christmas Fair at his old school, Athelstan Primary. Maureen Oakes, with whose sons Sean had often played as he grew up, worked at the school and had organised his visit. Says Maureen, 'We wanted someone to open the Fair, so I'd rung Rita Bean and asked her if she thought Sean would do it. He is so attached to Handsworth and will do whatever he can for the area and Sheffield and he said yes.

'It was the biggest turnout we have ever had. I had never seen so many parents come with their children to a school fair. The pupils – and their mothers – wouldn't leave him alone! But Sean is so natural and was really patient with everyone, posing for photographs and taking the time to talk to people. We made a lot of money that day from the huge crowd that he drew just by being there.

'And he hadn't changed a bit. His first words to me were, "Have you got a cigarette?" He's so modest too. Both my sons are stewards at Sheffield United Football Club and when Sean comes up to see the matches, he doesn't come as a celebrity who goes in the main entrance and heads for the executive suite. Sean queues up and goes through the turnstiles like normal.'

After his flying visit Sean returned to London. 1995 would ring a few changes in both his private and professional worlds. In some ways he would hit momentous heights. But not everything would be cause for celebration.

10

GOLDEN GOAL

THERE COULD NOT have been a role more tailor-made for Sean Bean than that of a young working-class bloke, whose dream of becoming a professional football player with Sheffield United comes true. In fact, it was *so* great a proposition that when producer Jimmy Daly, whose work includes *Highlander III*, left a message for Sean to ring him to discuss it, Bean thought that someone, as he put it, was 'taking the piss' and, initially, he ignored it. Making *When Saturday Comes*, however, would provide Sean with moments that count amongst the biggest thrills of his life and would add the 'working-class guy makes good' role to his crowded closet of screen personae.

Bean's star in 1995 was definitely blazing brightly, for his other feature film work saw him step, immediately afterwards, into the global limelight with the co-starring role of the silkily sinister villain in the latest James Bond blockbuster, *GoldenEye*.

Sean's *Sharpe* following would get their annual fix in April when the third series screened on British TV and, in what was becoming an established pattern, for most of the second half of the year he was committed to shooting a new series of adventures, thereby scoring successive hits on both the big and small screen.

The £1.3 million budgeted *When Saturday Comes* (which had begun life as *A Pint O' Bitter*) was the pet project of Jimmy Daly, himself a Sheffielder, and there were some autobiographical strands in the story of a brewery worker in a dead-end job. A talented footballer, he is offered a life-changing trial with a major league club but, because of a lack of self-confidence, blows it by going on a drunken binge the night before. He fights his way back through a series of personal problems and a family tragedy, all in the teeth of a critical and resentful father.

Between the germ of an idea to the movie hitting the screen, the project would be seven years in the making during which time Daly pursued a successful career as a producer in Los Angeles. Daly's American wife then, Maria Giese, wrote the screenplay and intended making her directorial debut with *When Saturday Comes*. Co-producers would be Meir Teper and *Highlander* star Christopher Lambert. But, as Daly later confessed, when it came to financing the film they wanted to come up with a star for the lead role that would help attract investors.

The story goes that while discussing the casting for *When Saturday Comes* when in a pub one night, Daly said that having seen Sean in *Patriot Games* it was a pity that he was Irish, only to have a mate splutter, 'Fuckin' hell! He's from Sheffield, you daft git!' The producer's prompt pursuit of Bean, however, almost foundered when, having traced his whereabouts to Bristol, he left messages that went unanswered.

In summer 1993 Sean had been making *A Woman's Guide to Adultery* but the message left in his hotel room, on a bit of scrap paper, to give a stranger a ring in America about starring in a film then called *A Pint O' Bitter* which revolved around a Sheffield lad getting to play for Sheffield United, smacked too much to him of a mates' wind-up. And it was not until he returned to London that he decided he ought to check it out, by which time Daly had been trying to make contact though Sean's parents in Sheffield.

Daly's tenacity prevailed and *When Saturday Comes*' principal photography started on 15 January 1995. To support Bean in the role of the central character of Jimmy Muir, the cast included John McEnery and Ann Bell as his parents, together with Craig Kelly as his younger brother; although this part almost went to another famous Sheffielder when Daly approached rock star Joe Elliott, lead singer with the giant heavy metal band Def Leppard, to play Russell Muir.

Joe recalls, 'I went to dinner a few times with Jimmy and Maria and they were well up for me being in the film playing Sean's brother who is killed in the pit. I was keen but I thought it might have been a bit tricky because I was then thirty-four and the character was twenty-four. But as it happened, I was busy in Spain with the *Slang* album and our producer made it clear, quite rightly, that there was no way I was going to be able to leave the studio for five weeks. So I had to turn it down.'

Elliott retained a connection with the film, however, when he wrote songs for the movie soundtrack, including the title track. Says Joe, 'When they asked could I submit some music I was definitely going to do that. The film was called *A Pint O' Bitter* then though and it wasn't until they changed the title that I had a song. I had the music and some of the lyrics but the chorus wouldn't come. There was just nothing cool about singing about a pint of bitter. But now I could tailor the song to these football lyrics, so I had "When Saturday Comes". I also had an instrumental – a kind of lament – which had been called "Song for Ronno" in memory of the late guitarist Mick Ronson, which was very Jeff Beck-ish, and it became "Jimmy's Theme".'

For Sean the joys inherent in making *When Saturday Comes* were infinite. Emily Lloyd portrayed his screen girlfriend, but Melanie Hill played his sister. Bean's mate Pete Postlethwaite returned to the wise fatherly figure, to take on the task as the football manager and talent spotter who wants to bring Jimmy Muir on. And, while ex-Leeds United player Mel Sterland played a team mate, for a life-long Blades fan, a sheer delight for Sean came when Sheffield United's legendary midfielder, Tony Currie, played the club's manager before whom Jimmy Muir has his first trial.

When Saturday Comes was filmed on location in Sheffield near Sean's old stomping ground, Handsworth, as well as at the Bramall Lane stadium. It brought Sean as close as he would ever get to the real thing when in preparation for the film, Sheffield United Football Club's then manager Dave Bassett allowed him and other cast members to train with the team, to play a few practice games and to join in the team talk in the dressing room. Bean was in seventh heaven as Dave Bassett recalls.

'As a fanatical Blade, Sean was really keen to join the team in training. He was very enthusiastic too, and got stuck in. But it was also strange, because here he was, a film star, and yet he was in awe of the players. It was a dream come true for him, even though he was clearly

apprehensive which was only natural. He was not a professional footballer and he was conscious all the time of being in their company. I
liked Sean very much. He's a down-to-earth, working-class lad who
likes his cigarettes and a beer – he's one of the boys. There was no arrogance, or airs and graces about him in the least.'

The climax of the movie comes when, having finally been signed
up by Sheffield United, Jimmy Muir is brought on as a substitute in
the second half of an FA Cup tie with Manchester United. He is soon
booked, but redeems himself when a good header from him sets up
one goal. He promptly scores a second, squaring the score at 2–2.
Then – in unabashed *Roy of the Rovers* tradition – he also ends up
scoring the winning goal from the penalty spot in the last kick of the
match.

By a twist of Fate, six days before filming officially commenced,
The Blades played Man United for real at Bramall Lane in the FA
Cup, Third Round and the film's climactic penalty scenes were actually
shot at half-time during this match. To Sean, this was tantamount to
agony and ecstasy; the latter in getting the chance to pull on the
famous red and white shirt and run out on to the hallowed turf before
a real crowd, and the former because nerves threatened to engulf him
at the very prospect. Bean baldly described his mounting anxiety as, 'I
were shitting me'self,' as the first half drew to an end, heralding the
moment when the film crew would get ready to roll.

Nerves, however, fled once he was out on the pitch. It was a night
game, with the powerful floodlights blazing over a packed stadium and
Bean's adrenalin was pumping. They had just fifteen minutes in which
to film and so could only set up about six shots of Jimmy Muir taking
his penalty but the atmosphere was electric.

Bean had supported the club since the night game when as a six-
year-old he had first gazed startled at the massive overhead floodlights
and now, albeit for a film, his fellow passionate Blade fans were rooting
for him. The Sheffield United supporters got behind one of their own
and gave Sean tremendous support. Swept up in the make-believe
mood they collectively gasped, 'Ooooooh!' when Sean missed, even by
the proverbial mile. But entering into the spirit of things, rhythmically
saluting the night air with their fists they, quite spontaneously and en

masse, began chanting the rousing encouragement, 'BEAN-O! BEAN-O! BEAN-O!'

It was an incredible sight and sound and an emotional experience for Sean personally, as well as professionally. He later declared, 'I can't imagine anything topping that.'

At the age of thirty-five, Sean convincingly portrayed a man ten years younger and he turned in a sensitive portrayal of someone at odds with a jealous father, who is protective of his mother, shy of commitment to his pregnant girlfriend and close to his younger brother. An actor not known for playing parts that require him to break down, Sean drew on personal past sadness to convey his reaction to Russell's death.

Sean was entirely tuned in to the mentality of the footballer, the team camaraderie and that whole culture of lads bonding and becoming wrapped up in the collective high spirits of celebration. And the love scenes with his screen girlfriend, as well as the post-match communal bath scenes, brought Sean Bean's familiar flesh back on screen. Initially he had wondered at the wisdom of such a sport-oriented film lying in the hands of a female director, but in the end he felt that the balance had actively benefited by it.

Sean had always wanted to make a movie in Sheffield, particularly one set in a familiar grass-roots world of boozers and betting shops and the whole experience took on a personal flavour. His father, Brian Bean, would occasionally drop by the set to see his son at work, while Sean roped in a few of his real friends to play Jimmy Muir's mates in a couple of bar scenes. Over the years they had often ribbed him about being an actor; now they had the chance to see Sean operate in his profession.

Sean enjoyed the unique opportunity and made the most of it. After the day's filming ended he and his friends would party for real in the pub, before ending up back at the hotel where Sean was staying, where they carried on drinking till after midnight; none of these sessions ever interfered with Sean rising at 6.00 a.m. the next morning to get back to work.

His roots were here and being among the warm-hearted earthy Sheffield people acted as an extra touchstone for him. He reflected,

'You can forget what things were like when times were rough and you were looking for a job.'

Sean felt a self-imposed pressure to get this role right. Everyone knew how close it was to his heart and maybe that is why his approach this time led him on to an unusual path. In the past, he had switched immediately out of character once a take was over, but not now as the film's cinematographer Gerry Fisher found.

'The moment Sean stepped on set he was Jimmy Muir and I quickly became aware of his desire to stay in character. For instance, if someone came up and offered him a cup of tea between takes he would answer as Jimmy. He was unwilling to let go. He wanted to retain his screen identity, to wear Jimmy Muir's problems, rather than jolt back to being Sean Bean, successful actor. Actors like Sean make the character's problems part of their demeanour.

'*When Saturday Comes* was shot in pretty cold and uncomfortable conditions because there were a lot of exterior shots, with football matches and training sessions. You would get up in the morning and wonder what the weather would throw at you today and we got the lot – loads of rain and snow. We did a live snow scene one day which was pretty tricky. You have a certain amount of footage to film and it might start with fresh snow but then turn warm and it has all melted by the time you come to shoot other scenes, which throws up headaches for continuity. On big budget movies you can snow a scene, but even that has varying success. We were always captive to the weather on this film and very often forlorn. My feet were soaked through and freezing but Sean had it worst of all. At least we had some cover. Sean was, nevertheless, willing to do whatever was necessary and he put up with all kinds of conditions with good cheer. There are actors I've worked with who would've revolted at some of the situations but Sean was always there on the button every day, eager to get going.'

The footage shot during the real life football match was insufficient for their needs so the producers had appealed through the local Press for extras to help film match crowd scenes. Three thousands fans turned up at Bramall Lane, appropriately kitted out, and patiently cooperated with being shepherded around the stadium to accommodate capturing the different angled shots.

ABOVE *Extremely Dangerous* was written specifically with Sean in mind for the lead, Neil Byrne. It became one of the classiest dramas on British television in 1999. The climactic scene when Byrne catches up with his enemy was filmed at Manchester airport with members of the public streaming by.

ABOVE Sean assumed the responsibility of portraying ex-SAS sergeant Andy McNab in the screen adaptation of McNab's bestselling book *Bravo Two Zero*. Andy approved of this casting, saying of Sean, 'I think he could have done the job in real life.'

ABOVE The star of *Essex Boys*, Sean is flanked left and right by writer/producer Jeff Pope and writer/director Terry Winsor at the film's gala premiere on 10 July 2000 at the Odeon, Southend, Essex.

A major talent who is much in demand Sean also possesses one of the most elusive and envied screen qualities, that of being both adored by women and admired by men.

Gerry Fisher says, 'We had been fortunate with that real game, especially since at that time Eric Cantona was playing with Manchester United. We had done as much as we could during the half-time with close angle shots and the crucial goal scoring scenes but we needed a small section for early material especially. So much in film is an illusion. One of the earliest lessons learned is that it's not necessary to have everything you *think* you are seeing.'

The film's tight budget meant long days of hard work. Fisher says, 'It was a happy experience though. Sean is a very concentrated person, in any situation. He's a very earthy man and not particularly demonstrative outside of a role. I think he brought a real honesty to the character. He had lived in that area, he knew the situation and, of course, is mad on Sheffield United. But Sean also has a great presence and great abilities. And there is clearly much more to come.'

Filming ended on 17 February and *When Saturday Comes'* world première was held a year later at the Warner Village cinema at the Meadowhall complex in Sheffield on 27 February 1996, before opening nationwide on 1 March. The promotion circuit for this movie entailed Bean giving the most Press interviews he ever had. But one PR idea was particularly inventive when Sean ended up featuring in a specially written story in the adult comic *Viz*.

Depicted in a series of cartoon-strip photos it followed the fortunes of a bespectacled nerd called Peter Pilkington who wants to have a makeover that will give him film star looks. It appeared in one of January's editions and Stevie Glover of *Viz* recalls how it came about.

'Sean's agent wrote to us to say that Sean was a big fan of *Viz* and that he would like to be in a photo story. We thought it was a joke at first but when we realised it was for real we were all very excited. Chris Donald, our editor at that time, worked on the story and then Sean came up to Newcastle to do the photo shoot.

'I was sent to Central Station to meet him, but I didn't know what he looked like. I had never watched *Sharpe*. However, the *Sun* had just run a big story on him so I went off to the station clutching my copy of the newspaper. Actually, I recognised his wife first. They got off the train and we met, were introduced and then headed to the office and it was dead weird.

'I didn't realise just how famous Sean Bean was. I had never been in the company of someone so famous. Wherever he went, people thronged around him. They stopped him continually and even when we were set up to take some photos in the street, people were walking blatantly between the camera and Sean, completely single-minded in their determination to get to him. And he was dead nice to everyone.

'We went on to take photos at the old *Viz* office and at a hairdressers, as well as the house belonging to the editor's dad. I was the posh bird in the story and there was one moment, photographed out the back of this house, when Sean and I had to be pictured on the back step together where I had to seduce him. Well when we got to that point, Sean didn't quite know what to do. He was sort of unsure. I was saying, "It's okay. Just look down my cleavage. C'mon, look at my tits." But no. Then Melanie who was laughing her head off, yelled over at him, "Go on Sean! Fill yer boots!" It ended up a really great laugh. We went back to the office afterwards for a drink and a chat. *Viz* had had the likes of Rodney Bewes and Harry Enfield in photo stories before. But we have never had a star as big as Sean and he was so unstarry.'

This natural manner is also mirrored by Sean's willingness to lend assistance to causes that touch him and in 1995 before leaving Sheffield after filming wrapped on *When Saturday Comes*, he had made a point of helping out the founder of a fledgling local charity.

While filming in the Ukraine towards the end of the previous year, his mother had sent him newspaper cuttings concerning Sincere Support, a support group that was being set up to help parents of sick children in a variety of ways. At its centre was Beverley Simpkins. Sean admired what she was aiming to do and he telephoned her to offer his support.

Says Beverley, 'Everyone in Sheffield knows how nice Sean is and he's known for wanting to help out people locally, so in that sense it wasn't a great surprise when he called, but at the time I was still shocked to hear from him personally. I grew up in the same area as Sean, we went to the same schools and we knew each other in passing. He said he wanted to help in any way he could, so I asked if he would take part in an appeal for the charity.

'He came to my office to film the appeal at the end of the video we were putting together and what hit me was how normal he was. When we were preparing for it we kept getting it wrong, but as soon as the camera began rolling he was suddenly in complete command and so professional. I remember standing there thinking that it was unbelievable to have Sean Bean in my office, doing this.'

When Sean returned to London in February 1995 he barely missed a step before he was off again. Filming of *GoldenEye* had been under way for some weeks when Sean joined the production.

Bean had already sampled MGM-UA/Eon Production's high-powered style when, one week into the *When Saturday Comes?* shoot, on Sunday 22 January, he had had to take time out to attend the lavish Press conference in London which had launched the latest Bond movie. Immediately afterwards Sean was returned by helicopter to Sheffield. The pilot treated Sean by circling three times overhead Bramall Lane to give him an aerial view of the stadium before going on to land. Sean's fear of flying had been sufficiently anaesthetised by the heady champagne supped at the film launch, which had enabled him to enjoy the experience.

The succession of movies based upon Ian Fleming's fictional British secret agent 007, James Bond had, by 1995, become the most successful film franchise ever and in its thirty-three-year history four actors had played the lead role beginning with Sean Connery, who was followed by George Lazenby, Roger Moore and Timothy Dalton. After his outings as the sophisticated lady-killer hero, Dalton had called it a day and the post had lain vacant for six years before being resurrected now with the new £25 million *GoldenEye*.

The long-awaited comeback Bond movie had originally been earmarked to commence production in summer 1994 and at the time casting had taken place Sean was being viewed in America as the most sexually potent actor to have come out of Britain for years. Bond producer Barbara Broccoli, daughter of the legendary Albert 'Cubby' Broccoli, had liked Sean as Richard Sharpe. She says, 'When the part became vacant after Timothy Dalton, Sean was obviously one of the actors we thought of for Bond. He is incredibly handsome and he's certainly got all the right attributes to be James Bond. But at that time he was a little too young.'

By the end of that year, though, Sean had been screen tested for, and had secured the major supporting role of 006, Alec Trevelyan. Barbara states, 'It was important to us to cast someone in the role who could be a contemporary of James Bond, and who could also be a darker character who turns out to be devious and double-crossing. Sean is a terrific actor, very physical, and he was totally believable as someone who was Bond's friend and trusted colleague. Equally, Sean was totally believable as the agent who had turned.

'We had to set up the relationship between the two characters quickly and early on in the sequence before the credits. We had to show these two men who worked in swift coordination and to portray in a matter of minutes the depth of their friendship and trust. And if that hadn't have worked, then the payoff wouldn't have been so effective when the betrayal came to light. So we needed someone for Alec who could carry that off. We considered a tremendous number of actors, but we knew early on that Sean was right. He has that edge. And we were really very happy that Sean agreed to take the part.'

By this time they were also thrilled to have secured the services of the blue-eyed, dark-haired, Irish-born heart-throb Pierce Brosnan as the fifth incumbent of the post of the smooth secret agent. Pierce topped the popularity polls for the part he had originally been offered in the mid-Eighties. His contractual commitments to the American television hit series *Remington Steele* had prevented him then from being able to take it up. Even in this popular light entertainment series he had clearly shone as the natural future candidate to play Bond. In many ways the passage of time had made him even better suited, as with maturity and film experience he was now a dab-hand at sliding out the witty one-liners. He had the ideal combination of roguish charisma, elegance and steel to be the perfect James Bond.

Sean Bean, meanwhile, already looked like a man who could do you serious damage and, strengthening his reputation as a fearsome top-notch screen villain here speaking with a cut-glass English accent, he portrayed a suave and silkily sinister adversary who posed a real threat to the hero's invincibility. Trevelyan and Bond were evenly matched and indeed, scarred cheek and all, Bean would give Brosnan an alarming run for his money as the dishy attraction in the blockbuster movie.

Behind the on-screen confidence, though, both actors had been apprehensive as Pierce Brosnan recalls, 'Sean and I met at a time in our lives that was important for both of us. It certainly was for me, stepping into the Bond role. I had already heard about Sean and his work in *Sharpe* and when we hooked up, it was good. I like Sean very much. There is no bullshit about the guy. His thick accent was a little tricky at first, but once we went to the pub, that was sorted out. I think we were both shit scared doing this movie. I know I was. Doing Bond? I didn't want to screw that one up.'

Co-scripted by Jeffrey Caine and Bruce Feirstein from a story by Michael France based on Fleming's characters, *GoldenEye*, co-produced by Broccoli and Michael Wilson, was directed by New Zealand-born Martin Campbell. All the essential ingredients were there – explosions, exotic locations, fabulously ridiculous gadgets, whiplash wit, charm, deadly action and beautiful women, some with risqué names: this time a female assassin called Onatopp who liked to kill her victims during lovemaking was played by Famke Janssen and Bond's Russian lover Natalya would be Izabella Scorupco.

With conniving Russians, a loud-mouthed Yank and upper-crust English men and women, from its explosive opening scenes when the two Secret Service agents infiltrate a Soviet Nerve Gas Facility, it was pure escapist entertainment as Bond battles to thwart the evil designs of an elusive shadowy figure code named Janus who is plotting to bring down the British Government and get super rich in the process by using a high-tech satellite weapon called GoldenEye.

With other co-stars including Joe Don Baker, Judi Dench, Robbie Coltrane, Alan Cumming, Samantha Bond and the late Desmond Llewelyn filming, which began on 16 January 1995, took place at Leavesden Studios in Hertfordshire as well as on location in Switzerland and the French Riviera, the sun-drenched exotic paradise of Puerto Rico where the climax was partly shot, and the imposing surroundings of St Petersburg in Russia. However, because of escalating costs the Russian shoot had to be cut back and the St Petersburg airport scene was actually filmed at Epsom Downs race course, outside London. Barbara Broccoli recalls, 'It was funny because Sean was excited at getting to go to all these exotic locations when, of course, as it turned out all his scenes were shot in the studio.'

The fact that Trevelyan and Bond begin as friends and trusted colleagues would bring an interestingly unique dimension to the traditional role of the Bond villain and the scenes between the two of them when Trevelyan turns out to be the mastermind criminal, are considered to rank among the film's highlights. The poignancy appealed to Pierce.

'It gave the film added depth,' he states. 'Certainly it was the only thing I could hold on to emotionally in this role – the fact that we had once been agents together and friends. The worst thing in the world is to have a mate that sticks it to you. It rocks your whole world and it was lovely in that sense to have that depth between our two characters.

'The corner-stone of the whole performance came in the beach scene when Bond comes to terms with the fact that he is on this mission to kill Trevelyan. For me, the rest of the story was the kind of stuff that had been well trodden before by Connery and the others. You always get the bullshit, can we really have a vulnerable Bond? Well, I think you can. And what Sean especially brought to Alec Trevelyan was a deep seated pain and anger, but also a sensitive vulnerability. There was a special longing to his countenance that was so effective.'

The poignancy was important, too, to Barbara Broccoli. She explains, 'Bond has dedicated his life to the service of his country and it is a severe blow to be betrayed by a friend and fellow agent. The idea is also horrific that he had been so close to someone and had not been able to spot the betrayal coming. That goes deep with Bond. Then, of course, when he goes up against Alec, Trevelyan knows entirely the way Bond works. So he really gets deep in there and it rattles Bond. It was a vital dimension to the whole movie.

'Originally Alec Trevelyan was scripted more in the nature of a mentor. Then somewhere along the line we changed his character to be a contemporary. Bond really meets his match with Alec and we felt that it would be more interesting that way – to show, in effect, the other – darker – side of Bond. Sean made the role of Alec Trevelyan something really special. *He* gave it all the interesting dimension it needed.'

The rapid pace of the action suited Bean. In discussions with Martin Campbell prior to shooting, he admired the director's meticulous attention to detail and welcomed his expressed need for there to be vital, blood-thumping energy in the sequences between the hero and the villain.

Ever an actor to revel in the physicality of a role, Sean particularly enjoyed the lengthy end scene when he and Pierce engage in non-stop hand-to-hand combat. For authenticity the two stars did most of the action themselves, having previously rehearsed and carefully choreographed it with the movie's fight arranger. But still accidents happen.

Says Brosnan, 'It was bloody hard work. We had rehearsed it over a six-week period, an hour or two here and there. But Sean's got nasty old elbows. He's a wiry bugger and in that kind of fast action fighting you can't help unintentionally hitting each other. So we'd each end up getting a dig in the jaw, or in the head.'

For Bean making this film had been a big change of pace. Gone was the high-energy anxiety attached to making small projects on limited budgets on which he thrives. This had a totally secure atmosphere but he thoroughly enjoyed being involved in such a giant production and in a gutsy role.

Pierce reveals, 'The Bond movies are extremely hard work if you want to do them well. I was on set every day and really I couldn't see the wood for the trees most of the time because it was such an intense experience. So Sean and I didn't get a lot of chances to socialise but we had a good old piss up together one night in Hampstead at my house. It was in the garden and was on May 16, my birthday. We both suffer from the same deep shyness that can sometimes make you seem aloof. But we became friends that night. That was the night we trusted each other.'

In addition to their friendship, Brosnan makes no bones about the depth of his professional respect for Bean. He says, 'Sean brings a lovely clarity to his work. He has such strength and a hard core flinty edge to him that comes from his childhood. He's a class act. He's a man who marches to his own drum. He's never let go of his roots, his accent or what he's about. There is that great dyed in the wool Sheffield lad quality to him. Sean is a peasant actor who can play a prince and I couldn't have had a better actor to act opposite me in *GoldenEye*.'

Barbara Broccoli declares, 'Sean and Pierce got on great and enjoyed each other's company and that set the tone for everyone else. Sean is an extraordinary, delightful person. He was very excited at getting the part in the movie. When the truth is, he was a big asset to us. He has this great attitude towards the job that makes it absolutely wonderful to work with him. He's a low-key person, highly professional and very dedicated, helpful and incredibly approachable. It's quite arduous making these films with all the fight scenes, blue screen acting and so on and people like Sean make your lives so much easier all round. I can't speak too highly of him. It was a great experience working with him. Sean is a major actor and a superb human being.'

Filming on the seventeenth Bond movie ended in spring and *GoldenEye* premiered on 13 November 1995, at Radio City Music Hall in New York. By then, Sean was in Turkey shooting the fourth series of *Sharpe* but he took a brief break to attend the event and *Sharpe*'s director Tom Clegg recalls the impact it made on Sean. 'Sean was absolutely thrilled when he was flown out to the New York première and when he came back he was completely star struck. I vividly recall him breathing in awed tones, "I was sitting next to Kathleen Turner!". '

GoldenEye went on general release in America on 17 November and was a smash hit; its opening weekend box office receipts were a staggering $26,205,007 which ensured it became the number one opener of any of the Bond movies to date.

GoldenEye also marked another pinnacle in Sean Bean's career, and in a role in which his image as a heart throb and his image as a villain, this time meshed. His down to earth appeal already established by *Sharpe* would be strengthened with the release of *When Saturday Comes*, for which he would have to handle substantial promotion, soon after all the coverage surrounding *GoldenEye*'s release.

Not always comfortable with performing the obligatory round of Press interviews, his responsibilities to *When Saturday Comes* would be easier for Sean, and his trademark grin became more in evidence; likewise, a more relaxed, natural look began to feature in his Press photographs too.

His elevated status shifted Sean into the happy position of being able to choose his roles. Bean will say, 'I just like acting.' But he could now have the scope of applying a code when it came to selecting work. Although renowned for playing violent figures, he has made it clear that he would draw the line at portraying a mass murderer; a sensitive subject matter he believes – especially if it relates to a real-life mass murderer – that ought never to be glamorised.

Although some of his studio portraits as Alec Trevelyan gave him some Hollywood gloss, despite the fact that Bean's profile had significantly heightened it would become refreshingly clear that it would be a complete waste of anyone's time to try to re-construct Sean Bean. Sean never has, nor ever will, see the need to suppress his native accent off screen.

Outside Sheffield he consciously makes himself more understandable, but in his hometown he enjoys the freedom to switch back. And whenever an issue is made of his Yorkshire accent, it need only be pointed out that it has served Sean well in his career with roles such as in *Sharpe*, *Lady Chatterley* and *When Saturday Comes*.

As it was, back in the summer of 1995 completion of his filming commitments to *GoldenEye* left Bean with time to turn his attentions to home life and leisure, which included trips to see his parents and his friends up North.

Sean's devotion to Sheffield United was again highlighted when it emerged that during *GoldenEye*'s Moscow première at the Dom Kino on 17 January 1996 when the glitzy event was in full throttle and he had met everyone he was supposed to meet, Sean slipped away to a quiet corner to telephone the sports desk at Hallam FM, a local Sheffield radio station, to find out how his team was faring in their game against Arsenal in the FA Cup, Third Round Replay. His shocked delight to discover that United had pulled off a 1–0 win spurred him into waiting on the line to join in, long-distance, with the station's after-match phone-in.

On the homefront, major changes were afoot. With their daughters growing up, Sean and Melanie left their Muswell Hill home of about eight years, to move into a seven-bedroomed mansion in Totteridge, North London; the accompanying couple of acres of land would also afford the family some increased privacy.

One of the attractions of this grand property for Sean was that the grounds were more than large enough to accommodate a big work shed which was perfect for him to shut himself away in for hours, making toys for the children or something useful for the house. Sometimes he was so content in there, that it wasn't easy for Melanie to prise him out, even to answer a summons to the telephone. He had never been fastidious about getting his hands dirty and would also set about re-landscaping the garden, digging, shifting boulders about and generally enjoying being outdoors in the fresh air.

Unfortunately, however, there was also another – and unwelcome – kind of atmosphere to upset this idyllic picture of rising prosperity, as within the walls of their new home his marriage to Melanie had begun to come under strain. Melanie reportedly later admitted that once she had missed him so much that she nearly went mad when Sean was away working for almost five months, and the fourth series of *Sharpe* was looming up ahead.

In the recent past alone, Sean's heavy work schedule had seen him filming in Russia from summer 1994 through to December, followed quickly by *When Saturday Comes* in Sheffield, with *GoldenEye* coming hard after that. All of which meant that their time together had been at a decided premium. And further pressure was added when what free time he did have, was split three-ways between home and family, pub and mates, and football.

Sean's personal views on particular issues, too, could possibly have played a part in the emotional unrest. With regard to Sean the national Press did tend to beat the 'Northern lad' image to death; one magazine went so far as to trumpet of Sean Bean, 'He is to political correctness what Conan, The Barbarian is to the Peace Movement.' But setting aside such extreme labelling, Sean himself occasionally did admit in interviews to holding the kind of viewpoints that these days come in for attack.

For instance, he was once quoted as admitting that while he wanted Melanie to get on in her career, should the boot be on the other foot and it was her work commitments that required her to be absent from home for four-month stretches, then she would have to take the children with her. As with his personal view that, in an ideal world, he believes a mother should stay at home during the formative years of a child's life, Sean did not try to dilute what could be seen as a chauvinistic standpoint.

At this point the strain on his marriage was still a private matter, although his unhappiness would become apparent when he joined the cast and crew to film the new *Sharpe* adventures which, ironically, was the first series to be partly shot in Britain, thereby cutting down the length of his absence abroad by five weeks.

Sharpe's Regiment, the first of the three films, would be filmed at various locations including Oxfordshire and a small island on the Essex marshes since the storyline takes Major Sharpe to England to investigate why his second battalion apparently existed only on paper, and along the way he uncovers dirty dealings in high places.

For this story Sean had, in effect, two love interests: Caroline Langrishe who played the intriguing Lady Camoynes, the first woman to bed Richard as opposed to the other way round; and Abigail Cruttenden as the pretty but timid Jane Gibbons who, as the abused niece of Sharpe's arch enemy Sir Henry Simmerson, was ripe for rescuing by the hero.

For the first time since Comandante Teresa had been written out, a leading lady would truly capture Sharpe's heart. In the second of the films, *Sharpe's Siege*, he would marry Jane and by the third film, *Sharpe's Mission*, the marriage was already going pear-shaped when, not cut out to be the wife of a serving soldier, she begins to flirt with other men when the loyal and faithful husband is away.

Abigail Cruttenden said of Sean afterwards, 'He has such a huge appeal to women. I think he's lovely.' But as Tom Clegg confirms, it was a purely professional relationship between the two. Says Tom, 'During this first series that Sean and Abigail acted together, Sean liked her, but there was nothing going on.'

Making *Sharpe's Regiment* once more brought new actors to add an infusion of fresh blood, as well as reuniting Sean with familiar faces including Julian Fellowes, whose character Major Dunnett in *Sharpe's*

Rifles had been killed off. Julian was back now as the Prince Regent and he recalls his experiences this time around.

'When I returned to play the Prince Regent, naturally enough everything had changed. The mood of the first series had been of a crazy, impossible-to-predict gamble. That had vanished and been replaced by the warming atmosphere of a smooth-running hit show. Some of the actors had also changed a little and a measure of temperament and over-security had entered the proceedings. But Sean was precisely the same – still worried about the latest results of his favourite football team, still as pleasant and un-actorish as before.

'There was a rather hilarious element in filming *Sharpe's Regiment* for me, at least. The Prince Regent is not exactly a low-key character, nor, I must confess, did I play him as such. "Very *brave*," said Caroline Langrishe, rather terrifyingly, as I came off the set after the first scene, and it is not in every screenplay that Sean has to be slobbered over by a fat man in make-up, never mind the wig that made me look like the loser in an Elvis lookalike contest. But apart from proving more of a corpser than I had suspected, he took it all in his stride.

'I remember when the first film [*Sharpe's Rifles*] was in chaos and everyone was being rushed to hospital right, left and centre and we first heard that Sean Bean would be coming out to play Dick Sharpe, I was in London and I asked various friends what it would mean. "Oh," they said, to a man, "He's perfect for the part, but you won't get on with him at all. You won't have the slightest thing in common." They could not have been more wrong. I don't know what we have in common particularly, other than a shared belief that acting is a job, like any other, but I enjoyed him enormously. He is talented and polite and very un-mad. In a successful actor, one cannot ask for more than – and seldom gets as much as – that.'

That shooting *Sharpe* had become more well-oiled helped to keep it on schedule, but the fact that the second and third films in this series would be set abroad, thereby necessitating two production bases, also meant that it was actually the most ambitious undertaking yet. The Ukraine had been arduous, but familiar. Turkey was a totally new country to the production team setting up base at locations around the towns of Antalya and Selifke but they had the matter under control.

Muir Sutherland recalls, 'We had our location manager out in Turkey overseeing preparations long in advance and we always worked a bit ahead. So that after we had finished filming in Britain everything would be set for us when we arrived in Turkey. There was never much time. We might arrive on the Wednesday and be starting to film on Friday.'

With no second unit, the pressure was on as usual and this time there was the added problem that because the terrain was mountainous, the light faded by late afternoon shortening the day and inducing a furious pace, and it was a common sight to see tractors busily pulling trailers transporting the crew and equipment over bumpy ground to the next site as fast as was possible, the long poles with the furry microphone covers poking up into the sky like chimney sweep brushes amid bodies so squeezed like sardines into the trailer that they lurched in unison with every rock bounced over.

Where *Regiment* had featured the familiar harrumphing Sir Henry Simmerson, *Seige* and *Mission* brought two other hateable adversaries for Sharpe in the shape of Ducos, Napoleon's chief spymaster played by Feodor Atkine, and the sneery Colonel Brand, the role handled by Mark Strong. In these two, once again Bernard Cornwell had drawn vivid villains to drive stories that inspired freshness every time.

Sean, too, whilst providing the viewer with the solid familiar base desired, brought new nuances to Richard Sharpe, a character he now knew almost as if he had been a real person. Bean admired Sharpe's integrity but he also closely associated with his rough, sometimes brutal, edge. He said, 'I like to see heroes portrayed as ordinary people, not saints.'

For a long time now in the minds of many Richard Sharpe and Sean Bean had become indivisible and as *Sharpe's* creator Bernard Cornwell admits, from a writing point of view it was no accident. Says Bernard, 'I did it deliberately. The books had been successful before, but became very successful with the TV series. It would have been perverse not to put a touch of Sean in there. So, yes, he changed the way I wrote. It was a natural consequence, but I hint at it – I don't go overboard. Having said that, I deliberately do not mention Richard's hair colour now!'

Turkey proved to be a more congenial environment all round as director Tom Clegg explains, 'The conditions were so much better and, of course, the hotels and restaurants were nicer. There was a bigger night life too, which gave the lads more to do when they were not working.'

Daragh O'Malley recalls, 'Turkey was a huge improvement. Sean and I were, for some odd reason, the only two people who hadn't fallen ill at some point in the Crimea. Then we got to Turkey and I got badly injured in a fight scene. It was shot late at night and I was accidentally kicked in the face. I had seven bones broken in my face and the infraorbital nerve was severed on the left side of my face. They were all set to fly me back to England but then it was discovered that because of my smashed sinus I wouldn't be allowed on board the pressurised cabin of a plane. So I had to be operated on by Turkish doctors. I was back on set in two weeks and they filmed all my shots from the right side. But I couldn't help thinking it was ironic that after having survived Russia, I go and get injured in Turkey.'

Over the years, the central cast and crew were used to arriving on set to start work on a new series and finding Sean the same as ever. Only this year something was different.

Director Tom Clegg reveals, 'Sean was devastated at his marriage breaking down. He was *so* unhappy. But we were all in the dark. We didn't know at first and everyone cared so much about him. It was very obvious that something was wrong and people were going up to him and anxiously asking, "Are you okay?" Sean was finding it very hard. He found difficulty concentrating on what he was doing which was just not him at all. We were all worried about him.

'I thought initially that he was just unhappy at being back abroad on location for so long and I wasn't the first to find out what was wrong. One of the other actors he was close to knew, and I think Malcolm [Craddock] knew before I did. But it was difficult to be able to help Sean. We made it clear, as best we could, that we would listen if he wanted to talk. But he is a very private man and not one who goes around talking about his private life.

'On top of that he had to work very hard. Then, of course, it worried him when he realised that it was affecting his work which put an even bigger strain on him. He would come to me privately and say anxiously, "You will tell me if I'm not doing well, won't you?" And I'd assure him, "Well, of course!" '

Ultimately, despite his personal distress, Sean ensured that he fulfilled his commitments. Filming on the fourth series finished before the year's end and *Sharpe's Regiment, Sharpe's Siege* and *Sharpe's Mission* screened in Britain between 1 and 15 May 1996.

1995 saw Melanie notch up another feature film role when she shot her scenes in *Brassed Off,* one of the best British movies ever made, in which as Sandra, she played the stressed-out wife of one of the central characters played by Stephen Tompkinson. That same year had also brought her three more television appearances in *The Widowing of Mrs Holroyd, Cruel Train* and *Circles of Deceit: Dark Secret.* The release of both *Brassed Off* and *When Saturday Comes* the following year increased her feature film credits, and since her appearance in *The Hawk* Melanie had wanted to move more into movie work.

On leaving Turkey, Sean had decided that, from now on, he was determined to spend more time with his wife and family; that he would no longer be prepared to go away for such long periods of time. But there may have been more to the brewing trouble than his lengthy absences.

When the rumour mill over the Beans' marriage gradually began to crank into action, there was speculation that what might be partly undermining the marriage was a supposed difference of opinion on the question of enlarging their family. Sean is said to have wanted another child. Whereas Melanie, who had already twice happily interrupted her career to have kids, it was thought, wanted to concentrate on her career.

Press rumours of discord between Sean and Melanie started when she had attended *GoldenEye's* London premiere at the Odeon in Leicester Square on 21 November with a family friend, and not Sean. Bean was still working in Turkey and they tried to play it down. But proof that one of the most stable and long-lasting relationships in showbusiness was falling apart would not be long in coming.

11

LOVE HURTS

THE PRESS ONSLAUGHT against Sean Bean, painting him as a Neanderthal man, began even before the official announcement on 2 April 1996 that he and Melanie were to separate. With rumours of marital discord already rife at the start of the year, eagle-eyed journalists had been on the lookout for clues in the couple's body language when they attended *When Saturday Comes'* première in late February in Sheffield and it was duly reported that while she mingled with guests, he headed off to a private function in the executive suite.

Soon afterwards an unnamed friend stressed publicly that the Beans did not want to go their separate ways and around this time it was reported that Sean was quitting *Sharpe* because his lengthy absences from home filming the hit series, year on year, were taking a toll on his personal life.

It was not only his commitments to filming these adventures, of course, that required Sean to work abroad and upcoming was his next major role as a cavalry officer in a big budget feature film that, ironically, would take him back to Russia for several weeks.

Shooting on *Leo Tolstoy's Anna Karenina* had commenced in February and as Sean was due to join the cast and crew in April, in March he got into training. Though he would never be a fitness fanatic, his many action roles meant that he was rarely out of condition. But it was essential to cut a tautly honed figure in uniform and so his exercise regime included running to keep himself in trim.

Bean had always led a low-profile off-set existence, something which came in handy now that he was under Press scrutiny, and he had a reputation in journalistic circles for being calmly tight-lipped about his private life. But then the lid blew off his personal problems with a *News of the World* feature at the end of March which showed Sean in an extremely poor light. Said to be relayed through a friend Melanie's alleged remarks showed her to be unhappy with life right then.

The central theme revolved around an accusation of selfish behaviour on his part as Sean was attacked for not helping out with the housework, for being away working for too long, and that when he *did* have spare time that he spent too much of it watching Sheffield United games and being wrapped up with football in general.

To further enhance the illustration, various newspapers, picking up on this feature, tagged on an earlier, unconnected, quote of Sean's when he had once stated, 'Scoring a goal for Sheffield United would be better than sex. If it was the winning goal in the FA Cup Final, definitely.' Stirred into the pot also surfaced the rumoured conflict of opinion over having another child.

It was a very one-sided depiction but in the face of intense media scrutiny, Sean remained resolutely silent on the subject, except, when pressed, to point out in general terms regarding Melanie's supposed revelations that allowance had to be made for a degree of misrepresentation by the Press, which perhaps had a tendency to report things out of context.

Bean would not argue with the fact that his heavy work schedule had had an effect on his family life and neither had he ever made a secret of his devotion to football and to The Blades. He had always been a man for whom certain things were intrinsically part of his make-up and as such, were deeply important to him.

As to the more personal allegations, only the two involved could know the truth. The one concrete fact was that on 2 April came the official news via a spokesman for the couple, that Sean and Melanie were to separate. The day before, Sean, Melanie and their two daughters had allowed themselves to be photographed in the garden of their home when the girls were enjoying a visit of three lion cubs brought over from a nearby wildlife centre as a treat. The picture of untrammelled domesticity, however, had been a facade and Sean is reported to have driven off soon after the photo was taken.

Far from the official announcement of their separation drawing a line under the situation, the much publicised breakdown of the Beans' marriage shifted up another gear and now it was claimed that husband and wife had been sleeping apart in their North London mansion pending Sean's departure for Russia to film *Anna Karenina*. Melanie was widely quoted as stating, 'When families break up, it is the end of your dreams.' And certainly, the sad state of affairs was a source of deep unhappiness to a couple whose long-standing relationship had been viewed as being among the most stable in the business. When Sean left Britain, Melanie and the children stayed in the family home.

Any hope that Bean might have had of blocking out the distress of marital collapse by escaping into work, however, was a forlorn one as he stepped straight into his first major studio leading role as Count Vronsky, the lovelorn romantic hero in the passion-charged nine-teenth-century classic tale *Anna Karenina* written by Count Leo Nikolayevich Tolstoy.

This new £25 million film adaptation of the timeless tragic love story of an aristocratic, beautiful but lonely young woman at the heart of Imperial Russian society who dares to defy convention by leaving her high-ranking husband for her dashing cavalry officer lover, only to suffer the consequences of a scandalised society's backlash and the torment of having to choose between her lover and her son, would be the first western film to be shot entirely in post-Soviet Russia. And filmed on location mainly in and around St Petersburg, with a small section also shot in Moscow, it would be a lavish production.

Produced by Oscar-winner Bruce Davey, the screenplay had been written by Bernard Rose, who would also direct. Although set against a sweeping backdrop, the story focuses on a small group of individuals and includes the parallel love story of characters Levin, a wealthy landowner, and Kitty, a sweet-natured society girl who has to get over her unrequited love for Vronsky to be able to love Levin, and the film-makers considered the correct casting of the central characters to be crucial to the film's appeal.

Their search for the ideal candidates resulted in respected stage and screen actor Alfred Molina playing Levin, and Mia Kirshner, a young actress whose film profile was increasing, as Kitty. While the part of

Anna's cuckolded husband, Russian Ministry official Alexei Karenin, went to veteran actor James Fox. When it came to pairing the two lead roles to portray the lovers snared in the grip of a powerful and all-absorbing passion, Bernard Rose knew his requirements exactly.

In Anna, he looked for an actress who was beautiful in an aristocratic way and who was able to project a vulnerability as well as an intoxicating air of mystery that was strong enough to drive a noble and, till then, career conscious, officer to heedless obsessional distraction. And they felt that they had found her in the French actress Sophie Marceau, who had recently worked with Mel Gibson in *Braveheart*.

When it came to the equally vital choice of actor to play the virile Count Vronsky, Bernard Rose zeroed in on Sean Bean immediately. Says John Hubbard of Hubbard Casting, 'Sean is a very strong, heroic type but, as with all great actors, he has a streak of vulnerability that makes women want to put their arms around him, want to give him their heart.

'He has, too, an extremely romantic image. Women feel he could be kind and gentle, as well as strong. And it's really quite rare in our business for an actor to have all the qualities that Sean encompasses.' It was then, because of all these qualities, plus the fact that Sean carried off uniformed roles with commanding aplomb, that Bernard Rose declared, 'I knew he'd be perfect for Vronsky.'

Bean had been very pleased to have been asked to portray this famous fictional romantic figure who relentlessly covets another man's wife and is so consumed by his feelings that at one point he marches into Karenin's home and carries his delicately wilting lover out, down a sweeping staircase and makes off with her. To grasp the essence of a romantic lead can be very rewarding, but it is also considered to be surprisingly hard to pull off.

Sean, though, was looking forward to picking up the cudgels now and from wearing the impressive Imperial Russian military uniforms with impeccable stern sophistication, to setting pulses hammering with evocative love scenes that included him undressing Anna as she sat compliantly in a chair, pushing her skirts and petticoats up as kneeling before her, he trails his lips to the top of her thighs, he had intended to deliver his best.

The story is one awash with emotion and one of the most poignantly effective scenes in the movie comes when Karenin and Vronsky are sitting outside Anna's sickroom. As the husband and the lover they both have a claim on the heroine, and Karenin's sheer dignity deepening Vronsky's inner turmoil makes for a charged moment. Recalling this scene James Fox says, 'I was very touched by Sean's reading of shame and confusion in the face of my response to the discovery of his affair with my wife. There is a dimension to all these things and I think Sean captured that extremely well.'

What Sean found particularly interesting about the legendary romance was the stage when, having been ostracised by society, their once luminous love, becomes a destructive thing as the flame of illicit passion is starved out by a neediness on Anna's part and a weariness on Vronsky's, over her constant insecurity.

Just as *Sharpe*'s filmmakers had found the bravery of the Russian stuntmen to be unparalleled, so *Anna Karenina*'s production team were to be startled at the valiant breakneck speed with which the Russian horsemen uncompromisingly competed in the movie's cavalry race scene. The production also benefited by having hired Russian ballet dancers as graceful extras for the ballroom scenes.

Probably the quirkiest moment came when during the section shot in Moscow in a square outside the Kremlin, despite having obtained all the required permits to do so, work was suspended when – so the story goes – Russian President Boris Yeltsin, flanked by a handful of officials, is said to have come out and asked the film crew to leave, as the noise was disturbing him.

The Arctic summer provided almost round-the-clock daylight, which assisted the production to keep on schedule and the six-month shoot ended in July. *Leo Tolstoy's Anna Karenina* opened in Britain on 23 May 1997 to mixed reviews, but the film offered all the emotional turmoil of a doomed love affair conducted in beautiful costumes, in sumptuous surroundings and complete with chugging steam trains and horse-drawn carriages amid picturesque flurrying snowfalls.

But throughout his many weeks in Russia, during his off-duty hours, it was difficult for Sean to block out thoughts of the situation back in Britain where, surrounding his official separation from

Melanie, the Press were wading into him with their attacks and his personal problems weighed heavy on him as Saskia Wickham, his co-star from *Clarissa* who played the character Dolly in *Anna Karenina*, recalls.

'It was a terribly difficult and unhappy time for Sean. I don't know how he got through it all, especially when filming this movie wasn't an especially good experience in some ways for him. Working on a British production, people are always friendly. But in a big American movie production there is very much a hierarchy in place which is designed to protect the stars, and I think Sean felt isolated. Looking back, I wish I had gone to his hotel door, knocked hard and asked. "Are you okay?" But it was difficult. We had worked so well together on *Clarissa* but my part in *Anna Karenina* was a small one and I was a bit over-awed by him now. He was the star. And, there's also this British reserve about not wanting to intrude on someone. Sean is a proud man and it was a very lonely time for him.'

At another time, in happier circumstances, Saskia feels that Sean would have been perfect for Vronsky. She states, 'Sean is my favourite British actor. He is wonderfully versatile and he has the danger and energy that's perfect for that character. But there were things that worried Sean. For instance, in the ballroom scene. The majority of the extras were actually professional ballet dancers and it would have been impossible for any actor to shine among them, let's face it. Sean took more and more dancing lessons for his scene when Vronsky – who is supposed to be the best dancer in the room – takes to the floor. He was meant to look so cool and great and I know that Sean was worried that, instead, he looked stiff and awkward.'

The experience had, however, made its particular mark on him in at least one warming way as *Sharpe* director Tom Clegg recalls, 'When Sean came back from filming *Anna Karenina*, he spoke about Sophie Marceau in a way that I had never heard him speak before. He enthused about her, thought she was fantastic and very beautiful and so on. His marriage to Melanie was over. They had made the official announcement of their separation and I think he was quite besotted with Sophie.'

On his return from St Petersburg Sean was once more living under the same roof as his estranged wife, as Melanie and the children were still living at the house in Totteridge. It was a temporary arrangement, until Melanie could find suitable alternative accommodation, and they were not living together as man and wife.

This stressful situation for them both was made worse when the Press latched on to the fact that Sean and Melanie had resumed living in the same house and by August, journalists' rampant speculation translated quickly into paper talk of a reconciliation, which had no foundation.

It strayed into absurd realms when, because of this same paper talk, if Sean – stalked by press photographers – was seen talking in a pub to any woman, he was immediately branded as two-timing Melanie, with whom he was not reunited. Clearly, the situation had to be resolved, but it would carry on in this unsettling vein for some time yet.

As it happened, before long, work whisked him away again. After their separation, Sean saw no need to continue with his earlier decision not to do another *Sharpe* and in May, much to the delight of millions of *Sharpe* fans, it had been announced that a fifth series starring Sean Bean was, after all, scheduled to go into production later that year.

Before that, however, Sean finally chalked up his début in the fourth medium of his craft – the radio play. He had the lead role in *The True Story of Martin Guerre* which he recorded for Radio 4 at the BBC's Maida Vale studios. For this he had joined other cast members Leslie Dunlop, Olivier Pierre, Jill Graham, Andrew Melville, Steve Hodson and Geraldine Fitzgerald to rehearse and record the two-part play dramatised by Guy Meredith, under director Janet Whitaker.

As Martin Guerre, Bean plays a man who, in the sixteenth century, arrives in the Pyrenean village of Artigat after a long absence and resumes life with his wife. She subsequently denounces him as an imposter, feeling she has damned her immortal soul by living with, and having children by, a man she knows is not really her husband. Guerre stands trial in a religious court and the play is based on the actual trial notes of the French judge who presided over this real-life case. It was an intriguing role that the director had felt would suit Sean.

Says Janet Whitaker, 'In the story the man who comes back from the war is a much nicer man than the one who went away and I needed one actor to play both parts, someone who could be the softer guy and also the tough man. Having seen some of Sean's earlier work, before *Sharpe*, I felt that he was particularly good at suggesting a sensitive tenderness, but at the same time having another side to him that is violent and aggressive. He is very adept at getting that switchback and so I rang his agent and subsequently sent the script. Sean was very struck by the story. It's one that has fascinated many people for a long time and there have been a few interpretations of it. It's gripping stuff.

'In some ways it was tough for him because, although his was the lead role, he was surrounded by a lot of actors who were very experienced in radio. But Sean worked hard at the part. There are actors who have come this far in their careers who then consider radio to be a doddle, but Sean came to me early on, somewhat sheepishly actually – he sort of sidled quietly up to me and said, "I haven't done a radio play before. I hope I'll be okay."

'He turned in a powerful performance. He's an actor who throws himself so much into a role. His concentration was deeply impressive. I was particularly struck by the real energy and power he brought to it and I don't mean just shouting. He brought real force to the role. There was one moment which stood out for me. He had a speech that was nine pages long when he was confessing to his wife all about what had made him perpetrate the deceit and Sean was concentrating so incredibly hard that he was literally shaking by the time he finished.'

The experience is one that Janet remembers fondly. 'I wanted to work with him again, this time on *Wuthering Heights*. Sean would make the perfect Heathcliff, but he was busy with costume fittings for *Anna Karenina*. *Martin Guerre*, though, had given him a chance to show two sides and he contrasted them beautifully. Sean has strength and tenderness and I would like to see him in more serious roles. Personally, I feel that he has not always been used correctly by directors because, from what I saw in this play, Sean Bean is a far more consummate actor than he has yet been given the credit for.'

The True Story of Martin Guerre was broadcast on 21 and 28 June 1996. That summer also saw the fruits of more television narration work when Sean recorded the voice-over for an ITV *Survival Special: Creatures of the Magic Water*, a documentary about wildlife in the Brazilian rainforest which was transmitted on 10 July. He then narrated the first of two BBC 2 series called *Decisive Weapons* that concentrated on the advances that had been made down the years in the technology of warfare. The first series of six weekly episodes began on 18 September 1996, with the second series showing from 8 September the following year.

As those first episodes were being transmitted filming of the fifth – and to date, final – Sharpe series was under way, again split between Turkey and Britain; this time the Turkish shoot came first.

The UK locations were the Yorkshire moors and at a cotton mill at Hebden Bridge, near Bradford. And as everyone assembled, there was a palpable feeling that this series should be special. The long associations formed over the years would ensure this, even as with familiar tenacity they bent their attention to bringing to life *Sharpe's Revenge*, *Sharpe's Justice* and *Sharpe's Waterloo*.

Daragh O'Malley declares, 'I think an actor gets paid for all the waiting around and for getting along with people. The acting, I think, is for free. Looking back over the five series of *Sharpe*, it had all been very draining, and emotionally so too. It had been difficult on relationships because of being away from home for such long stretches at a time. And it had been the commitment to the work we were doing that kept us going. Actors who'd come and gone to film scenes might have been horrified at conditions but they could afford to treat it as an adventure. For the likes of Sean and I, we were there for four-, nearly five-month stretches unremittingly.'

Daragh singles out one aspect regarding Sean's quieter off duty moments. 'Sean is a wonderful artist – he studies art. Over the years he often did sketching and drawing. He drew pictures of Sharpe and Harper at Waterloo, I know, but I never got to see the finished product. I don't know if he will ever display his work some day.'

As always, each adventure satisfyingly delivered all the requisite action and Sharpe's lovelife was given a tantalising development when, finally facing up to his screen wife's infidelity, the hitherto faithful husband decides to take a lover too. The French woman called Lucille, whose charms until then he had resisted, was played by Cecile Paoli. And it is with Cecile that – in terms of romance – Sean shot one of the most macho moments over the five series when the hero, once uncertain with women, kicks open her bedroom door, growling the wholly inadequate apology, 'Beggin' yer pardon ma'am, but yer door was locked.'

This masterful approach, adored by *Sharpe*'s female following, also took Cecile by surprise. She says, 'When Richard has to force his way into my bedroom Sean really went for it. He had to, otherwise it would have looked ridiculous. But still, I didn't expect him to do it quite that way. I had been waiting all day for this scene and I got such a shock when Sean kicked the door open and with such startling energy, that I laughed delightedly and we had to do it again.

'I loved the very straightforward way that he worked in all our scenes together. He is a very strong, but also graceful, actor and he makes love scenes very pleasurable. Off set he was nice, but there was a remoteness about him too, because he does enjoy the company of his male friends. And also, by the time the series progressed he was very much in love with Abigail who became his real-life wife.'

While Sean was shooting *Sharpe*, matters had indeed developed a step further. Erroneously being accused of two-timing an estranged wife, with whom he had not been reconciled, had gone on long enough and needed to be dealt with. And so, on Sean's behalf a spokesman released a second statement dated 3 October 1996 which read:

'The decision to separate was made some time ago and neither Sean nor Melanie have changed their opinion since this. Sean and Melanie are now living separately and as independent individuals.'

To reinforce this, that same day Melanie and the girls moved out of the family home in Totteridge and into a house in Finchley. Melanie and Sean, in addition to having two lovely daughters, to whom both are devoted, would remain on friendly terms. But each one was now openly a free agent, and there was no longer any room for Press confusion.

Being a free agent, in Sean's case, would not last long. The man who had once declared that it was a mistake for an actor to fall for his leading lady, now did precisely that when his screen wife, returning to series five of *Sharpe*, became the next special woman in Bean's life.

The bubbly, bright-eyed and buxom beauty Abigail Cruttenden had enjoyed a varied television career prior to joining *Sharpe* in series four, with roles that included playing a princess in *Hans, My Hedgehog*, one of the episodes in *The Storyteller* series (the same series in which Sean had played a prince in *The True Bride*), Nell Gregory in *Intimate Contact*, Miss Violet Merville in the series *The Casebook of Sherlock Holmes* and Belinda in the mini-series, *Love On a Branch Line*. And while, on set, she portrayed Richard Sharpe's cheating wife, she and Sean had, off set, now picked up the threads of romance for real. But they would go out of their way to be discreet about it, as Tom Clegg recalls.

'This series, something had changed. Sean never waltzed into the bar, making any kind of announcement that he and Abigail were together. He never talked about it. But you would notice that, for the first time, he was talking at the bar with a woman. You'd begin to notice that they would come down together, or at least, one would arrive not long after the other. And the gaps between them individually leaving would equally be small.

'But the penny really dropped for me when we had been shooting around Bradford and Sean came to me. He had a couple of tickets to see Sheffield United play and he asked if I wanted to come and I said, "Yes." Then he added, "Oh, by the way, Abigail is coming too." I said, "Fine." And then it hit me and I thought, "Sean taking a woman to see Sheffield United? This is immense!" '

Sharpe had been such a big part of Sean's life that after filming drew to a close in December he confessed to experiencing a degree of real sadness. Producer Muir Sutherland remembers, 'It was so chilly in Yorkshire, with snow everywhere and it wasn't an easy film to shoot. But there was a feeling, similar I guess to that feeling when you come to leave school finally, of letting go, parting from people with whom you'd been good friends for so long. And we had all been mates so it was only natural to feel some sorrow. We'd been a good team. There were no bastards on the show. Usually you get at least one.'

Daragh O'Malley states, 'There was a sadness when we finished. It's strange because you get so close to people, especially working in something that had come around every year for five years. Then it comes to a point when you realise that that's it – you won't be seeing them again. But for me it didn't really sink in properly until the following year. I was doing other work but I became aware suddenly when July and August came around that I wasn't preparing as usual to head out to join the cast and crew of *Sharpe*. The conditions had often been tough but still it was a team effort and I'm pretty grateful to Muir Sutherland and Malcolm Craddock.'

Ultimately, it may not, of course, be the end of the story. Bernard Cornwell's bestseller, *Sharpe's Tiger*, is a prequel to the television series when Richard Sharpe is a raw young private in the 33rd Regiment under Lt. Col. Wellesley and is set in India at the siege of Seringapatam and there has been talk of filming this adventure. Bernard Cornwell says, 'There was a suggestion that Sean couldn't be cast as Richard because Sharpe would be so much younger, but that would be a definite non-starter. The fans would never accept it.'

Speaking on behalf of the worldwide members of The Sharpe Appreciation Society, its secretary Christine Clarke agrees. 'I can honestly say that if the producers ever decided to make another *Sharpe* film, there is no other actor that could fill Richard Sharpe's shoes. Sean's athleticism, fencing ability and sheer magnetism would make it impossible to consider anyone else. To us, Sean Bean *is* Richard Sharpe.'

Muir Sutherland hopes that there will be more *Sharpe* films. 'We have asked Sean if he would come back as Richard Sharpe and he has said yes. So it's something that is hopefully on the agenda.'

Bean is, rightly, very proud of his association with *Sharpe* and over the years he earned the deepest respect from those closest involved. Bernard Cornwell, who sent Sean a personal letter of appreciation for the way he portrayed Richard Sharpe over the five series, says, 'Sean is plainly terrific in the role and I am hugely grateful to him, as well as being full of admiration.'

Muir Sutherland says, 'Sean brought such a gritty determination to the role. Sharpe is a maverick and Sean, in some ways, is too. He's a man of the people and there could not have been anyone better suited for Sharpe than Sean. He was also always easy to work with, never gave us any problems. He's an excellent bloke all round.'

While director Tom Clegg declares, 'The whole five series, it was a deep joy. I really looked forward to every one of them because they were brilliant pieces to work on. Sean and I got on well. He could have bought another drink or two maybe – he's a bit tight on the drinks. But seriously, I cannot speak too highly of him. Richard Sharpe is the best role he has ever done, in my view. And I thought he and the series should have got some award. But we were up against the likes of *Cracker* and *Prime Suspect*. Still I think it would have been deserved.' *Sharpe's Revenge*, *Sharpe's Justice* and *Sharpe's Waterloo* were screened between 7 and 21 May 1997.

More than any other role, Richard Sharpe had done most to establish Sean Bean as one of Britain's favourite stars. Now Sean was closing that chapter in his professional life just as the irrevocable step of Melanie's departure in October had ended the longest chapter in his personal life. But there was much to look forward to and 1997 was to bring new and exciting developments in his life.

12

A NEW LEADING LADY

THE MOMENT THAT the new woman in Sean Bean's life moved into his home was captured by a lurking paparazzo, whose tenacious surveillance paid off when early in 1997 he snapped removal men shifting Abigail Cruttenden's furniture into Sean's North London mansion. And there was a bonus photo opportunity when the long lens pictured Bean lending the men some assistance with a particularly heavy sofa. Abigail, the privately educated middle-class daughter of an advertising executive, by making this commitment, reinforced the belief among the couple's friends that she and Sean were deeply in love and that wedding bells could be on the cards.

As it was, Sean and Melanie had yet to be divorced but by early summer appropriate proceedings were under way. For her part, Melanie had also moved on personally and professionally she would soon become a favourite once again in a new television series as Rita Dolan in *Playing the Field*, which was, ironically – considering her perceived views on the dominating influence of soccer in her private life – all about a female football team.

Abigail's television profile would heighten throughout the year when, in addition to appearing in the fifth series of *Sharpe*, other roles included that of Heather Mallender in *Into the Blue*, Annabel Lynes in *Bribery and Corruption* and Blanche Ingram in a new TV version of the Charlotte Brontë classic *Jane Eyre*.

While for Sean, May's transmission of the new *Sharpe* series on television (which series, like its predecessors, would be seen all over the world), was followed immediately by the UK cinema release of the movie *Leo Tolstoy's Anna Karenina*. In the first four months of 1997, though, the only work he undertook was recording the narration for an Anglia Television documentary called *There's Only One Barry Fry*, about the colourful football manager of the same name which ITV subsequently broadcast on 24 May.

Otherwise he concentrated on settling into home life with a new partner. Contrary to common perception, Sean does not only ever devote his free time to football and to drinking with his mates. He is inquisitive about a lot of things. A sense of history appeals to him, he likes the ambience of old churches and he reads avidly. He is both artistic and practical with his hands, and is a devoted dad. He also enjoys a stimulating, varied career that takes him around the world, working among, and relating to, a cosmopolitan mix of people and he is interested in the whole process of filmmaking, with possible aspirations of, one day, turning to directing.

During the summer of 1997 Sean started training for an exciting new project that he had lined up, but he was also always open to a potentially good prospect and when he was approached at the start of July by director Julian Grant about appearing in a film called *Airborne*, he liked the sound of it.

Co-written by Toronto-based Julian Grant and Tony Johnston, *Airborne* was to be directed by Grant and produced by John Gillespie for Alliance Communications Corporation and Le Monde Entertainment. Julian (now producer/director of the *Robocop: Prime Directives* feature films) would live up to his well-deserved reputation for working wonders on limited budgets when with $3 million he and the production team put together a taut, high-octane thriller with spectacular special effects.

The central cast featured Steve Guttenberg, breaking out of the kid-friendly role he was most associated with, Colm Feore, Kim Coates and Torri Higginson, and Julian was looking to Britain to fill a significant cameo role. He explains, 'I wanted to get the best actor possible for each role. I had seen Sean in *Sharpe* and also in *Patriot Games* and *GoldenEye* and was very impressed with him. He was a phenomenal talent in Europe and I wanted to increase the calibre of my film by putting together an international cast and I thought that Sean was the natural choice for this role. I approached him and we chatted on the telephone and although it was a problem working out his availability, I managed to get him for one week.

'It was for the character of Toombs that I had particularly wanted to expand outside of the typical North American actor and Sean had the refinement that I was looking for. He read the whole script, which is nice – some actors only read their own part – and he decided he liked it, that it would be fun and he wanted the part, so he came over to Toronto.'

Airborne is an intense cat-and-mouse thriller that starts with the theft from a sensitive research laboratory of a deadly biological virus that can jump species, by a highly-motivated terrorist team led by Toombs. The virus is to be put up for sale on the international arms black market and a special ops squad led by McNeil (Steve Guttenberg) known as Mach One is assigned the task of getting it back. The plot gets complicated when members of the Mach One team are picked off and the remaining agents become suspicious as to exactly which side their own government department is on.

As the merciless mercenary Toombs, Bean was, in some ways, 006 revisited in the debonair English flair with which he cloaked his efficient ruthlessness. The director declares, 'Sean brought class and panache to the role. He was perfect as the charming, but deadly, rogue.'

The feature film was brimful of gunfights, explosions, an out-of-control car – even the gruesome sight of a man being quick frozen by liquid nitrogen and whose limbs then snap off. But the most breathlessly daring sequence happens early in the movie when in pursuit of the terrorists the Mach One agents manoeuvre their stealth plane and manage to board the terrorists' plane mid-air.

Julian reveals, 'We did that plane sequence inside a small lumber yard, the same place, in fact, as *Robocop* is made. *Airborne* took just twenty-five days to shoot in and around Toronto and the Ontario area which was really where I live and therefore very convenient. We also shot at some outlying airfields.'

Another Julian Grant hallmark is his meticulous preparation. He says, 'Whether for actors, directors or whoever, all the best work is done in advance. If you're smart you don't wait until you are on the set. It's with strict preparation that you are much more likely to capture lightning in a bottle.

'I did storyboards for everything, so everyone knew what was needed. Sean and I would sit down and chat a little bit about how we wanted a scene to go and day after day he came in prepared and ready to shoot. Sean knew that because it was a $3 million budget we needed to do the best we could, as fast as we could, and he made sure that he was very accommodating. He even watched all the footage already filmed so that he could ensure that his scenes matched in.

'He was also extremely comfortable with firearms, careful and very precise. Some actors can be pretty cavalier with firearms, but he respected our safety standards which, speaking as a producer and a director, was a blessing. He has the undoubted ability to assume the skin of a character with authority and it is done, with Sean, through an intense vigilance that shows in his eyes.'

Julian was grateful too that, in Sean, he had no spoilt temperament to have to waste time handling. He says, 'A lot of actors are "line coun-ters", only interested in spouting dialogue all day long. But I didn't get any complaints from Sean that Toombs didn't have enough lines. Great actors embody a character and that's what Sean does to a T. And at the end of the day these are the ones that stand out, the characters people remember. Working with Sean was a classic case of the bigger the star, the nicer they are.'

Weeks later Julian hooked up again with Sean in London as he explains, 'There was some dialogue replacement required and I flew over to sort out the imperfections so Sean and I met up in Soho to re-do these. Afterwards, we nipped to a nearby pub for a quick drink before the car came and Sean was immediately swamped with people. In a split second about twenty had already gathered around our table and by the time it was time to go, I thought he would be lucky to get out of there. But he was so natural with everyone.

'I had to laugh though. Here was a guy in denims with his hair all mussed up and wearing plimsolls that had a great big hole in one of the toes and the crowds were mobbing him. And the unique thing about it was, he was genuinely in awe of his own appeal and popu-larity. He'll have a long career because of his talent and the fact that he concentrates so hard on the work. But also because, he is not ever likely to get caught up with being seen in the right places, being photographed for all the right magazines and that whole scene.'

Airborne premiered at the Fant-Asia Film Festival in Montreal on 19 July 1998, followed days later in Toronto, and was released in Britain in November. Julian Grant reveals, '*Airborne* was intended as a low-budget *Mission: Impossible* and it did enormously well. It sold to 117 territories, which is pretty much the whole world. And the distributor clawed in tons of dough, which is what it's all about.'

When Bean left Canada on completion of his scenes, he headed straight to Africa to resume training for his next project, but he did not forget Julian Grant. The director recalls, 'Sean called me from South Africa to say how much he had enjoyed working on *Airborne*. I really appreciated that.'

Performing one of his deft turnarounds, Sean went straight from playing a ruthless killer on the wrong side of the law, to portraying a deadly-skilled fighter on the right side when, in August 1997, principal photography began on a screen adaptation of the international bestselling book *Bravo Two Zero*, written by ex-SAS Sergeant Andy McNab.

During the Gulf War in January 1991, Sgt. McNab led an eight-man élite SAS squad in a daring top-secret mission behind Iraqi lines to sabotage the mobile launchers for the devastating scud missiles which Saddam Hussein had aimed at Israel's capital Tel Aviv, and to locate and destroy the fibre optic cables along the country's main supply route thereby cutting the crucial command communication lines between Baghdad and North West Iraq. The team's call sign was 'Bravo Two Zero' and they would become the most highly decorated British patrol since the Boer War.

But things went horribly wrong when, due to a blunder, they were left with the wrong equipment, radio links that didn't work and were given the wrong coordinates which meant that they were dropped into 'Scud Alley' between two divisions of Iraqi troops, some 3,000 soldiers. Soon detected, the men courageously had to fight their way to the Syrian border – a distance of over a hundred miles and across the Euphrates river. Only five of the squad survived the ordeal and

McNab, plus two of his patrol, were captured by the Iraqi military. In the hands of the secret police, they endured systematic, prolonged torture and interrogation in Baghdad.

Naturally, this tale of amazing skill, endurance and heroism, was a magnet for film companies. But it became clear quickly to McNab that many of these film companies sought little more than the title *Bravo Two Zero* and had agendas to turn the story into a star vehicle for some actor. It was imperative to Andy that, while he appreciated the need to make it entertaining, it had to document the true facts. He and his men were not gung-ho Rambo characters, but highly-trained specialist soldiers on a real-life mission and to McNab's mind the BBC – which could not hope to compete with the money being dangled by major film companies – came up with the best treatment.

Screenwriter Troy Kennedy Martin collaborated for an intensive couple of months with McNab on a screenplay and *Bravo Two Zero* would be co-produced by Anant Singh and Helena Spring and directed by Tom Clegg, fresh from the *Sharpe* series. As Clegg reveals, the idea of casting Sean Bean as Andy McNab had been on the cards for a long time.

'I had to go to an interview with the BBC where I met with a few people including Helena Spring and executive producer Ruth Caleb and we talked about *Bravo Two Zero*, which they had been going to film about a year earlier and for which they had at that time had Sean in mind for the lead. They asked me what I would think of him as Andy McNab and I replied, "Yes, so long as you accept that he will be older than Andy is and don't give Sean a Cockney accent." They said, "Well, you know him. Will you talk to him?" So I rang Sean and we arranged to go out to dinner to discuss the role. He ended up saying, "Yeah. I'll do it." And that was it.'

Tom Clegg felt that Sean also had the advantage of possessing huge street cred. And Andy McNab described Bean as ideal casting. He said, 'Sean understood the responsibility of the role. I think he could have done the job in real life.'

Sean was already drawn to the appeal of these shadowy saviours and during training, he would come to greatly admire and respect the work of the SAS. He later remarked, 'It takes a certain mentality to be

able to do the job they do. There is a real element of madness to it.'
And having read the book on its release, he had been familiar with,
and impressed by, the story. But perhaps the strongest appeal for him
lay in the very human aspects that were built into the heroism.

Basic fitness training for the role got under way in July and Tom
Clegg reveals, 'It was the South African equivalent of the SAS who
were involved in the pre-training exercises.' Among other things, these
tough taskmasters put the actors through a rigorous regime to build up
their stamina levels and it was a physically draining crash course but
Bean admitted, 'It was good to have somebody kicking you up the
arse, or you wouldn't have done it.'

When shooting started on 12 August 1997 in South Africa's
Northern Cape province, McNab was on set every day as consultant.
The director says, 'Andy was constantly on hand to give advice whilst
we were shooting. We filmed on the fringes of the Kalahari Desert at a
place called Uppington.' After four weeks spent there, the production
moved to Johannesburg for three weeks and finally to Britain for one
week at London's Twickenham Studios, ending in early October.

From their first meeting and throughout the filming as Andy acted
as military adviser, Bean and McNab got on well. It pleased the former
SAS sergeant that Sean could immediately handle the weaponry
convincingly, but Bean found extra feeding in simply watching
McNab at work, noting, for example, the deftness needed to reload
magazines in a crisis.

It was a stimulating role and Sean indeed took his responsibilities
very seriously. This was not the first time he had played a real person,
but it was his first chance to spend a long time with the man he would
be portraying on screen and, because Sean was eager to understand
what made McNab tick, they talked a lot in the evenings. No one felt
it necessary to try to make Sean look or sound like Andy and instead
Sean concentrated closely on capturing the fingerprint of McNab's
personality; it was an on-going collaboration which the star has
described as having been invaluable.

The most delicate area understandably related to the torture scenes
and before filming them Tom, Sean and Andy spent several nights in
deep discussion. Sean needed to discover how McNab mentally

managed to sustain himself throughout this persistent inhumane suffering, but he was also acutely aware that it might be hard for Andy to relive the horror.

However, the director recalls, 'Andy was not upset so much about that. He was more upset when he could hear his friend Dinger being tortured. But we talked a great deal about his own experiences. And of course, you are never going to get everything about what went on during the torture. Just like you are never going to get everything about the way the SAS works, obviously, so the actors were not going to be able to follow strict SAS procedures. Nobody knows the whole truth.'

To play the crack unit Bean was joined by actors Steve Nicolson, Rick Warden, Richard Graham, Kevin Collins, Ian Curtis, Jamie Bartlett, Robert Hobbs and Ron Senior, Jnr. Robert Whitehead portrayed the Iraqi Colonel and other roles were handled either by real Iraqi soldiers or South Africans. Tom Clegg recalls, 'It was a lads-own thing all over again, and a great atmosphere of camaraderie quickly developed. Sean was the star, but he likes fair treatment for all and this was very much a team piece, where everyone was holding their own.

'As ever Sean would muck in and do anything that was asked of him. He entered into it 100 per cent and did a great job. I felt that he was especially good at showing the vulnerability of this SAS sergeant who was sometimes, in effect, saying, "I'm not right all the time. I don't always have all the answers." Sean was very good indeed at showing when the doubts crept in, which, of course, is one of his strengths as an actor.'

Bravo Two Zero was transmitted as a two-part BBC 1 drama on 3 and 4 January 1999. Says Tom Clegg, 'Sean was disappointed in the fact that originally they had promised that this would be a theatrical release, but in the end the decision was made not to go ahead with it as a feature film.' Nevertheless, Bean had enjoyed the whole experience enormously and while the role added to his tough guy screen credits, he had appreciated the opportunity of stretching his abilities and exploring deeper levels within a performance.

When Sean returned home in October, tired but exhilarated, he faced two important events in his private life in the following month.

Back in August his and Melanie's divorce had been granted, which paved the way for a new start for them both. Sean never had sought to publicise any part of his private life but he was especially cagey now. And when he and Abigail married on Saturday 22 November 1997, they did so secretly; even arriving for the simple low-key civil ceremony at Hendon Registry Office at 8.00 a.m., one hour before normal opening hours. Their union was then blessed the following day at St Andrew's Church in Totteridge and the Press found out about it only after the event.

For his third wedding Sean was smart in a dark suit, collar and tie with a carnation buttonhole, while twenty-nine-year-old Abigail in a low-cut traditional long wedding gown, smiled serenely from beneath the heavy garland-style headdress she wore. She was attended by Sean and Melanie's daughters, ten-year-old Lorna and six-year-old Molly, as bridesmaids and the wedding guests included Abigail's mother and a brother, as well as Sean's parents who, with other Bean family members and close friends, had bussed by luxury coach down from Sheffield to London for the hush-hush ceremony.

The newly-weds' honeymoon period would be interrupted when they had to travel from the Lake District to Sean's hometown less than one week later when Sheffield Hallam University awarded Sean a general honorary doctorate. News that he would be receiving this honour had first surfaced in August and Sean excited much attention when on Friday morning, 28 November he came to Sheffield City Hall to collect his degree during a ceremony attended by students and their proud families.

Natasha Wagstaff of Sheffield Hallam University recalls, 'Sean was a very humble guy who seemed almost too shy for his profession. He endeared himself to us by wondering why so many people were in the academic procession that day. I didn't have the heart to tell him that the platform was almost double its normal size, due to many wanting to share a stage with him.' Sean's citation, which was read at the ceremony, was warm and – as university graduation citations go – in places, a little risqué. Extracts from it read:

'Sheffield City Hall seats three thousand four hundred people. Today there's several hundred more lining the pavements outside and they're not queuing for the Vice Chancellor's autograph. If you had any difficulty getting in through the front door to find your seat, blame Sean Bean. For Sean is one of Sheffield's most glamorous products. He has starred in over a dozen feature films and more than twenty television dramas. He looks especially wonderful in those skin tight breeches he wears for *Sharpe*, and as part of the city's export drive, he certainly beats the stainless steel penknife.

'Of all his roles, Richard Sharpe – that swashbuckling, sexy man of action – remains his favourite. He admits that there's always something of yourself in each character you play – and he plays strong men to perfection. But whether he's a romantic hero or a villain, his art conceals his art. His approach may appear casual and laid back, but he is dedicated in his quest for perfection and completely serious about the craft of acting.

'Sean's body is now well known to most of us. When he played Mellors in the TV adaptation of *Lady Chatterley's Lover*, his bottom became a national treasure, earning him the popular title of "Rear of the Year".

'He is proud of his Sheffield roots and has become a true ambassador for the city. To many people, Sean Bean *is* Sheffield. Sheffield Hallam is a university committed to serving the local community and to encouraging part-time and day release education for those who might have missed their chance at school. Sean Bean is an international superstar who embodies those principles, whose own drive, determination and conviction in his own abilities have taken him from an unpromising educational beginning, to the heights of his profession. He is a shining talent and Sheffield Hallam University has the honour to confer the degree of Doctor of the University *honoris causa* upon Sean Bean.'

Among others being honoured with doctorates or fellowships were TV science children's presenter Johnny Ball, broadcaster, author and former MP, Matthew Parris, four Sheffield citizens, and distinguished scientists Professor Sir Harold Kroto, Ken Pounds and Professor John Tarn.

Professor John Tarn says, 'Sean attracted much more attention and interest than probably all the rest of us put together!' While Professor

Sir Harold Kroto, who had recently been awarded the Nobel Prize for Chemistry, remembers, 'Being a famous celebrity, Sean arrived just before the event and was whisked about in all directions. The two of us were sitting side by side on the stage during the presentations and as the students filed past, a significant number of young female students took the opportunity to kiss Sean Bean. Occasionally, one or two, who must have forgotten their glasses, missed and kissed me!'

Sean Bean, Doctor of the University, beamed proudly afterwards for photographs, impressive in his burgundy with silver trim graduation robe and mortar board and he also patiently signed autographs before he and Abigail slipped away to spend the rest of the weekend in Sheffield.

Sean's final filming commitment of 1997 had been another role in a major movie as one of the co-stars in the Hollywood suspense thriller *Ronin* starring American superstar Robert De Niro. The United Artists movie, based on a screenplay by J.D. Zeik, was produced by Frank Mancuso, Jnr, and directed by John Frankenheimer. De Niro was backed by an international cast that included French star Jean Reno, Swedish actor Stellan Skarsgard and German ex-ice-skater Katerina Witt. Jonathan Pryce played an Irish terrorist and Sean, an English former special forces type.

Ronin – which means a masterless samurai warrior – is set in post-Cold War times and concentrates on a small group of former intelligence agents who have been brought together by an anonymous figure to work as hired guns, and are detailed to locate and sieze a mysteriously important, heavily-guarded briefcase. The complex thriller, complete with shoot-outs and noisy car chases was also, in part, a moral examination of the motives, past and present, of the individual ex-agents.

John Frankenheimer later declared of the film, 'A lot of things are left unsaid.' While producer Frank Mancuso added, 'The audience is left to decide whether or not to buy what any character says at any given moment.' And certainly with regard to Sean's character, Spence, a weapons expert and initially one of the agents, the viewer ends up confused as to whether Spence had truly been ex-SAS, or a complete fraud.

Bean had a clearer fix on the character's mentality and in expressing his own analysis of Spence he once offered, 'He talks a good fight and brags about his capabilities. But when it comes to the crunch, he's been through the horror of this experience before, and it gets to him.' As the edgy Spence who continually provokes Robert De Niro's character Sam, Sean enters the action at the start, but exits the film after half an hour.

Shooting commenced on 3 November in the Aubervilliers suburb of Paris and moved, a fortnight later, to Arles, before the production left to set up base in Nice. After the Christmas break, production resumed in the new year on the soundstage at Studios Eclair in Epinay and in all *Ronin*, shot at a brisk pace, took four months to film.

The film received its world première on 12 September 1998 at the Venice Film Festival, which Sean attended, as he also did *Ronin*'s Los Angeles première eleven days later which MGM hosted at the Academy of Motion Picture Arts and Sciences in Beverly Hills.

His involvement with *Ronin* had not necessitated too long an absence from home and he and his new bride looked forward to celebrating Christmas 1997 together. Mindful of the mortal pressure his heavy workload had placed on his previous marriage, Sean would spend substantially more time with Abigail throughout the coming year. Now a well-established star, he was able to afford the luxury of easing his foot off the pedal a little – the chance to give this marriage the best start yet.

13

BEAN THERE, DONE THAT

FOR THE FIRST TIME in a decade, Sean Bean purposefully slowed down the pace of his professional life and throughout 1998, instead of spending long spells away from home filming on location, he contented himself with carrying out narration or reading work for a series of television and radio programmes between March and December.

The first was for a Channel 5 documentary called *The Real Monty*. The hit movie *The Full Monty*, starring Robert Carlyle, had focused on a fictional group of unemployed Sheffield men who start stripping for a living. This documentary, directed by Phillip Jones, examined the reality behind the lives and work of real male strippers and it featured a Sheffield-based agency called Prime Cuts. To producer Aileen McCracken, Bean was the obvious choice as narrator.

'I had strong views on wanting Sean Bean to do the work. *The Real Monty* was about men from Sheffield who take their clothes off for work. Sean is a Sheffielder who had a reputation for screen nudity. So we approached his agent and checked out his availability and when it was all sorted out, we sent Sean the script. The documentary had been filmed around Attercliffe and Darnall, which was not far from where he had grown up, so he knew the locale, the pubs which featured in the piece and that kind of thing and he really enjoyed doing it.' Recorded on 16 March 1998, *The Real Monty* went out three days later.

At the other end of the scale, Sean's last recording commitment of the year came with the voice-over for the role of the priest in *The Canterbury Tales*, the episode called *The Nun's Priest*, one of six animated versions of Chaucer's Canterbury Tales which was shown on BBC 2 between 21 and 23 December. The series picked up awards, including the 1999 Emmy Award for best achievement in animation and the BAFTA Award for best short animated film. *The Nun's Priest* also won a Welsh BAFTA.

In between, Sean had obliged BBC Radio 4 twice, firstly by reading Stan Barstow's *A Kind of Loving* for the popular long-running 'Book at Bedtime' slot which aired between 11 and 22 May. Then, between 7 and 13 September he could be heard reading *Lyrical Ballads*, the work of romantic poet William Wordsworth and his friend and collaborator Samuel Taylor Coleridge. A classic from a different era saw Sean cap his radio work by reading in eight weekly parts, from Alan Sillitoe's novel *Saturday Night and Sunday Morning* for BBC Radio 2 between 7 August and 25 September.

And in television narration terms his three remaining jobs were all sport related, starting with ITV's programme *World Cup Rock 'n' Goal Years* screened on 12 July 1998, and BBC 1's review of soccer's top tournament on 2 December titled *Where Were You: Passion, Pride* and *Penalties*, both about football and programmes that sandwiched a *QED* special on the World Free Diving Championships called *Call of the Deep*, again for BBC 1 which was transmitted on 10 November.

While Bean's distinctive tones seemed to be heard everywhere, because recording these narration pieces barely cut into his time, he was left free to devote the bulk of his attention to home life. And proof that he and his new wife were starting to put down roots came when it emerged on 24 May, six months into their marriage, that Abigail was expecting a baby.

With a new wife and now a child on the way Sean decided to sell the Totteridge mansion and move house. He and Abigail chose Hampstead, an exclusive suburb popular with film and television celebrities, but also an area that they both liked, which was handy for London's West End and where, moreover, they had found their dream home.

The four-bedroomed £1.5 million Spanish-style villa was shielded by ten-feet high perimeter walls which would afford better privacy and the house is said to feature, romantically, a huge open fireplace. It also came complete with an underground garage. Moving into the villa in September, they just had time to put their personal stamp on the place and prepare their nursery, when Abigail was admitted to a private hospital. She was roughly eleven days overdue and had to be induced. Sean was present at the birth, to share emotionally in the experience, and he has described witnessing the arrival on 6 November 1998 of their baby girl as stunning. At 9 pounds 3 ounces, Evie Natasha was a big baby for the petite Abigail but both mother and child were declared to be doing well. Sean, who dotes on his elder girls, Lorna and Molly, now had another daughter to cherish.

At just thirty-nine, on the face of it, Sean seemed to have been around the block a few times already but although he was on his third marriage, a new father for the third time and living in his second luxury home, he was far from being jaded. On the contrary, life had a fresh invigorating feel to it. He was also rested, and by the end of the year was eager to return to work.

Essex Boys was a major feature film directed by Terry Winsor, who co-wrote it with producer Jeff Pope. This Granada Films production would reunite Bean, seven years on, with the team behind *Fool's Gold* with whom he had enjoyed a good working relationship, and with whom he was looking forward to hooking up a second time. Again it would be in the role of a gangland villain, but this time his character, that of Jason Locke, was a fictional one (as were all the characters); the movie itself, although inspired by a single true event, was also a work of fiction.

The real-life inspiration had come from the gruesome murders of three suspected drug dealers whose blood-spattered bodies were discovered slumped in a Range Rover parked in a lonely lane in Rettendon, Essex in early December 1995. For these killings two men were subsequently each given triple life sentences.

Essex Boys was to be a dark edgy thriller, often uncompromisingly brutal and set in the seedy world of organised crime. At its centre is the vibrant figure of Jason Locke, a dangerously unpredictable gangster who comes out of prison ready to settle an old score. Fuelled with resentment at having been the fall guy for his mates, all of whom have prospered in the meantime he is also paranoid that his beautiful wife has been unfaithful to him during his incarceration.

Heading up his own gang, Locke is ruthlessly determined to reassert his authority as an underworld kingpin and to do this he nails a large consignment of ecstasy tablets with a huge street value that will make him rich. However, unknown to him, the batch is contaminated. He takes some himself, with tragic consequences for his mistress, and in the meantime teenagers are landing, in waves, in hospital. With his reputation shot to pieces Locke goes on the rampage and thus develops a tale of double-dealing and death after which, when eventually the smoke clears, a surprising figure is left standing.

The two-month shoot began on 28 February 1999 and took Bean and the rest of the cast, to a number of Essex locations including Tilbury, Jaywick Sands, Clacton-on-Sea, Southend, Brightlingsea, Canvey Island and Epping Forest. Because there are no studio complexes in Essex, the interior scenes were to be shot in the vast space of the disused Bata shoe factory which had been adapted by the production team.

Other cast members included Tom Wilkinson, Charlie Creed-Miles, Larry Lamb, Michael McKell, Billy Murray, Gareth Milne, Amelia Lowdell and Terence Rigby. *ER* actress, the voluptuous Alex Kingston, who makes for an explosive pairing with Sean, is Jason Locke's wife, Lisa, a devious and foxy lady. While the role of Locke's blonde-haired mini-skirted mistress, Suzy Welch, went to little known actress Holly Davidson, the nineteen-year-old sister of Jude Law's actress wife, Sadie Frost.

Peopled by vividly drawn, high-octane characters *Essex Boys* is a fast-moving, gripping action drama designed to absorb the audience throughout and as such proved to be a strong magnet to Bean. For in addition to portraying a character with a strong part in the plotline, Jason Locke also had a colourful back story that engendered interesting convoluted complexities with which to get to grips, including his insecurities over his feisty wife with whom he has a violent relationship, and thus the part provided Sean with the kind of scope he more than ever craved the chance to explore.

To Terry Winsor and Jeff Pope, who had nursed the project for some time, although the film had not been written with any specific actor in mind, Sean, now a long-established pro at depicting heartless excess within frightening control, had always seemed to be the natural choice for Jason Locke.

Terry confirms, 'Sean was never far away from our minds, especially when we got down to thinking of everything that the role was going to involve. But there was the fact that by now he had done the likes of *GoldenEye*, and we thought we wouldn't ever see him again.

'Sean makes Jason Locke so utterly believable and he is a very nasty character. It's not that Locke was a cardboard villain in the writing, but Sean breathed such life into the part, as he did into the entire script. He made me believe in Jason Locke. I don't know how much vulnerability you can have sympathy for in such a tough and ruthless guy, but it's there a little.

'Sean also brought that fantastic visual presence of his to the screen and the camera just sucks him up. It's incredible to see and I enjoyed immensely watching him physically in the film. Sean is a good-looking guy – a bloke's bloke yet women go mad for him. It's another unique thing about Sean Bean.'

In addition to their other work, Pope and Winsor had a history of collaborating successfully in the making of crime films for television, but *Essex Boys* progressed into the bigger realms of the increasingly popular genre of the fully-fledged gangster feature movie. Filming in Essex allowed them to tap into locations as yet unexploited in film-making terms, and because this area was where the real murders that had inspired the movie had taken place, it also inbued proceedings with a surreal spirit of authenticity.

The filmmakers were conscious that they risked touching a few raw nerves locally but generally speaking, the making of the movie aroused interest rather than hostility, and the fact that they had moved away from the real-life murders calmed down any potential problems.

Says Terry, 'In police terms, Essex is crime county. Over the last ten years or so villains have moved out of London into the county – a second generation of villains without that almost mythical community spirit of say The Krays. There are no bounds nowadays, I guess because of the drugs. *Essex Boys* is really an accumulation of stories, all kicked off by that one true event.'

Unconventionally, in addition to normal rehearsals before principal photography began, rehearsals were also held midway through, during the Easter recess, after the characters had taken on a life of their own. This particularly benefited Alex Kingston whose commitments to *ER* meant that she commuted to Britain from America to film *Essex Boys* between shooting the hit medical drama in LA.

Terry Winsor explains, 'We shot scenes in the first period that didn't involve Alex. Then at Easter we went into rehearsals with her and subsequently we shot all her scenes in the second section. Alex and Sean are very interesting together. There is a fantastic mutual respect there. Each one was petrified of the other to start with and in the rehearsal room things were a bit tense. Everyone wanted to be the best and there was a little bit of posturing going on. Then, as soon as we started properly all that tension left and they sparked off one another.'

One particular moment stands out for the director. 'Jason violently throws Lisa down into the mud and when we came to shoot this scene Alex went up to Sean and said, "Now I'm very strong Sean. I work out and everything, so I'm fit. I'm really going to fight you and force you into doing your best to overpower me."

'Well Sean, of course, was right into the part, wasn't he! Alex didn't – couldn't – realise his strength and the immense power Sean has when he is in character and what a shock she got. There she was resisting him hard and then suddenly, Wow! Sean just took hold of her and wallop! She was flung like a doll over and down into the mud. The sheer shock on Alex's face was something to see.'

As Jason Locke, Sean puts himself through the mill to portray the man's many complexities. Bean explained, 'Everything he does is an over-the-top show of strength to disguise his frailty and increasing paranoia.' And he ploughed all his energies, mental and physical, into creating a realistic portrayal that went the full mile and then some as Terry Winsor illustrates.

'There is always so much going on with Sean in a performance. There's a scene when he has throttled a girl to death and afterwards is sitting on the floor staring in front of him, and that sounds simple enough. But as I was watching him, I began pushing closer and closer to him wondering, What are you going to do? There's a thousand things going on in your head. I can see it. How are you going to react? And all this came from the way Sean was looking right then. It is almost a biblical scene. There is a sense of seeing something out of the Old Testament. There was real beauty in it, about the way Sean was holding his body, the look in his eyes, in his face.'

When filming wrapped on 26 April 1999, for Sean it marked the completion of another very happy collaboration with the producer and director team. Terry states, 'We loved working together again. We just clicked.' Nine days before the end of the shooting schedule the film-makers surprised Sean with a big cake to mark his fortieth birthday. Such a powerful film, peppered with powerful performances meant that expectations ran high for *Essex Boys* but in the meantime, as the film entered post production, Sean took a few weeks off, in which to recharge his batteries.

Some of this time he spent in Sheffield where he had recently become involved in a pioneering project called the Sheffield Employment Bond, a social investment scheme designed to enable individuals, companies and collectives to invest in the city by buying a five-year zero-interest bond. The aim was to help regeneration by supporting new 'real' jobs for the local unemployed and to strive for a better quality of life in Sheffield. Sean launched the scheme in April.

One of the scheme's organisers, Martin Clark, recalls how Sean's involvement came about. He says, 'The connection came through Richard Caborn, Labour MP for Sheffield Central. He was then Minister for Regeneration and he and I met as his portfolio was relevant to what we were about. I asked him if he could think of a celebrity who might help get this project some profile. Richard often met Sean at Sheffield United games and he said he would talk to him about it the next time he saw him.

'One day a little later I arrived at my office and lo and behold one of our most timid secretaries said, "Sean Bean just called. He's calling back in ten minutes." She had been too overawed to think of getting a number or anything, the call had just made her day. But I wondered if it was for real. Anyway ten minutes later, sure enough Sean rang. I explained all about our plans and he thought it would be good and wanted to know more. He's a thoroughly genuine bloke who feels a real sense of duty towards Sheffield.

'After that we talked several times on the phone but we met for the first time when I went to the set of *Essex Boys* as Sean had agreed to a Press Association photographer taking some publicity shots. I was a bag of nerves at the prospect of meeting him in the flesh but despite the fact that clearly there was a lot of work going on on the film set, Sean broke off filming and couldn't have been more attentive.

'He was dressed in a sharp suit for his role as Jason Locke and on his forearm there was a tattoo of West Ham Football Club done in make-up. He was extremely worried that this could come out in the photo in the Sheffield newspapers and, while the photographs were being taken, he kept tugging his sleeve down to make sure it stayed hidden.

'He also shot some footage for the promotional video and his empathy for the plight of the unemployed, you could see, was very real. Sean was the first to officially sign up for a bond and his contribution was substantial. Certainly it was not throwaway money so he really put his money where his mouth was. It was a great boost to us to have his help publicising it.'

Sean's pride in Sheffield and its people is well known locally and it was not only in public ways that he lent his support as his former Brook Comprehensive school teacher Ian Footitt illustrated when he revealed, 'There was a girl in my class who had been involved in a very serious road accident a few years ago in which she nearly died. I went to see her in hospital and as soon as I arrived she showed me proudly a card and gift that she had received from Sean. He'd come up to see United play and heard about the accident that night at the Handsworth Working Men's Club.

'Another time a young lady whose ambition it is to become an actress went round to Sean's parents' house to ask if Sean could give her any advice. When Sean was next home his mum and dad asked the girl round and he sat with her on the sofa and talked to her for a long time about acting, answering her questions, telling her what to expect, what to avoid and generally reassuring her.'

And it is his unassuming manner, after all these years, that strikes a chord with another of Sean's ex-teachers, Rotherham College drama tutor Paul Daniels who states simply, 'Sean hasn't let fame change him at all. When he comes back to Sheffield you don't have to widen the doors to let him in.'

Having launched the Sheffield Employment Bond, Bean was now ready to move on to his own next commitment; one that would continue the trend that saw him being reunited with familiar faces to handle top quality dramatic roles in which he turned in exceptional performances.

14

THE TALENTED
MR BEAN

WITH *ESSEX BOYS* in the can, 1999, in television appearance terms, would bookend with another two powerful performances. *Bravo Two Zero* had been screened on BBC 1 in January and during the summer, Bean was about to take on a role that had been conceived with him in mind.

It had started when experienced screenwriter Murray Smith came up with an outline for an original drama series that was a cut above the normal and Smith's agent took a synopsis of the work along to Michael Foster, who had been Sean's theatrical agent for years but who had newly changed profession and entered the world of production.

The sketch of a story that began with a convicted murderer escaping his guards by leaping from a speeding night train to go on the run whilst trying to discover who really slaughtered his wife and child might easily have been dismissed as a take-off of the classic *The Fugitive*. But Michael Foster recognised that there was much more to both the proposed psychological drama and to the central character of Neil Byrne, and he was eager to meet for talks with the writer.

When he did, Foster wanted the project and instantly agreed with Smith's view that Sean would be perfect for Byrne, so they prepared to approach the star with the proposition. In the meantime, not yet having been directly involved in production, Michael Foster knew that he would be on a very steep learning curve and so to help him he brought in a partner in the shape of Malcolm Craddock, with whom (as Sean's agent) Foster had worked closely for the five years of making *Sharpe*.

To be called *Extremely Dangerous* the drama was always destined to

be a four-part series for television, rather than a feature film –
although it had all the ingredients – because TV provided a bigger
guaranteed audience. By the time the director, Sallie Aprahamian,
entered the frame, Sean Bean was already installed in the starring role.

Married with a daughter, Neil Byrne has been living a double life
when, as a Government undercover agent, he infiltrates an organised
crime syndicate. When his family are brutally murdered Byrne goes
down for the crime, but whilst in prison he is fed lures from the
outside, apparently through some cryptic hieroglyphs drawn in the
margin of a paperback which had been anonymously sent to him.

When he escapes custody, his one thought is to trace and deal with
his family's real killer and he needs all his wits and skills as an ex-agent
to evade detection along the way by his former underworld associates
who now know him for a plant; his own covert Government agency
that appears to have deleted his existence officially from their files; and
the law in the particular shape of a tenacious no-nonsense Scottish
police Chief Inspector on whose patch Byrne had made his daring bid
for freedom.

Sean thought it a brilliant script and he loved the psychological
dimension that distinguished *Extremely Dangerous* from being just
another action drama. One of the hooks for Sean was the challenge of
getting inside Byrne's head, a man who is driven to find the truth
whilst being disturbed by flashbacks of the sickening murder scene and
having to fight off waves of guilt over the tension caused between
himself and his wife over the risks he was taking in leading a
dangerous double life.

The drama was set in Manchester but when the eight-week shoot
commenced on 14 June 1999 very little time was actually spent there;
most of the filming was done at various London locations. Bean's
supporting cast included Nitin Ganatra, Juliet Aubrey, Ralph Brown,
Alex Norton, William Chubb, Tony Booth, Douglas Rao, Ron
Donachie and John Biggins. Sean had previously worked – though not
closely – with Juliet Aubrey in *Jacob* and Alex Norton in *Patriot Games*
but, for the main part, none of the cast were acquainted with one
another, which to Bean, resulted in giving the production an extra
beneficial edge.

Sean was raring to get stuck in to the role as the director, Sallie Aprahamian, recalls, 'He was absolutely determined to get the thing right and to that extent would endlessly enquire as to how to make it better. From a director's point, working on a star vehicle is usually quite complicated, but not with Sean. He made it simple by working hard, being earnest and very committed.

'What had attracted us both to the drama was that Neil Byrne had two sides to him. There was the action man who was going to get whoever killed his family, but there was also the dark inner stuff going on that came from the fact that he felt indirectly responsible for their slaughter. And just how these two sides co-existed quite fascinated Sean.

'The emotional world between an actor and a director on a psychological drama is much more interesting than on purely an action drama. Of course fight scenes are technically demanding, but they don't draw on the actor's relationship with the director. Sean can do mean and moody, walking backwards. And he was really interested with this piece, in stretching himself. He wanted to see what he could do with the role, how it could be different. He and I are very different as people and yet there was a common desire to do something special with this material and that was exciting.'

With three sets of people coming after Neil Byrne, still the drama's best scenes were those involving Byrne and the owner of a taxi business, called Ali Khan, played superbly by Nitin Ganatra. They were scenes with a rich sub-text which both Sean and Nitin handled with subtle deftness.

Nitin recalls the first day he joined the set. 'I was nervous because when you come in mid-shoot everyone else has got into the rhythm of filming. My first impression of Sean was that he was quite shy. In fact, his shyness can give people the wrong impression because he is not aloof.

'After the read-through of our first scene together Sean hadn't spoken at all and when I went into the make-up caravan, we were sitting side by side. Although he nodded hello, that was it. I thought, Right. How do I deal with this? We have a lot of scenes to do and I'd like us to get on. So, when the make-up lady said something to me about liking the way I read my lines in the read-through, to break the ice I replied, "I just hope that the other actors can keep up with me." Sean looked at me and immediately laughed, and from that point on everything was fine.'

Nitin's knack with the quick quip appealed to Sean as did his natural style of approach. Says Nitin, 'On my first day I went looking for Sean at one point because I wanted to speak to him about our scenes but when I found the caravan he was in, there was a guy standing guard out front who said, "You can't just knock on his door!" But I did anyway and went in and Sean was so grateful. He would much rather have companionship. He's a star, but he is a normal bloke and he doesn't want to be isolated.'

Ali Khan becomes Neil Byrne's one true ally and Nitin reveals, 'Sean and I became friends during the shoot too. He keeps a respectful distance, but he never hesitated to talk to me and I never felt that I had to pussyfoot around him. He enjoyed the way I would spar verbally with him on set. I think he was relieved to have someone be like that with him.'

Bean's way of working came as a surprise to Nitin. He explains, 'Sean is so serious when he is acting. He's constantly trying to figure things out, endlessly making sense of what he is doing. And I don't think he will do it until he's comfortable with it. He doesn't smile very often either which means that there are a lot of furrowed-brow looks.

'He's not a methody guy. I mean, if he was playing someone with a limp, when it was over he would just walk away normally – he wouldn't do a Daniel Day-Lewis and stay in the wheelchair, kind of thing. But he concentrates hard and that's line by line. Even on what would seem to others to be throwaway lines. He's forever questioning, making each line work for him.'

That this intensity could sometimes overtake him became clear to Nitin early on. He recalls, 'In our opening scene when I give Byrne a no-questions-asked job driving for my firm and I ask him if he knows Manchester, he replies, "Like the back of my hand." I ask him to describe it. And he describes the back of his hand. Well Sean was concentrating so hard on it that I ended up having to say to him, "Sean! It's a fucking gag. Stop it, you're killing the joke man!" Some of the crew were a bit shocked that someone should speak to the star like that. But Sean looked at me for a moment then said, "I know," and we fell about laughing.'

Almost every scene involving these two threw up a highlight during filming. Nitin goes on, 'There was a moment when I have to stitch a gash on Bryne's arm. Beforehand, I had been given a plastic arm to practise on and it was a thin piece of plastic scarring and a thick needle and I thought, this is easy. When it came to shooting the scene Sean had a great huge thick plastic scar on his arm and I had a thin needle and I thought, How am I going to do this? I was digging this needle into him and stabbing myself at the same time. Sean was trying to help me saying very quietly, "I think you should try going up the way." After it was over when they came to peel it off, it turned out that I had gone right into his arm, had sewn his arm. I went to Sean and said, "Why didn't you tell me?" He just replied in his tough guy voice, "Oh, it's all right, it's all right." '

What had not helped the actors was that stitching Byrne's arm was not supposed to be the real focus of a scene that was rife with the unspoken currents washing between the two characters. Nitin confirms, 'This was the moment when the viewer's not sure if I know, or am about to find out, that Byrne is a wanted man. Byrne can't be sure of me and is trying to figure out what I might do if I do know. It was a key tense scene and it had also been a high pressure day anyway. Sean doesn't like to rush scenes and there was an element of people trying to rush this important moment, so he was getting really uptight about it. So was I.'

There was also a high point when Byrne comes to rescue Ali Khan from being cruelly tortured by the villains. Nitin reveals, 'Ali always had a punch line and I didn't have one for this last scene. I felt that there should have been an exit line and I suggested this to the director. Sallie said, "Well if you can think of anything, say it."

'Sean wasn't aware of this when we came to shoot the scene, so when he saves me and, all bloodied and battered, I limp outside with him, when I came out with something like, "I hope you haven't scratched my car," Sean clocked it right off, thought I was impro-vising and burst out laughing. His response was so natural and typical of the style of our screen friendship that they actually kept that first take.'

Over the weeks their screen rapport reflected that off screen. Nitin states, 'We had a laugh and enjoyed joking together and swapping stories. And we respected each other professionally. He was a bit surprised at our first rehearsal when he saw that I was pitching it at such a high level but he gauged it right away. It quickly clicked with him that I wanted to play Ali Khan in this way and he went with me on it, which shows great generosity in an actor.

'In my close-ups, Sean gave just as much to his performance as when the camera had been on him. You can get stars who, once they've done their close-up, they don't put as much energy into it for your close-up and you're left thinking, C'mon. Give me something to work with. Sean though responded to me. I would respond back and so it went. He's possibly very competitive, but amicable with it. There was never any upstaging going on. We talked a little about our scenes and would sometimes do a couple of line runs. But mainly we preferred to leave the stuff for the camera. To have analysed the way we responded to one another could have killed it.'

One of the drama's most energised scenes occurred when two young armed hoodlums try to hold up Ali Khan in the mini cab office when Byrne is there and it was a scene that became dramatic in real life. Nitin declares, 'That was quite a moment. There were about thirty people crammed around that small office and when Sean, as Byrne, in that claustrophobic setting lost his temper and dealt with the pair the whole space became absolutely electric! It was *incredibly* violent to watch.

'Sean's quite a big bloke and when Byrne smashes the kid's head against the cold cabinet door that was a real accident. Sean had got into the part so much that his energy was astonishing and the real glass in the door shattered and showered all over the poor guy. The split second that happened Sean snapped out of being Bryne and he was *so* concerned for the kid. The kid was all right but Sean was really shaken up by the whole experience.'

Extremely Dangerous's director Sallie Aprahamian also singles out this particular scene, 'That fight scene when Byrne goes berserk on the young hoods is a classic example of one that Sean and I discussed a lot. I'm aware that violence is used as entertainment and I am not really into that. And Sean wanted to discuss Byrne's reaction – to query why it went way beyond what was needed. We debated it a lot and came to the conclusion that his extreme reaction when he nearly kills the pair for trying to rip off the cab owner, stemmed from a protectiveness towards his only friend, the depth of the grief he was nursing and the stress under which he was living. He was keeping so much together, but on this one level he was out of control and Sean was deeply tuned into this dimension.'

Handling the psychological aspects of a character is different for every actor as Alex Norton, who embodied the tenacious and shrewd Scottish DCI Wallace who was determined to feel Byrne's collar, explains, 'Personally I think it works best when you work instinctively because it's on the set where you really find your character, rather than from reading words on a page, and feelings come up, even as you rehearse. There's no point, in fact, coming up with the definitive performance in advance because the director may have an entirely different view of how it should go, as may the other actors around you. So it's got to be a fluid thing which makes it rich with possibilities.'

Bean revelled in handling a multi-faceted role and his favourite scenes were those with Nitin Ganatra. Nitin says, 'We were sitting chatting one day near the end of the shoot in one of the cars just after we had shot the scene when we swap cars and it was then that Sean told me that our scenes were his favourite. And I know they were thinking at one stage of cutting some of the scenes but Sean insisted on having them kept in, entirely.

'Sean also saw these encounters as showing another side of Neil Byrne. After all the running around, scaling walls, outwitting people, making miraculous escapes and handling the rough stuff he found it refreshing to show some depth of character, this human element and the friendship with another man.'

For Ganatra, working with Sean had thrown up a few surprises. He explains, 'Because I'm a bit of a learn-aholic, I wondered what I could learn from this guy. And it was funny because when I came home after my first day, my girlfriend and some mates were waiting and they immediately asked, "Well? What's he like?" And I said, "There I was, working really hard in our first scene together and Sean didn't look like he was doing anything!" And that's true. You can't actually see what he's doing, yet it translates immediately on to the screen. Now you can't learn that. It can't just be a technique. That's a real gift. And it's one that very few actors have. The only other actor I think is like that is Robert De Niro. Sean has incredible screen presence.'

He goes on, 'There's also an energy about Sean, something very volatile about him. He looks like he's going to explode!' On that score it hardly helped that Sean was trying to give up smoking. Ganatra laughs, 'It was tough on him. He'd given up and was puffing furiously on one of those plastic inhalators. And not only am I a chain smoker, but he had to smoke as Byrne. It was killing him! He's one of those guys who doesn't have to strenuously work out, which is a tragedy for people like me constantly watching their weight. But he was complaining that, with not smoking, he had put on a stone.

'Over the course of the shoot ladies would drop by and ask for his autograph and he was always very gentlemanly towards them. I've known some actors who are disappointingly hoity-toity in those situations. There are never any tantrums with Sean either. If he had a genuine problem with something, then he would say. But he would still try to make the director's notes work. He's an actor who tends to trust the director's notes.

'His sensitivity stood out too. There was a moment when I had to say, "I'm a Paki," and he immediately questioned this. But I liked it. I thought, More irony, please, for my character. I count myself very fortunate to have been playing his friend in *Extremely Dangerous*.'

That Bean invested much mentally and emotionally in his performance would become clear in the finished product and it was also physically draining for everyone involved, particularly since the original ten-week schedule had been shaved to eight weeks. The director states, 'It was such a demanding shoot. For the kind of piece it was, in fact, it was shot miles too fast which meant putting in incredibly long days. There were some stunts that should have taken about three days, but had to be done in half a day. It was very taxing.

'Sean did almost all of his own stunts, all the fights and the chase sequences. He will basically do anything that is not going to risk his life, naturally – he's very game. We did have a good double, but as Sean says no double walks the way you do. So even in the chases where the double would normally be used a lot, Sean would be in there doing them.'

The climax of the drama sees Neil Bryne in outdoor clothes being weighted down with chains and viciously hauled into a swimming pool, at the mercy of his former underworld associates; a scene Sallie Aprahamian vividly recalls filming. She stresses, 'That was a tough one. This would have been an ideal chance to use Sean's double for many of the wide shots, or the shots solely on Ralph Brown (who played Joe) and, as the star, Sean would have been well within his rights to have wanted us to use the double as much as possible. But he knew it was a vitally important moment and he actually wanted to experience the whole thing. He wanted to be acutely aware of the anxiety of getting out of the pool and because he was very finely tuned in to everything that was supposed to be going on, he wanted to do it all. He came out of the pool at the end, soaking wet and exhausted, but with not a single word of complaint.'

It would look all the more realistic for Sean's total involvement, but it had not been easy to achieve. Sallie reveals, 'There was a Perspex table on the bottom of the swimming pool which Sean could *just* touch with the tips of his toes whenever he got tired of treading water and the chains wrapped around his body were made of plastic to make them a bit lighter. We used a stunt man for the first moment when Byrne is yanked suddenly from the side into the pool but that was because we insisted on that, not that Sean refused to do that bit.'

Despite it being exhausting work, Aprahamian says that Bean remained tireless in his daily analysis of progress. 'When we wound down at the end of filming each day with a beer in one of the caravans Sean would still be talking about the part and asking, "Did the scenes work today?" ' She adds, 'He's a quiet, very private man but very well liked by everyone, especially the crew being a man's man.'

Alex Norton came away from the experience with yet further respect for Bean. 'There was such a lot to do in such a short space of time but Sean is a real worker and he does what he does bloody well. He brought a real dignity to Neil Byrne. Sean has this great quality of reality about him. Harrison Ford has said that he likes to play guys who are not invincible heroes and Sean is the same. If Byrne had been a killing machine – an Arnold Schwarzenegger type – nobody would have cared what happened to him. But Sean brought out sympathy for his character and made you realise that he *had* to do what he was doing to clear his name and find the killers.

'Sean was absolutely wonderful in *Extremely Dangerous*. He is a very generous spirited actor. There is never an attitude about him that says, "This is my shot, this is my scene." A star who, let's face it, is being paid all the money, is entitled to say, "Focus on me more. I'm the money." But you'll find it's the second rankers who are the me, me, me type. Real stars don't have to prove anything that way, and Sean is real star quality. The end scene between Byrne and my character I felt was a bit ambivalent. Personally, I couldn't quite work out what I was supposed to be conveying when I just walk off and leave Byrne to his own devices. But it worked.'

For William Chubb who played Ericson, Byrne's former Government agency boss and a key figure in the thriller, his memory focuses on filming the vital airport scene between their characters. He recalls, 'We filmed that scene in a corridor at Manchester airport which was obviously a very public place. There's always a lot of waiting about between takes while people set about preparing the lighting etc., for the next take and this confrontation when Byrne catches up with Ericson, although on screen it lasted about five minutes, took about two hours to shoot.

'In that time, scores of people were streaming by to catch their flights and many were quick to recognise Sean, so between takes he would be surrounded. And what really impressed me was the immense patience he showed as he dealt with numerous approaches. He was extremely good about it all and signed countless autographs, allowed people to be photographed beside him. He's a wonderful actor but he's also so good with people.'

After filming ended in mid-August Sallie was frequently struck during the editing process with certain aspects of Sean's performance.

She maintains, 'It doesn't often happen but sometimes it's when you are piecing the shots together that suddenly you see something that really grabs you. Sean is not a tricksy actor. And there were moments in close-ups, especially when he was alone in a scene, when there was something in his eyes, or in the sadness I could feel coming from him, that just kept me watching him closer and closer on the monitor and each time I saw something a little different in there.

'I told Sean that I would like to work with him again some day – only on something in which he wasn't hitting anyone. He laughed at that bit. I know there is a safety in Sean hitting people, but what really gives him that special ingredient and draws his absolutely huge female following, is his vulnerability.'

This classy thriller, with its psychological elements, still satisfyingly delivered plenty of action, as well as a slight romantic flavour when, at one stage, Byrne becomes closer than a brother-in-law ought to be to Juliet Aubrey's character. And when *Extremely Dangerous* was transmitted on ITV between 11 November and 2 December 1999 Sean Bean's long-awaited return to the small screen that year was trailered in the press and in television publicity for the drama with the announcement, 'He's back!'

Sean had been out of the country a full month by the time *Extremely Dangerous* began transmission but he must have been pleased by news of its popularity. He would also miss his third, albeit very brief and certainly unique, UK TV appearance of 1999.

Game for a laugh, when he had been approached by the makers of the award-winning BBC 1 situation comedy *The Vicar of Dibley*, starring Dawn French, Sean had agreed to make a guest appearance as himself in an espisode to be part of the new series produced by Sue Vertue and directed by Gareth Carrivick.

In *Spring*, Dawn French's character, Geraldine Granger, vicar of St Barnabus Church, has received a marriage proposal from an admirer. Her fantasy, however, is that Sean Bean would come romantically bursting into the church determined to stop her from marrying anyone else. It was a fun scenario which took hardly any time to film as Dawn recalls.

'We picked a different hero at the start of each series of *Vicar* and his framed photograph would go up on the wall next to a photo of Jesus. One series it was Mel Gibson, another was Robson Green – it was whoever was the flavour at the time. So we had decided on Sean Bean for this series and we hoped that when it came to the episode when I was going to get married that Sean would agree to be in it and he did.

'It was all very quickly done. In fact, we only met for about an hour. It was odd for us and I am sure for him too, but he came along in the middle of the day and shot his scenes. He was very game and didn't mind in the least being the hunk factor. I thought he was extremely down to earth and, I felt, really quite shy but very charming.' *Spring*, with Sean Bean's surprise cameo, which he recorded in September before leaving the country, was shown on 27 December 1999.

Around the world there were just days left before the historic start of a new millennium and much thought was being devoted to times past, present and future. For several weeks, Sean had been on the other side of the globe in New Zealand working on a movie which was set in a fantasy world all of its own.

John Ronald Reuel Tolkien, born in 1892 in Bloemfontein, South Africa had studied in Birmingham and Oxford, where he became a professor of English language and literature. As a novelist his most famous books were *The Hobbit* published in 1937 and *The Lord of the Rings* almost two decades later, in three volumes entitled *The Fellowship of the Ring, The Two Towers* and *The Return of the King*.

Set in the mythical Third Age of Middle Earth the sagas of good versus evil were played out with a mixture of hobbits, elves, trolls, orcs and humans. Good is represented in *The Fellowship of the Ring* by a young hobbit named Frodo Baggins, while evil incarnate is the Dark Lord Sauron. The story tells of a dangerous quest across Middle Earth by Baggins to destroy a magic ring of great evil before Sauron, its original maker, can retrieve it. Baggins is accompanied on this mission by a select group called the Fellowship whose job it is to protect him from the pursuing evil forces, the orcs.

These classics of fantasy literature had been popular with generations of readers since their publication in the mid-1950s. Then in Los Angeles on 7 October 1999 New Line Cinema executives officially announced that, with a £190 million budget, they were to make a trilogy of feature films based on these novels, to be filmed one after the other, starting with *The Fellowship of the Ring*; principal photography would begin in Wellington four days later.

From a screenplay co-written by Peter Jackson, Fran Walsh, Stephen Sinclair and Philippa Boyens, the movie would be co-produced by Peter Jackson, Tim Sanders and Barrie Osborne and directed by Jackson. Its cast, drawn from an international pool of actors, in addition to Sean Bean is said to include Elijah Wood, Cate Blanchett, Brad Dourif, Christopher Lee, Sir Ian Holm, Liv Tyler, Sir Ian McKellen and Sean Astin.

News of Bean's possible involvement with this movie had first appeared as early as June 1997 when Press reports hotly tipped him for the part of the swordsmith Strider. At that stage Bean's agent would not confirm this, but did confirm that Sean was talking to American producers about a variety of projects. All that could be said about the trilogy was that Sean would be interested in a part in it.

As it happened, Sean landed the significant role of one of the human characters called Boromir, the son of the ruler of the kingdom of Gondor, as John Hubbard of Hubbard Casting, the agency handling the UK casting of *The Fellowship of the Ring*, recalls. 'In the book when the people have their meeting where it is decided which of the group will go with Frodo with the Ring to the Mountain of Doom, Boromir is appointed as one of the escorts. However, along the way, he is seduced by the Ring and tries to steal it from Frodo. Afterwards, he is cut up by guilt and his conscience is so heavy that he goes out and faces an attack by the orcs, like one man against thousands. It's a self sacrificing act.

'Boromir is an incredibly brave man, but fallible. He wanted the power that the Ring could give him, not for personal greed but to help his country. But, of course, he has broken the trust placed in him and he sees that his only way out is to lay down his life honorably. Because of all this Boromir, then, is one of the most intriguing characters in the whole thing and we did extensive casting for him. Sean Bean emerged as undoubtedly the best. Again it was this mix of his of being able to portray the heroic type but with a streak of vulnerability. As will be seen, Sean is *so* right for Boromir.'

The movie – a massive production with magnificent sets and employing a staggering 20,000 extras – was shot entirely in New Zealand in the contrasting scenic locations of vast and verdant pastures, the rocky volcanic terrain in the North and the snowy Southern Alps. As Boromir, Sean adopts an attractively untamed style with straggly hair and sports a close beard and moustache.

Filming finished in February and two months later New Line Cinema executives, after watching an advance showing of an eighteen-minute section of the movie, declared themselves ecstatic with the results. In May 2000 Sean returned to New Zealand to wrap up some final scenes and as shooting then got under way for the second instalment of the trilogy, the projected release date of *The Fellowship of the Ring* was said to be Christmas 2001. Meanwhile, having fulfilled his commitment to the movie for now, Sean came home in time to concentrate on the upcoming release of his latest film *Essex Boys* which premiered at the Odeon, Southend, Essex on 10 July 2000 and opened nationwide four days later. Box-office receipts over its opening weekend sent *Essex Boys* straight into the UK film charts at number nine and favourable reviews were swift in coming.

TV film critic Jonathan Ross called it 'Powerful and acutely observant.' *Heat* magazine found it 'compelling and classy' and the *News of the World* announced 'Do not miss this.' While *Uncut* declared '*Essex Boys* is as close as it gets to the real face of organised crime', and, perhaps predictably, the very nature of the film's subject matter sparked controversy; the day after its première Sean found himself countering allegations that *Essex Boys* glorified violence. He stated, 'What violence there is, is there for a specific purpose.' His powerfully scary performance in the film, meanwhile, was widely praised. *Empire* applauded an 'excellent performance from Sean Bean as loose canon Jason Locke', and other critics followed suit.

It was amid the hectic round of promotional obligations for his new movie that some startling news broke – Sean was reported to have revealed that his marriage to Abigail had ended in divorce.

Astonishingly, this major development had managed to remain a closely guarded secret for several months and it caught all by surprise to read that the Beans, married in November 1997, had gone their separate ways in 1999. In line with Sean's preference for privacy regarding his personal life, however, very few details emerged and – in terms of celebrity splits – the coverage remained almost discreet, certainly low-key.

In his professional life, it is a safe bet that Sean will rack up another striking performance in *The Fellowship of the Ring*. The confidence he engenders in directors and producers alike that he will deliver the goods is remarkable and has uniformly percolated for some time throughout the film and television world, making his professional standing rock solid.

From making his début at age twenty-four, in the intervening seventeen years Sean has amassed a fair-sized body of work. And he has a shining future ahead. For, although Bean is the first to confess that to date he has not capitalised, as perhaps he ought to have done, on his big screen successes, especially in America, he does not lack ambition. Financially secure now, his main concern is to be selective with his roles, choosing challenging ones that will explore the full range of his capabilities as never before and it is guaranteed that he will always stand out.

His RADA tutor Euan Smith says, 'Sean is a very powerful actor when he turns it on. He has been so successful because of his talent obviously, and because of his individuality which will always mark him out. But also, I think, partly because he has a certain *look*. It's a bit like when Albert Finney had a look for his time. He is very distinctive.'

What is also different about Bean is how genuinely grounded a star he is. In a glamorous world of make-believe and fantastic egos, Sean Bean is very real and, moreover, he is seen to be. With the ability to assume the skin of any character on set, off set he has the confidence to retain his own identity.

Sean values dearly the times he can spend living a normal existence, whilst appreciating that yet there are inevitable differences. His friend and the director with whom Bean has most often worked, Tom Clegg, says, 'Sean is a complex man. He likes being a star. He likes the first-class travel, the nice hotels and he demands good money but at the same time he doesn't like it to intrude on his life. I would say to him, "You know, you can't have it all ways Sean." He's a reluctant star in the sense that he doesn't like to let fame affect the way he lives his life.'

Socially, Sean largely shuns fashionable London. Instead, he likes the ordinariness of going to the pub and his far from excitable manner means that he copes easily should people flock around him. But he is just as content to be left alone to prop up the bar counter unnoticed like the next man. Tom Clegg says, 'He's very good if anyone wants his autograph and he'll talk to people quite happily if they come up to him. But he does like some privacy and although he is never rude, he can be monosyllabic as a way of letting people know when he wants to be by himself.'

Allowing this kind of access brings its own risks. If someone wants to congratulate Sean on his work, he appreciates it. However, he is not precious. If anyone baldly – even rudely – criticises his work, he is quite unperturbed. The only type Bean will consciously avoid is the drunk. With his tough-guy screen image, there will always be a chance that someone could try to turn ugly.

This kind of self-control comes from being a self-contained man. He feels no urge to broadcast his personal views but if they are solicited, he can be disconcertingly direct in a world increasingly preoccupied with political correctness. Euan Smith declares, 'Sean is no fool. He always could see clean through people.' While Tom Clegg adds, 'You have to work hard to earn Sean's trust.'

It is hardly surprising then that – in contrast to some celebrities who will throw a party for 'hundreds' of their friends – Sean is happy to count a small but tight and trusted circle of people as being close to him; they number among them his life-long Sheffield mates and a few London friends.

A believer in the 'see all, say nowt' philosophy, nothing much goes past Bean. When it comes to his private life he keeps the world at bay – charming during the Press interviews that form the various PR obligations, but at the same time erecting an invisible, yet tangible, barrier that has left many a journalist quietly frustrated and wondering just how he skilfully managed to give nothing away about his personal world.

It is a mistake to pigeon-hole Sean Bean simply as a Northern man with a passion for football, the lads and a pint. He is a far more rounded individual than that. The restless young lad with a short temper has matured into an intrinsically kind and thoughtful man. And his many serious and nasty villainous roles belie a guy with a well-developed wry, and often self-deprecating, sense of humour.

From the gamin spirit of the drama student with a quirky taste for eccentric fun, to the regular laugh capable of rallying the forlorn troops in early morning trips to location in the grim Crimea, it is natural then that he has become universally popular among those with whom he has worked. And that is in addition to being a highly accomplished actor with an impressively broad range, who is deeply respected throughout the industry and is deservedly much in demand.

On screen and off, he exudes with natural authority an intriguing blend of strength and sensitivity which endows him with one of the most elusive and envied of screen qualities – that of being both adored by women and admired by men. Sean Bean is a major talent and an ever-rising star. And widespread though the admiration is of his work to date, there is a unanimous conviction that we have not yet seen the very best of Bean.

But whichever new heights he is destined to scale, one fact will irrefutably remain the same and it is one that he himself, once best expressed when he said in his inimitable way, 'I'm still Sean that me mates went to school with, not Sean the film star. And that's the way I prefer to be.'

CREDITS

The following is a list of Sean's professional appearances in film and theatre and TV, and his one radio play.

FILM

CARAVAGGIO (1986)
Director: Derek Jarman
Producer: Sarah Radclyffe
Screenplay: Derek Jarman
Sean's character: Ranuccio Thomasoni
Cast: Nigel Terry, Tilda Swinton, Michael Gough, Nigel Davenport

STORMY MONDAY (1988)
Director: Mike Figgis
Producer: Nigel Stafford-Clark
Screenplay: Mike Figgis
Sean's character: Brendan
Cast: Tommy Lee Jones, Melanie Griffith, Sting, James Cosmo

HOW TO GET AHEAD IN ADVERTISING (1989)
Director: Bruce Robinson
Producer: David Wimbury
Screenplay: Bruce Robinson
Sean's character: Larry Frisk
Cast: Richard E. Grant, Rachel Ward, John Shrapnel, John Levitt

WAR REQUIEM (1989)
Director: Derek Jarman
Producer: Don Boyd
Screenplay: Derek Jarman
Sean's character: German Soldier
Cast: Tilda Swinton, Nigel Terry, Owen Teale, Lord Olivier

WINDPRINTS (1990)
Director: David Wicht
Producer: Michael Games
Screenplay: David Wicht
Sean's character: Anton van Heerden
Cast: John Hurt, Marius Weyers, Lesley Fong, Eric Nobbs

THE FIELD (1990)
Director: Jim Sheridan
Producer: Noel Pearson
Writer: John B. Keane
Sean's character: Tadgh McCabe
Cast: Richard Harris, John Hurt, Brenda Fricker, Tom Berenger

PATRIOT GAMES (1992)
Director: Phillip Noyce
Producers: Mace Neufeld and Robert Rehme
Writer: Tom Clancy
Sean's character: Sean Miller
Cast: Harrison Ford, Anne Archer, James Fox, Patrick Bergin.

SHOPPING (1994)
Director: Paul Anderson
Producer: Jeremy Bolt
Screenplay: Paul Anderson
Sean's character: Venning
Cast: Jude Law, Sadie Frost, Sean Pertwee, Jonathan Pryce, Melanie Hill

BLACK BEAUTY (1994)
Director: Caroline Thompson
Producers: Peter MacGregor-Scott
and Robert Shapiro
Writer: Anna Sewell
Sean's character: Farmer Grey
Cast: David Thewlis, Jim Carter,
Peter Cook, Eleanor Bron

GOLDENEYE (1995)
Director: Martin Campbell
Producers: Barbara Broccoli and
Michael Wilson
Screenplay: Jeffrey Caine and
Bruce Feirstein
Sean's character: Alec Trevelyan
Cast: Pierce Brosnan, Izabella
Scorupco, Judi Dench, Desmond
Llewelyn

WHEN SATURDAY COMES (1996)
Director: Maria Giese
Producer: Jimmy Daly
Screenplay: Maria Giese
Sean's character: Jimmy Muir
Cast: Pete Postlethwaite, Emily
Lloyd, Craig Kelly, Tony Currie

LEO TOLSTOY'S ANNA KARENINA (1997)
Director: Bernard Rose
Producer: Bruce Davey
Writer: Leo Tolstoy
Sean's character: Count Vronsky
Cast: Sophie Marceau, James Fox,
Alfred Molina, Saskia Wickham

AIRBORNE (1998)
Director: Julian Grant
Producer: John Gillespie
Screenplay: Julian Grant and Tony
Johnston
Sean's character: Toombs
Cast: Steve Guttenberg, Colm

Feore, Kim Coates, Torri
Higginson

RONIN (1998)
Director: John Frankenheimer
Producer: Frank Mancuso
Screenplay: J.D. Zeik
Sean's character: Spence
Cast: Robert De Niro, Jean Reno,
Stellan Skarsgard, Jonathan Pryce

ESSEX BOYS (2000)
Director: Terry Winsor
Producer: Jeff Pope
Screenplay: Terry Winsor and Jeff
Pope
Sean's character: Jason Locke
Cast: Alex Kingston, Charlie
Creed-Miles, Tom Wilkinson,
Holly Davidson

THE FELLOWSHIP OF THE RING (2001)
Director: Peter Jackson
Producers: Peter Jackson, Tim
Sanders, Barrie Osborne
Writer: J.R.R. Tolkien
Sean's character: Boromir
Cast: Elijah Wood, Cate Blanchett,
Christopher Lee, Sir Ian Holm

TELEVISION

PUNTERS (AKA, JOEY AND SPANKSY)
Channel: BBC
Director: Chris Mensul
Producer: Andrée Molyneaux
Screenplay: Stephen Wakelam
Transmission: 27 November 1984
Sean's character: Lurch
Cast: Mick Ward, Tom Davidson,
Peter Howitt, Janet Dale

WINTER FLIGHT
Channel: Channel 4
Director: Roy Battersby
Producers: Robert Douet and
Susan Richards
Screenplay: Alan Janes
Transmission: 20 December 1984
Sean's character: Hooker
Cast: Reece Dinsdale, Nicola
Cowper, Gary Olsen, Timothy
Bentinck

THE BILL: EPISODE 'LONG ODDS'
Channel: ITV
Director: John Michael Phillips
Producer: Thames Television
Writer: Geoff McQueen
Transmission: 6 November 1984
Sean's character: Horace Clark
Cast: Gary Olsen, Eric Richard,
John Salthouse, Tony Scannell

THE PRACTICE: EPISODES 'I CAN HANDLE IT' AND 'THE TRAGEDY OF HEROIN'
Channel: ITV
Director: Pedr James and Dave
Richards
Producer: Sita Williams
Screenplay: Janey Preger
Transmission: 13 and 20 June 1986
Sean's character: Terry Donlan
Cast: John Fraser, Brigit Forsyth,
Rob Edwards, Amanda York

EXPLOITS AT WEST POLEY
Channel: ITV
Director: Diarmud Lawrence
Producer: Pamela Lonsdale
Screenplay: James Andrew Hall
Transmission: 31 August 1990
Sean's character: Scarface
Cast: Anthony Bale, Brenda Fricker,
Charlie Condou, Jonathan Jackson

JIM HENSON'S THE STORYTELLER: EPISODE 'THE TRUE BRIDE'
Channel: Channel 4
Director: Peter Smith
Producer: Duncan Kenworthy
Screenplay: Anthony Minghella
Transmission: 23 July 1989
Sean's character: Prince
Cast: Jane Horrocks, John Hurt,
Robert Hamilton, Frederick Warder

TROUBLES
Channel: ITV
Director: Christopher Morahan
Producer: London Weekend
Television
Writer: Charles Sturridge
Transmission: 1 and 8 May 1988
Sean's character: Captain Bolton
Cast: Ian Richardson, Ian
Charleson, Emer Gillespie

MY KINGDOM FOR A HORSE
Channel: BBC
Director: Barbara Rennie
Producer: BBC
Writer: John Godber
Transmission: 12 March 1991
Sean's character: Steve
Cast: Andrew Livingston, Jane
Clifford, Bryan Pringle, Sheila
Hancock

SMALL ZONES
Channel: BBC
Director: Michael Whyte
Producer: Terry Coles
Writer: Jim Hawkins
Transmission: 4 March 1990
Sean's character: Vic
Cast: Catherine Neilson, Suzanna
Hamilton, Barrie Houghton,
Angela Walsh

THE FIFTEEN STREETS
Channel: ITV
Director: David Wheatley
Producer: Ray Marshall
Writer: Catherine Cookson
Transmission: 30 August 1989
Sean's character: Dominic O'Brien
Cast: Owen Teale, Clare Holman, Leslie Schofield, Anny Tobin

LORNA DOONE
Channel: ITV
Director: Andrew Grieve
Producers: Anthony Root and Alan Horrox
Writer: R.D. Blackmore
Transmission: 26 December 1990
Sean's character: Carver Doone
Cast: Polly Walker, Clive Owen, Billie Whitelaw, Miles Anderson

TELL ME THAT YOU LOVE ME
Channel: BBC
Director: Bruce MacDonald
Producer: Sara Curtis
Writer: Adrian Hodges
Transmission: 8 September 1991
Sean's character: Gabriel Lewis
Cast: Judith Scott, James Wilby, Michael Cochrane, Rowena Cooper

IN THE BORDER COUNTRY
Channel: Channel 4
Director: Thaddeus O'Sullivan
Producer: Channel 4
Writer: Daniel Mornin
Transmission: 2 March 1991
Sean's character: Smith
Cast: Saskia Reeves, Juliet Stevenson, Sean McGinley, John Kavanagh

PRINCE
Channel: BBC
Director: David Wheatley
Producer: Ruth Baumgarten
Writer: Julie Burchill
Transmission: 6 October 1991
Sean's character: Jack Morgan
Cast: Janet McTeer, William Armstrong, Jackie McGuire, Marie Clifford, Celia Montague

CLARISSA
Channel: BBC
Director: Robert Bierman
Producer: Kevin Loader
Writer: Samuel Richardson
Transmission: 27 November–11 December 1991
Sean's character: Robert Lovelace
Cast: Saskia Wickham, Jeffry Wickham, Jonathan Phillips, Sean Pertwee

INSPECTOR MORSE: EPISODE 'ABSOLUTE CONVICTION'
Channel: ITV
Director: Antonia Bird
Producer: Deirdre Keir
Screenplay: John Brown
Transmission: 8 April 1992
Sean's character: Alex Bailey
Cast: John Thaw, Kevin Whately, Jim Broadbent, Richard Wilson

FOOL'S GOLD
Channel: ITV
Director: Terry Winsor
Producer: Jeff Pope
Screenplay: Terry Winsor and Jeff Pope
Transmission: 14 November 1992
Sean's character: Micky McAvoy
Cast: Brian Croucher, Trevor Byfield, John Labanowski, Larry Lamb

LADY CHATTERLEY
Channel: BBC
Director: Ken Russell
Producer: Michael Haggiag
Writer: D.H. Lawrence
Transmission: 6–27 June 1993
Sean's character: Oliver Mellors
Cast: Joely Richardson, James Wilby, Shirley Anne Field, David Sterne

SHARPE SERIES 1 TO 5
Channel: ITV
Director: Tom Clegg
Producers: Muir Sutherland and Malcolm Craddock
Writer: Bernard Cornwell
Sean's character: Richard Sharpe

Series 1:
Sharpe's Rifles, transmission 5 May 1993
Sharpe's Eagle, transmission 12 May 1993

Series 2:
Sharpe's Company, transmission 25 May 1994
Sharpe's Enemy, transmission 1 June 1994
Sharpe's Honour, transmission 8 June 1994

Series 3:
Sharpe's Gold, transmission 12 April 1995
Sharpe's Battle, transmission 19 April 1995
Sharpe's Sword, transmission 26 April 1995

Series 4:
Sharpe's Regiment, transmission 1 May 1996
Sharpe's Siege, transmission 8 May 1996
Sharpe's Mission, transmission 15 May 1996

Series 5:
Sharpe's Revenge, transmission 7 May 1997
Sharpe's Justice, transmission 14 May 1997
Sharpe's Waterloo, transmission 21 May 1997

A WOMAN'S GUIDE TO ADULTERY
Channel: ITV
Director: David Hayman
Producer: Beryl Vertue
Writer: Carol Clewlow
Transmission: 29 November–13 December 1993
Sean's character: Paul
Cast: Theresa Russell, Amanda Donohoe, Ingrid Lacey, Fiona Gillies

SCARLETT
Channel: CBS (USA)
Director: John Erman
Producer: Robert Halmi
Writer: Alexandra Ripley
Transmission: 13 November 1994
Sean's character: The Earl of Fenton
Cast: Joanne Whalley-Kilmer, Timothy Dalton, Colm Meaney, Stephen Collins

JACOB
Channel: TNT
Director: Sir Peter Hall
Screenplay: Lionel Chetwynd
Transmission: 4 December 1994
Sean's character: Esau
Cast: Matthew Modine, Juliet Aubrey, Joss Ackland, Irene Papas

BRAVO TWO ZERO
Channel: BBC
Director: Tom Clegg
Producers: Anant Singh and
Helena Spring
Writer: Andy McNab
Transmission: 3 and 4 January
1999
Sean's character: Andy McNab
Cast: Steve Nicolson, Rick
Warden, Richard Graham, Kevin
Collins

EXTREMELY DANGEROUS
Channel: ITV
Director: Sallie Aprahamian
Producers: Michael Foster and
Malcolm Craddock
Writer: Murray Smith
Transmission: 11 November–2
December 1999
Sean's character: Neil Bryne
Cast: Nitin Ganatra, Alex Norton,
Juliet Aubrey, William Chubb

THEATRE

ROMEO AND JULIET
Theatre: Watermill Theatre,
Newbury, Berks
Director: Euan Smith
Writer: William Shakespeare
Run: 10–28 May 1983
Sean's character: Tybalt
Cast: Kathryn Hunter, David
Maylan, John Levitt, Gerrard
McArthur

THE LAST DAYS OF MANKIND
Theatre: Citizens' Theatre,
Glasgow
Director: Robert David
MacDonald

Writer: Karl Kraus
Run: 16–24 September 1983
Sean's character: Journalist
Cast: Ciaran Hinds, Lorcan
Cranitch, Gary Oldman

ROSENKAVALIER
Theatre: Citizens' Theatre, Glasgow
Director: Philip Prowse
Writer: Hugo von Hofmannsthal
Run: 30 September–15 October
1983
Sean's character: An animal seller
Cast: Ciaran Hinds, Lorcan
Cranitch, Gary Oldman

DAVID AND JONATHAN
Theatre: The Redgrave Theatre,
Farnham, Surrey
Director: Stephen Barry
Writer: William Douglas Home
Run: 12–30 June 1984
Sean's character: Jonathan
Cast: John McAndrew, George
Waring, Suzie Cerys, Mike Shannon

DEATHWATCH
Theatre: Young Vic, London
Director: Roland Rees
Writer: Jean Genet
Run: 18 April–4 May 1985
Sean's character: Lederer
Cast: Jimmy Chisholm, Vincenzo
Ricotta, Gary Lilburn

TRIPLE BILL OF PLAYS
Theatre: Royal Court, Theatre
Upstairs, London
Director: Simon Curtis
Play No 1: *Who Knew McKenzie*
by Brian Hilton
No 2: *Stalemate* by Emily
Fuller
No 3: *Gone* by Elizabeth
Krechowiecka

Run: 26 June–20 July 1985
Sean's character: Play No 1: Terry,
No. 2: an estate agent, No. 3: Arf
Cast: Elizabeth Bell, Lesley Sharpe,
Jonathan Phillips, Hetta Charnley,
Alan Leith

ROYAL SHAKESPEARE COMPANY (1986–1987)
Plays performed in Stratford Upon
Avon, Newcastle and London
1. Romeo and Juliet
Writer: William Shakespeare
Director: Michael Bogdanov
2. A Midsummer Night's Dream
Writer: William Shakespeare
Director: Bill Alexander
3. The Fair Maid of the West
Writer: Thomas Heywood
Director: Trevor Nunn
Sean's character: 1) Romeo: 2)
Robin Starveling: 3) Spencer
Cast: Niamh Cusack, Michael
Kitchen, Robert Demeger, Richard
Moore, Imelda Staunton, Pete
Postlethwaite, Paul Greenwood,
Joe Melia, Donald McBride

KILLING THE CAT
Theatre: Royal Court, Theatre
Upstairs, London
Director: Sue Dunderdale
Writer: David Spencer
Run: 23 August–15 September
1990
Sean's character: Danny
Cast: Henry Stamper, Sally Rogers,
Kate McLoughlin, Valerie Lilley

In addition to carrying out a
variety of narration work for
television and radio Sean also took
the lead role in the radio play:-

THE TRUE STORY OF MARTIN GUERRE
Channel: BBC Radio 4
Director: Janet Whitaker
Dramatised By: Guy Meredith
Aired: 21 and 28 June 1996
Sean's character: Martin Guerre
Cast: Leslie Dunlop, Olivier Pierre,
Jill Graham, Andrew Melville

Sean appeared in the following
short films:
1. *The Loser* (Channel 4) (Date
unknown)
2. *Samson and Delilah* (Channel
4) 3 January 1987
3. *Wedded* (BBC) 29 August 1990

Sean also made a cameo
appearance as himself in *The Vicar
of Dibley*, (BBC) shown on 27
December 1999

PICTURE CREDITS

INDEX